Out of his definitive six-volume work on Lincoln and his times, Carl Sandburg has written this superb 430,000 word biography. These volumes have sold over 1,200,000 copies in high-priced editions. Now for the first time they are published in an inexpensive three-volume paperback edition. Here is Volume I, *The Prairie Years*. Volume II contains *The War Years (1861-1864)*; Volume III, *The War Years (1864-1865)*.

CARL SANDBURG was born in Galesburg, Illinois, on January 6, 1878. He graduated from Lombard College in Galesburg, and received honorary degrees from Harvard, Yale, New York University, Northwestern, Knox College, Wesleyan University, Syracuse University, Lafayette, Rollins, Augustana and Dartmouth. At thirty he married Lillian Steichen, sister of the great photographer. He was Secretary to the Mayor of Milwaukee, private in the U.S. Army, newspaper correspondent, editorial writer, film writer, folk song recitalist, poet and Lincoln biographer. In addition to the Pulitzer Prize for Poetry (1950) and the gold medal for history given by the American Academy of Arts and Letters (1952), Sandburg won several literary awards. His published works began with CHICAGO POEMS (1915), REMEMBRANCE ROCK, his only novel, appeared in 1948. ABRAHAM LINCOLN: THE PRAIRIE YEARS was first published in 1926, and THE WAR YEARS in 1939. He died in 1967.

VOLUME I

THE PRAIRIE YEARS

CARL SANDBURG

Abraham Lincoln

THE PRAIRIE YEARS *and* THE WAR YEARS

in three volumes

A Laurel Edition

Published by
Dell Publishing Co., Inc.
1 Dag Hammarskjold Plaza
New York, NY 10017
Copyright, 1954, by Carl Sandburg
Copyright, 1925, 1926, by The Pictorial Review Company
Renewed by Carl Sandburg
Copyright, 1926, by Harcourt Brace Jovanovich, Inc.
Renewed by Carl Sandburg
Copyright, 1939, by Harcourt Brace Jovanovich, Inc.
Copyright, 1936, 1937, 1938, 1939, 1964, 1965, 1966, 1967
by Carl Sandburg
Laurel ® TM 674623, Dell Publishing Co., Inc.

Reprinted by Arrangement with
Harcourt Brace Jovanovich, Inc.
New York, NY 10017
Printed in U.S.A.
Previous Laurel Edition #4812
New Laurel Edition
First Printing—September 1974
Second Printing—December 1974
Third Printing—June 1975
Fourth Printing—September 1975
Fifth Printing—March 1978
Sixth Printing—May 1981

Dedication

To Harry and Marion Dolores Pratt, a handsome team of Lincoln scholars, who gave time and care to the new manuscript of the Prairie Years, wherefore the author is responsible for possible inaccuracies or errors—

To Paul M. Angle, a hardened veteran in the Lincoln field, a man of good will who can be relentlessly logical while hoping he is not "magisterial" in tone—

To Benjamin P. Thomas, a ballplayer and farmer who is a man of learning and integrity, possessed by Lincoln's dream of "man's vast future," a citizen with a deep and keen anxiety about the American Dream—

To Allan Nevins, whose four-volume *Ordeal of the Union* and *Emergence of Lincoln* are a massive and vivid presentation of the fourteen-year national scenes in which Lincoln moved in silence or speech till his first inaugural—

To the departed friends Lloyd Lewis, Oliver Barrett, Alf Harcourt, Stevie Benét, Jim Randall, Douglas Freeman, Henry Horner, Jake Buchbinder, whose shadows linger and whose fellowship endures—

To Edward Steichen, whose projected photographic exhibition "The Family of Man" will register his faith joined to Lincoln's in the unity of mankind and the hope of "freedom for all men everywhere"—

To my wife, Paula, whose counsel was ever of help and whose many ready and cheerful attentions are a part of this book—

To Catherine McCarthy, whose exacting toils in the compression of a six-volume work into one volume, whose skills, perspicacity and devotion are beyond praise, who merits an armful of roses in token of affectionate regard.

To the faithful toilers on an incessantly changing manuscript: Helga Sandburg Golby, Marjorie Arnette Braye, Mari Jinishian, Mrs. Carl Sandburg.

CONTENTS

VOLUME I—THE PRAIRIE YEARS

Prologue 10
Preface 17
1. Wilderness Beginnings 21
2. New Salem Days 50
3. The Young Legislator 79
4. Lawyer in Springfield 104
5. "I Am Going To Be Married" 128
6. Running for Congress 143
7. Congressman Lincoln 164
8. Back Home in Springfield 180
9. Restless Growing America 198
10. The Deepening Slavery Issue 221
11. The Great Debates 231
12. Strange Friend and Friendly Stranger 245
13. "Only Events Can Make a President" 258
14. "Mary, We're Elected" 277
15. The House Dividing 301
16. "I Bid You an Affectionate Farewell" 314

VOLUME II—THE WAR YEARS, 1861-1864

1. America Whither?
   —Lincoln Journeys to Washington 9
2. Lincoln Takes the Oath as President 33
3. Sumter and War Challenge—Call for Troops 54

4. Jefferson Davis—His Government 77
5. Turmoil—Fear—Hazards 84
6. Bull Run—McClellan—Frémont
      —The Trent Affair 100
7. The Politics of War—Corruption 129
8. Donelson—Grant—Shiloh—*Monitor* and
      Merrimac—"Seven Days"—The Draft 151
9. Second Bull Run—Bloody Antietam—Chaos 177
10. The Involved Slavery Issue
      —Preliminary Emancipation Proclamation 195
11. McClellan's "Slows"—Election Losses
      —Fredericksburg—'62 Message 212
12. Thunder over the Cabinet—Murfreesboro 227
13. Final Emancipation Proclamation, '63 244
14. "More Horses Than Oats"—Office Seekers 253
15. Hooker—Chancellorsville—Calamity 265
16. Will Grant Take Vicksburg? 283
17. Deep Shadows—Lincoln in Early '63 290
18. The Man in the White House 317
19. Gettysburg—Vicksburg Siege
      —Deep Tides, '63 351
20. Lincoln at Storm Center 374
21. Chickamauga—Elections Won, '63 386
22. Lincoln Speaks at Gettysburg 400
23. Epic '63 Draws to a Close 415
24. Grant Given High Command, '64 433

VOLUME III—THE WAR YEARS, 1864-1865

25. Will His Party Renominate Lincoln? 455
26. Jay Cooke—Cash for War
      —Hard Times and Flush 474
27. Chase Thirsts to Run for President 486
28. Spring of '64—Blood and Anger 504

29. Grant's Offensive, '64—Free Press
      —Lincoln Visits the Army   523
30. The Lincoln-Johnson Ticket of the
      National Union Party   532
31. Washington on the Defensive
      —Peace Babblings   545
32. "The Darkest Month of the War"
      —August '64   566
33. The Fierce Fall Campaign of '64   587
34. Lincoln's Laughter—and His Religion   607
35. The Pardoner   635
36. The Man Who Had Become the Issue   659
37. Election Day, November 8, 1864   686
38. Lincoln Names a Chief Justice   693
39. The "Lost Army"—The South in Fire
      and Blood—War Prisons   697
40. The Bitter Year of '64 Comes to a Close   720
41. "Forever Free"
      —The Thirteenth Amendment   738
42. Heavy Smoke—Dark Smoke   744
43. The Second Inaugural   768
44. Endless Executive Routine   775
45. Lincoln Visits Grant's Army
      —Grant Breaks Lee's Line   785
46. Richmond Falls—Appomattox   803
47. "Not in Sorrow, but in Gladness of Heart"   816
48. Negotiations—An Ominous Dream   821
49. The Calendar Says Good Friday   827
50. Blood on the Moon   839
51. Shock—The Assassin
      —A Stricken People   856
52. A Tree Is Best Measured when It's Down   874
53. Vast Pageant—Then Great Quiet   885
      Sources and Acknowledgments   896
      Index   905

Prologue

The Congressional Record *for February 12, 1959, carries the following reproduction of Carl Sandburg's address to a joint session of Congress commemorating the 150th anniversary of the birth of Abraham Lincoln.*

THE SPEAKER. And now it becomes my great pleasure, and I deem it a high privilege, to be able to present to you the man who in all probability knows more about the life, the times, the hopes, and the aspirations of Abraham Lincoln than any other human being. He has studied and has put on paper his conceptions of the towering figure of this great and this good man. I take pleasure and I deem it an honor to be able to present to you this great writer, this great historian, Carl Sandburg. [Applause, the Members rising.]

MR. SANDBURG. Before beginning this prepared address, I must make the remark that this introduction, this reception here calls for humility rather than pride. I am well aware of that.

Not often in the story of mankind does a man arrive on earth who is both steel and velvet, who is as hard as rock and soft as drifting fog, who holds in his heart and mind the paradox of terrible storm and peace unspeakable and perfect. Here and there across centuries come reports of men alleged to have these contrasts. And the incomparable Abraham Lincoln born 150 years ago this day, is an approach if not a perfect realization of this character. In the time of the April lilacs in the year 1865, on his death, the casket with his body was carried north and west a thousand miles; and the American people wept as never before; bells sobbed, cities wore crepe; people stood in tears and with hats off as the railroad burial car paused in the leading cities of seven States ending its journey at Springfield, Ill., the hometown. During the 4 years he was President he at times, especially in the first 3 months, took to himself the powers of a dictator; he commanded the most powerful armies till then assembled in modern warfare; he enforced conscription of soldiers for the first time in American history; under imperative necessity he abolished the right of habeas corpus; he directed politically and spiritually the wild, massive turbulent forces let loose in civil war, a war [to avoid which] he argued and pleaded for compensated emancipation of the slaves. The slaves were property, they were on the tax books along with horses and cattle, the valuation of each slave written next to his name on the tax assessor's books. Failing to get action on compensated emancipation, as a Chief Executive having war powers he issued the paper by which he declared the slaves to be free under military necessity. In the end nearly $4 billion worth of property was taken away from those who were legal owners of it, property confiscated, wiped out as by fire and turned to ashes, at his instigation and executive direction. Chattel property recognized and lawful for 300 years was expropriated, seized without payment.

In the month the war began he told his secretary, John Hay:

My policy is to have no policy.

Three years later in a letter to a Kentucky friend made public, he confessed plainly:

I have been controlled by events.

His words at Gettysburg were sacred, yet strange with a color of the familiar:

We cannot consecrate—we cannot hallow—this ground. The brave men, living and dead, who struggled here, have consecrated it, far beyond our poor power to add or detract.

He could have said "the brave Union men." Did he have a purpose in omitting the word "Union"? Was he keeping himself and his utterance clear of the passion that would not be good to look back on when the time came for peace and reconciliation? Did he mean to leave an implication that there were brave Union men and brave Confederate men, living and dead, who had struggled there? We do not know, of a certainty. Was he thinking of the Kentucky father whose two sons died in battle, one in Union blue, the other in Confederate gray, the father inscribing on the stone over their double grave, "God knows which was right"? We do not know. His changing policies from time to time aimed at saving the Union. In the end his armies won and his Nation became a world power. In August of 1864 he wrote a memorandum that he expected in view of the national situation, he expected to lose the next November election. That month of August was so dark. Sudden military victory brought the tide his way; the vote was 2,200,000 for him and 1,800,000 against him. Among his bitter opponents were such figures as Samuel F. B. Morse, inventor of the telegraph, and Cyrus H. McCormick, inventor of the farm reaper. In all its essential propositions the southern Confederacy had the moral support of powerful, respectable elements throughout the north, probably more than a million voters believing in the justice of the southern cause. While the war winds howled he insisted that the Mississippi was one river meant to belong to one country, that railroad connection from coast to coast must be pushed through and the Union Pacific Railroad made a reality. While the luck of war wavered and broke and came again, as generals failed and campaigns were lost, he held enough forces of the north together to raise new armies and supply them, until generals were found who made war as victorious war has always been made, with terror, frightfulness, destruction, and on both sides, North and South, valor and sacrifice past words of man to tell. In the mixed shame and blame of the immense wrongs of two crashing civilizations, often with nothing to say, he said nothing, slept not at all, and on occasions he was seen to weep in a way that made weeping appropriate, decent, majestic. As he rode alone on horseback near Soldiers Home on the edge of Washington one night his hat was shot off; a son he loved died as he watched at the bed; his wife was accused of betraying information to the enemy, until denials from him were necessary. An Indiana man at the White House heard him say, "Vorhees, don't it seem strange to you that I, who could never so much as cut off the head of a chicken, should be elected, or selected, into the midst of all this blood?" He tried to guide General Nathaniel Prentiss Banks, a Democrat, three times Governor of Massachusetts, in the governing of some 17 of the 48 parishes of Louisiana controlled by the Union armies, an area holding a fourth of the slaves of Louisiana. He would like to see the State recognize the emancipation proclamation:

> And while she is at it, I think it would not be objectionable for her to adopt some practical system by which the two races could gradually lift themselves out of their old relation to each other, and both come out better prepared for the new. Education for the young blacks should be included in the plan.

To Gov. Michel Hahn, elected in 1864 by a majority of the 11,000 white male voters who had taken the oath of allegiance to the Union, Lincoln wrote:

> Now you are about to have a convention which, among other things, will probably define the elective franchise, I barely suggest for your private consideration, whether some of the colored people may not be let in—as for instance the very intelligent and especially those who have fought gallantly in our ranks.

Among the million words in the Lincoln utterance record, he interprets himself with a more keen precision than someone else offering to explain him. His simple opening of the House divided speech in 1858 serves for today:

> If we could first know where we are, and whither we are tending we could better judge what to do, and how to do it.

To his Kentucky friend, Joshua F. Speed, he wrote in 1855:

> Our progress in degeneracy appears to me to be pretty rapid. As a Nation we began by declaring that

"all men are created equal, except Negroes." When
the know-nothings get control, it will read "all men are
created equal except Negroes and foreigners and Catholics." When it comes to this, I shall prefer emigrating
to some country where they make no pretense of loving
liberty.

Infinitely tender was his word from a White House balcony to a crowd on the White House lawn:

> I have not willingly planted a thorn in any man's
> bosom.

Or to a military Governor:

> I shall do nothing through malice; what I deal with
> is too vast for malice.

He wrote for Congress to read on December 1, 1862:

> In times like the present men should utter nothing
> for which they would not willingly be responsible
> through time and eternity.

Like an ancient psalmist he warned Congress:

> Fellow citizens, we cannot escape history. We will
> be remembered in spite of ourselves. No personal sig-
> nificance or insignificance can spare one or another of
> us. The fiery trial through which we pass will light us
> down in honor or dishonor to the latest generation.

Wanting Congress to break and forget past traditions his
words came keen and flashing:

> The dogmas of the quiet past are inadequate for the
> stormy present. We must think anew, we must act
> anew, we must disenthrall ourselves.

They are the sort of words that actuated the mind and
will of the men who created and navigated that marvel of
the sea, the *Nautilus,* and her voyage from Pearl Harbor
and under the North Pole icecap.

The people of many other countries take Lincoln now for
their own. He belongs to them. He stands for decency, hon-

est dealing, plain talk, and funny stories. "Look where he came from—don't he know all us strugglers and wasn't he a kind of tough struggler all his life right up to the finish?" Something like that you can hear in any nearby neighborhood and across the seas. Millions there are who take him as a personal treasure. He had something they would like to see spread everywhere over the world. Democracy? We cannot say exactly what it is, but he had it. In his blood and bones he carried it. In the breath of his speeches and writings it is there. Popular government? Republican institutions? Government where the people have the say-so, one way or another telling their elected leaders what they want? He had the idea. It is there in the lights and shadows of his personality, a mystery that can be lived but never fully spoken in words.

Our good friend, the poet and playwright Mark Van Doren, tells us:

> To me, Lincoln seems, in some ways, the most interesting man who ever lived. He was gentle but this gentleness was combined with a terrific toughness, an iron strength.

And how did Lincoln say he would like to be remembered? Something of it is in this present occasion, the atmosphere of this room. His beloved friend, Representative Owen Lovejoy, of Illinois, had died in May of 1864, and friends wrote to Lincoln and he replied that the pressure of duties kept him from joining them in efforts for a marble monument to Lovejoy, the last sentence of Lincoln's letter, saying:

> Let him have the marble monument along with the well-assured and more enduring one in the hearts of those who love liberty, unselfishly, for all men.

Today we may say, perhaps, that the well-assured and most enduring memorial to Lincoln is invisibly there, today, tomorrow, and for a long time yet to come. It is there in the hearts of lovers of liberty, men and women—this country has always had them in crisis—men and women who understand that wherever there is freedom there have been those who fought, toiled, and sacrificed for it.

I thank you. [Applause, the Members rising.]

BENEDICTION

THE SPEAKER. The benediction will be pronounced by Dr. Frederick Brown Harris, Chaplain of the U. S. Senate.

DR. HARRIS. Our Father God, from this national sacrament of gratitude and memory, with the winged words of a prophet of our day lodged in our hearts, with the light of Thy countenance lifted upon us,

Send us forth into this testing, trying time with the faith and patience of Thy servant, Abraham Lincoln—like him—

> To be true to all truth the world denies,
> Not tongue-tied by its gilded lies;
> Not always right in all men's eyes,
> But faithful to the light within.

Amen.

Preface

As a growing boy in an Illinois prairie town I saw marching men who had fought under Grant and Sherman; I listened to stories of old-timers who had known Abraham Lincoln. At twenty in 1898 I served in the 6th Illinois Volunteers, our expedition to Porto Rico being commanded by General Nelson A. Miles, a brigadier general in some of the bloodiest battles of the Army of the Potomac in 1864. Our uniforms were the same light blue trousers and dark blue jackets with brass buttons as worn by the troops of the Army of the Potomac. We took swims in the Potomac River and had our first salt water swim in Charleston Harbor in sight of Fort Sumter.

The Lincoln lore of that time and place was of the man in his Illinois background and settings. When for thirty years and more I planned to make a certain portrait of Abraham Lincoln, it was as the country lawyer and prairie politician. But when I finished my *Prairie Years* portrait, Lincoln the Man had grown on me so that I went on to write *The War Years*. Now twenty-eight years after publication of the two-volume *Prairie Years* and nearly fifteen years after publication of the four-volume *War Years*, I have tried to compress the essential story of Lincoln the Man and President into one volume.

I have in this work, of course, consulted and made use of such new materials and researches as throw added light on the life and personality of Lincoln. Since the writing of *The Prairie Years* in the early 1920's there have been some thirty years of fiercely intensive research on the life of Lincoln before he became president. In no thirty-year period since the death of Lincoln has so rigorous and thorough an examination been given the facts and myths of the life of Lincoln. Listed separately at the end of volume 3 are my

"Sources and Acknowledgments." One may with no harm quote from Paul M. Angle: "I am convinced that annotation irritates almost everyone except professional historians . . . Still, if he is to play fair with his readers, the historical writer can hardly omit all mention of the materials he has used." Or from James G. Randall the cryptic: "Perhaps in general footnotes should be held guilty unless proved innocent." In all but four instances the texts as written by Lincoln, or as published, are followed literally without the use of [sic]. In three of these instances Lincoln stuttered in writing, but it is certain he did not stutter in speaking.

Walt Whitman saw Lincoln as "the grandest figure on the crowded canvas of the drama of the nineteenth century." In the story of a great pivotal figure at the vortex of a vast human struggle, we meet gaps and discrepancies. The teller of the story reports, within rigorous space limits, what is to him plain, moving, revealing. Every biographer of Lincoln is under compulsion to omit all or parts of Lincoln letters and speeches that he would like to include; this in part explains why any Lincoln biography is different from any or all other Lincoln biographies; each must choose and decide what sentences or paragraphs shed the light needed for the Lincoln portrait and story. Supposing all could be told, it would take a far longer time to tell it than was taken to enact it in life.

Here and there exist Lincoln letters not yet published but there are no expectations that they will throw important fresh light. As recently as February 1954 came the first publication of letters of Lincoln to Judge David Davis, which I have used herein as throwing slightly deeper gleams on Lincoln as a master politician. A national event was the opening at midnight on July 26, 1947, the "unveiling" as some termed it, of the long secret Robert T. Lincoln Collection in the Library of Congress. The next five days I did my best at reporting in seven newspaper columns for a syndicate what was revealed in the 18,300 letters, telegrams, manuscripts, miscellaneous data. The fourteen Lincoln scholars and authors present agreed that while no new light of importance was shed on Lincoln, the documents deepened and sharpened the outlines of the massive and subtle Lincoln as previously known. When I mentioned to Paul Angle a cynical editorial writer referring to us as "hagiographers" (saint worshippers), Paul said, "We could use a few real saints in this country now. And it's nice to live in a country where you can pick the saints you prefer to worship so long as you don't interfere with other saint worshippers."

Having read the million-word record of Lincoln's speeches and writings several times, Roy P. Basler sets forth, "The more fully Lincoln's varied career is traced . . . the more his genius grows and passes beyond each interpretation." Yankee Gamaliel Bradford put it briefly: "He still smiles and remains impenetrable."

To Joseph Fifer, Civil War soldier and later governor of Illinois, his favorite tribute to Lincoln was anonymous till after a six-year search he found that Homer Hoch of Kansas spoke it in the House of Representatives February 12, 1923:

"There is no new thing to be said about Lincoln. There is no new thing to be said of the mountains, or of the sea, or of the stars. The years go their way, but the same old mountains lift their granite shoulders above the drifting clouds; the same mysterious sea beats upon the shore; the same silent stars keep holy vigil above a tired world. But to the mountains and sea and stars men turn forever in unwearied homage. And thus with Lincoln. For he was a mountain in grandeur of soul, he was a sea in deep undervoice of mystic loneliness, he was a star in steadfast purity of purpose and service. And he abides."

On the 100th birthday anniversary of Lincoln, Brazilian Ambassador Joaquin Nabuco said: "With the increased velocity of modern changes, we do not know what the world will be a hundred years hence. For sure, the ideals of the generation of the year 2000 will not be the same of the generation of the year 1900. Nations will then be governed by currents of political thought which we can no more anticipate than the seventeenth century could anticipate the political currents of the eighteenth, which still in part sway us. But whether the spirit of authority, or that of freedom, increases, Lincoln's legend will ever appear more luminous in the amalgamation of centuries, because he supremely incarnated both those spirits."

CARL SANDBURG

Connemara Farm
Flat Rock, North Carolina
May 5, 1954

Chaper 1

Wilderness Beginnings

In the year 1776, when the 13 American colonies gave to the world their famous Declaration of Independence, there was a captain of Virginia militia living in Rockingham County named Abraham Lincoln. He had a 210-acre farm deeded to him by his father, John Lincoln, one of the many English, Scotch, Irish, German, Dutch settlers who were taking the green hills and slopes of the Shenandoah Valley and putting their plows to unbroken ground long held by the Indians. These Lincolns in Virginia came from Berks County in Pennsylvania and traced back to Lincolns in New England and Old England. There was a strain of Quaker blood in them; they were a serene, peaceable, obstinate people.

Abraham Lincoln had taken for a wife Bathsheba Herring, who bore him three sons, Mordecai, Josiah and Thomas, and two daughters, Mary and Nancy. This family Abraham Lincoln moved to Kentucky in 1782. For years his friend Daniel Boone, coming back from trips to Kentucky, had been telling of valleys there rich with black land and blue grass, game and fish, tall timber and clear running waters. It called to him, that country Boone talked about, where land was 40 cents an acre. Abraham Lincoln sold his farm; they packed their belongings and joined a party heading down the Wilderness Road through Cumberland Gap and up north and west into Kentucky. Abraham Lincoln located on the Green River, where he filed claims for more than 2,000 acres.

One day about two years later, he was working in a field with his three sons, and they saw him in a spasm of pain fall to the ground, just after the boys heard a rifle shot and the whine of a bullet. The boys yelled to each other, "Indians!"

Mordecai ran to a cabin nearby, Josiah started across fields
and woods to a fort to bring help. Six-year-old Tom stooped
over his father's bleeding body and wondered what he could
do. He looked up to see an Indian standing over him, a shining bangle hanging down over the Indian's shoulder close
to the heart. Then Tom saw the Indian's hands clutch upward, saw him double with a groan and crumple to the
ground. Mordecai with a rifle at a peephole in the cabin had
aimed his shot at the shining bangle. Little Tom was so
near he heard the bullet plug its hole into the red man.

Thomas Lincoln, while growing up, lived in different
places in Kentucky with kith and kin, sometimes hiring out
to farmers, mostly in Washington County. Betweenwhiles
he learned the carpenter's trade and cabinetmaking. In his
full growth he was about five feet nine, weighed about 185
pounds, his muscles and ribs close-knit. His dark hazel eyes
looked out from a round face, from under coarse black
hair. He could be short-spoken or reel off sayings, yarns,
jokes. He made a reputation as a storyteller. He had little or
no time for books, could read some, and could sign his
name.

Thomas Lincoln at 19 had served in the Kentucky state
militia. At 24 he was appointed a constable in Cumberland
County. The next year he moved to Hardin County and
served on a jury. He was trusted by a sheriff and paid by
the county to guard a prisoner for six days. In the county
jail he could see men bolted behind bars for not paying their
debts and at the public whipping post both white and black
men lashed on their naked backs. He saw prisoners in the
stocks kneeling with hands and head clamped between two
grooved planks; if a prisoner was dead drunk he was laid
on his back with his feet fastened in the stocks till he was
sober.

In 1803 Thomas Lincoln for "the sum of 118 pounds in
hand paid" bought a 238-acre tract near Mill Creek, seven
miles north of Elizabethtown, the county seat of Hardin
County. In March 1805 he was one of the four "patrollers"
appointed in Hardin County to seize suspicious white char-

acters or Negro slaves roving without permits. In March 1806 he was hired by Bleakley & Montgomery, storekeepers in Elizabethtown, to take a flatboat of their merchandise down the Ohio and Mississippi Rivers to New Orleans, earning 16 pounds in gold and a credit of 13 pounds in gold. Account books of the store had him occasionally buying "two twists of tobacco," one pound for 38 cents, and one pint of whisky for 21 cents.

And the books show that in May 1806 he went on a buying spree, purchasing "four skeins of silk," "five yards of linen," "four yards of coating," "one-fourth yard of scarlet cloth," several yards of "Jane" and of "Brown Holland," "three and one-half yards of cassemere," "one and one-quarter yards of red flannel," dozens of buttons, and other sundries. Earlier that year he had bought an aristocratic beaver hat for one pound six shillings and a pair of silk suspenders for $1.50. He was courting a woman he meant to marry and was buying clothes and dress goods intended for his bride and himself.

Thomas Lincoln was in love and his wedding set for June 12, 1806, at Beechland in Washington County. Nancy Hanks, the bride-to-be, was a daughter of Lucy Hanks and was sometimes called Nancy Sparrow as though she was an adopted daughter of Thomas and Elizabeth Sparrow whose house was her home.

Lucy Hanks had welcomed her child Nancy into life in Virginia about 1784. The name of the child's father seems to have vanished from any documents or letters that may have existed. His name stayed unknown to baffle and mystify the seekers who for years searched for records and sought evidence that might bring to light the name of the father of the girl child Nancy Hanks.

Lucy traveled to Kentucky carrying what was to her a precious bundle. She was perhaps 19 when she made this trip. She could toss her bundle into the air against a far, hazy line of blue mountains, catch it in her two hands as it came down, let it snuggle to her breast and feed, while she asked, "Here we come—where from?" If Lucy was married when Nancy was born it seemed that her husband either died and she became a widow or he lived and stayed in Virginia or elsewhere. In either case she and their child had to get along as best they could without him.

Of how and where she lived in the years she was raising Nancy not much was remembered or recorded. There were those who said later that it was another Lucy Hanks, not the mother of Nancy, who was indicted November 24, 1789, by a grand jury in Mercer County Court for loose and shameless conduct with men. Months passed and there was no record of a trial of the Lucy Hanks indicted. In those months there came deeply into the life of the mother of Nancy a man named Henry Sparrow, Virginia-born, about her own age, a Revolutionary War veteran who had seen Lord Cornwallis' army surrendered to George Washington. Since his father's death in 1789 he had been caring for his widowed mother, sister and younger brother.

On April 26, 1790, Henry Sparrow, with a brother-in-law, John Daniel, gave bond for a license of marriage between himself and Lucy Hanks. On this same day Lucy Hanks, one of the few women of the time and locality who could read and write, wrote a certificate:

> I do sertify that I am
> of age and give my appro-
> bation freely for henry
> Sparrow to git out Lisons
> this or enny other day
> Given under my hand
> this day
> April 26th 1790
> day
> Lucey
> Hanks

Undersigned as witnesses were Robert Mitchell and John Berry, perhaps the same John Berry who had served on the jury that had indicted one Lucy Hanks. In the following May the Mercer County Court in the case "against Lucy Hanks, deft [defendant]" made a presentment recorded, "for reasons appearing to the court the suit is ordered to be dis-

continued." Whatever they meant by their indictment was
wiped out as though she had changed for the better or they
had been wrong in naming her in an indictment.

Nearly a year passed and Lucy Hanks and her way of living pleased Henry Sparrow. He wanted her for a life companion and, having their license that was issued April 26,
1790, they were, on April 3, 1791, married by the Baptist
preacher, the Reverend John Bailey. Lucy Hanks Sparrow
proved herself a woman of strengths and vitality, of passion
for life and brave living. Of her eight children that came she
saw to it in those days of little schooling that all of them
learned to read and write, and two became preachers of
reputation.

June 12, 1806, came and the home of Richard Berry at
Beechland in Washington County saw men and women on
horseback arriving for the wedding of 28-year-old Thomas
Lincoln and 22-year-old Nancy Hanks. The groom was
wearing his fancy beaver hat, a new black suit, his new silk
suspenders. The bride's outfit had in it linen and silk, perhaps a dash somewhere of the "one-fourth yard of scarlet
cloth" Tom had bought at Bleakley & Montgomery's. They
had many relatives and friends in Washington County and
the time was right to go to a wedding, what with spring
planting and corn plowing over and the hay harvest yet to
come. Nancy Hanks was at home in the big double log
cabin of the Berrys. She had done sewing there for Mrs.
Berry and it was Richard Berry who had joined Thomas Lincoln in signing the marriage bond, below his name writing
"garden," meaning guardian. The six Negro slaves owned
by Richard Berry were busy getting ready the food and
"fixins" to follow the wedding ceremony. The Reverend
Jesse Head arrived on his gray mare. He was a man they
rhymed about:

> His nose is long and his hair is red,
> And he goes by the name of Jesse Head.

A hater of sin, he liked decency and good order and could
pause in a sermon to step from the pulpit and throw out a
disorderly mocker who had had a few drinks. The bride and

groom stood up before him. He pronounced them man and wife and wrote for the county clerk that on June 12, 1806, Thomas Lincoln and Nancy Hanks had been joined together in the holy estate of matrimony "agreeable to the rites and ceremonies of the Methodist Episcopal Church."

Then came "the infare." One who was there remembered, "We had bear meat, venison, wild turkey and ducks, eggs wild and tame, maple sugar lumps tied on a string to bite off for coffee or whisky, syrup in big gourds, peach and honey, a sheep barbecued whole over coals of wood burned in a pit, and covered with green boughs to keep the juices in; and a race for the whisky bottle." Quite likely Henry Sparrow and his wife, Lucy Hanks Sparrow, rode over from Mercer County to join the wedding company. For them, as for the bride and groom, the solemn event of the day had a peculiar loveliness and Lucy could have a glad heart.

The new husband put his bride on a horse and they rode away on the red clay road along the timber trails to Elizabethtown to make a home in a cabin close to the county courthouse. At Bleakley & Montgomery's, Tom bought a half set of knives and forks, a half-dozen spoons, thread and needles, three skeins of silk, three pounds of tobacco—the silk for Nancy, the tobacco for himself. Tom worked as a carpenter, made cabinets, door frames, window sash and an occasional coffin. A child's coffin cost three dollars, a woman's six and a man's seven.

Tall, slender, dark-complexioned Nancy Hanks had happiness that year of 1806. One summer day she had news for her husband—a baby on the way! They rode out more often perhaps to the Little Mount Baptist Church where they were members and spoke prayers more often of hope for the child to come. Perhaps an added dark zeal came in the brief grace Thomas spoke at meals.

On February 10, 1807, the child came wellborn and they named her Sarah. Nancy washed and nursed her baby, made her wishes and prayers for the little one. It could be she was sad with sorrows like dark stars in blue mist, with hopes burned deep in her that beyond the everyday struggles, the babble and gabble of today, there might be what her brightest dreams told her. She read their Bible. One who knew her well said she was "a ready reader." She was a believer and knew—so much of what she believed was yonder—always yonder. Every day came cooking, keeping the fire going, scrubbing, washing, patching, with little time to think or sing of the glory she believed in—always yonder.

She saw her husband in trouble in law courts. He took a contract to hew timbers and help put up a new sawmill for Denton Geoghegan, spent days of hard work on the job. When Geoghegan wouldn't pay him, Tom filed suit and won. Geoghegan then started two suits against Lincoln, claiming the sawmill timbers were not hewn square and true. Tom Lincoln won both suits.

When he bought his second farm, 348½ acres on the South Fork of Nolin Creek, 18 miles southeast of Elizabethtown, he paid Isaac Bush $200 in cash and took on a small obligation due to a former titleholder. This in 1808 made Tom Lincoln owner of 586½ acres of land, along with two lots in Elizabethtown and some livestock.

In May and the blossom-time of 1808, Tom and Nancy with the baby moved from Elizabethtown to the farm of George Brownfield, where Tom did carpenter and farm work. Near their cabin wild crab-apple trees stood thick and flourishing with riots of bloom and odor. And the smell of wild crab-apple blossoms, and the low crying of all wild things, came keen that summer to Nancy Hanks. The summer stars that year shook out pain and warning, strange and bittersweet laughters, for Nancy Hanks.

The same year saw Tom Lincoln's family moved to his land on the South Fork of Nolin Creek, about two and a half miles from Hodgenville. He was trying to farm stubborn ground and make a home in a cabin of logs he cut from timber nearby. The floor was packed-down dirt. One door, swung on leather hinges, let them in and out. One small window gave a lookout on the weather, the rain or snow, sun and trees, and the play of the rolling prairie and low hills. A stick-clay chimney carried the fire smoke up and away.

One morning in February 1809, Tom Lincoln came out of his cabin to the road, stopped a neighbor and asked him to tell "the granny woman," Aunt Peggy Walters, that

Nancy would need help soon. On the morning of February 12, a Sunday, the granny woman was at the cabin. And she and Tom Lincoln and the moaning Nancy Hanks welcomed into a world of battle and blood, of whispering dreams and wistful dust, a new child, a boy.

A little later that morning Tom Lincoln threw extra wood on the fire, an extra bearskin over the mother, and walked two miles up the road to where the Sparrows, Tom and Betsy, lived. Dennis Hanks, the nine-year-old boy adopted by the Sparrows, met Tom at the door. In his slow way of talking Tom Lincoln told them, "Nancy's got a boy baby." A half-sheepish look was in his eyes, as though maybe more babies were not wanted in Kentucky just then.

Dennis Hanks took to his feet down the road to the Lincoln cabin. There he saw Nancy Hanks on a bed of poles cleated to a corner of the cabin, under warm bearskins. She turned her dark head from looking at the baby to look at Dennis and threw him a tired, white smile from her mouth and gray eyes. He stood watching the even, quiet breaths of this fresh, soft red baby. "What you goin' to name him, Nancy?" the boy asked. "Abraham," was the answer, "after his grandfather."

Soon came Betsy Sparrow. She washed the baby, put a yellow petticoat and a linsey shirt on him, cooked dried berries with wild honey for Nancy, put the one-room cabin in better order, kissed Nancy and comforted her, and went home, saying she would come again in the morning.

Dennis rolled up in a bearskin and slept by the fireplace that night. He listened to the crying of the newborn child once in the night and the feet of the father moving on the dirt floor to help the mother and the little one. In the morning he took a long look at the baby and said to himself, "Its skin looks just like red cherry pulp squeezed dry, in wrinkles."

He asked if he could hold the baby. Nancy, as she passed the little one into Dennis' arms, said, "Be keerful, Dennis, fur you air the fust boy he's ever seen." Dennis swung the baby back and forth, keeping up a chatter about how tickled he was to have a new cousin to play with. The baby screwed up its face and began crying with no letup. Dennis turned to Betsy Sparrow, handed her the baby and said, "Aunt, take him! He'll never come to much."

Thus the birthday scene reported years later by Dennis Hanks whose nimble mind sometimes invented more than he saw or heard. Peggy Walters, too, years later, gave the scene as her memory served: "I was twenty years old, then, and helping to bring a baby into the world was more of an event to me than it became afterward. But I was married young, and had a baby of my own, and I had helped mother who was quite famous as a granny woman. It was Saturday afternoon when Tom Lincoln sent over and asked me to come. They sent for Nancy's two aunts, Mis' Betsy Sparrow and Mis' Polly Friend. I was there before them, and we all had quite a spell to wait, and we got everything ready. Nancy had a good feather-bed under her; it wasn't a goose-feather bed, hardly anyone had that kind then, but good hen feathers. And she had blankets enough. A little girl there, two years old, Sarah, went to sleep before much of anything happened.

"Nancy had about as hard a time as most women, I reckon, easier than some and maybe harder than a few. The baby was born just about sunup, on Sunday morning. Nancy's two aunts took the baby and washed him and dressed him, and I looked after Nancy. And I remember after the baby was born, Tom came and stood beside the bed and looked down at Nancy lying there, so pale and so tired, and he stood there with that sort of hang-dog look that a man has, sort of guilty like, but mighty proud, and he says to me, 'Are you sure she's all right, Mis' Walters?' And Nancy kind of stuck out her hand and reached for his, and said, 'Yes, Tom, I'm all right.' And then she said, 'You're glad it's a boy, Tom, aren't you? So am I.' "

Whatever the exact particulars, the definite event on that 12th of February, 1809, was the birth of a boy they named Abraham after his grandfather who had been killed by Indians—born in silence and pain from a wilderness mother on a bed of perhaps cornhusks and perhaps hen feathers—with perhaps a laughing child prophecy later that he would "never come to much."

In the spring of 1811 Tom Lincoln moved his family ten miles northeast to a 230-acre farm he had bought on Knob Creek, where the soil was a little richer and there were more neighbors. The famous Cumberland Trail, the main pike from Louisville to Nashville, ran nearby the new log cabin Tom built, and they could see covered wagons with settlers heading south, west, north, peddlers with tinware and notions, gangs of slaves or "kaffles" moving on foot ahead of an overseer or slave trader on horseback, and sometimes in dandy carriages congressmen or legislative members going to sessions at Louisville.

Here little Abe grew out of one shirt into another, learned to walk and talk and as he grew bigger how to be a chore boy, to run errands, carry water, fill the woodbox, clean ashes from the fireplace. He learned the feel of blisters on his hands from using a hoe handle on rows of beans, onions, corn, potatoes. He ducked out of the way of the heels of the stallion and two brood mares his father kept and paid taxes on. That Knob Creek farm in their valley set round by high hills and deep gorges was the first home Abe Lincoln remembered. He told later how one Saturday afternoon other boys planted the corn in what was called "the big field" of seven acres. "I dropped the pumpkin seed. I dropped two seeds every other hill and every other row. The next Sunday morning there came a big rain in the hills, it did not rain a drop in the valley but the water coming down through the gorges washed ground, corn, pumpkin seeds and all clear off the field."

Again there were quiet and anxious days in 1812 when another baby was on the way; again came neighbor helpers and Nancy gave birth to her third child. They named him Thomas but he died a few days after and Sarah and Abe saw, in a coffin their father made, the little cold still face and made their first acquaintance with the look of death in a personal grief in their own one-room cabin.

Four miles a day Sarah and Abe walked when school kept and they were not needed at home. In a log schoolhouse with a dirt floor and one door, seated on puncheon benches with no backs, they learned the alphabet A to Z

and numbers one to ten. It was called a "blab school"; the
pupils before reciting read their lessons out loud to themselves to show they were busy studying. Their first teacher
was Zachariah Riney, a Catholic, and the second one, Caleb
Hazel, a former tavernkeeper. Under them young Abe
learned to write and to like forming letters and shaping
words. He said later that "anywhere and everywhere that
lines could be drawn, there he improved his capacity for
writing." He scrawled words with charcoal, he shaped them
in the dust, in sand, in snow. Writing had a fascination for
him.

Tom Lincoln worked hard and had a reputation for paying his debts. One year he was appointed a "road surveyor"
to keep a certain stretch of road in repair, another time was
named appraiser for an estate, and an 1814 tax book listed
him as 15th among the 98 property owners named. In 1816
he paid taxes on four horses. In 1814, however, because of
a flaw in title he sold his Mill Creek farm for 18 pounds less
than he had paid for it; the tract survey in one place read
"west" where it should have read "east." Another suit involved his title to the Nolin Creek farm, still another aimed
to dispossess him of the Knob Creek farm. Meantime slavery was on the rise and in 1816 there were 1,238 slaves on
the tax lists of Hardin County, one taxpayer owning 58
Negro slaves, men, women and children, on the books
valued along with horses, cows and other livestock. So when
Tom Lincoln in 1816 decided to move to Indiana it was, as
Abe later wrote, "partly on account of slavery; but chiefly
on account of the difficulty in land titles."

In December 1816, Tom Lincoln with Nancy, Sarah,
Abe, four horses and their most needed household goods,
made their breakaway from Kentucky, moving north and
crossing the Ohio River into land then Perry County, later
Spencer County, Indiana. They traveled a wild raw country,
rolling land with trees everywhere, tall oaks and elms,
maples, birches, dogwood, underbrush tied down by ever-
winding grapevines, thin mist and winter damp rising from
the ground as Tom, with Abe perhaps helping, sometimes
went ahead with an ax and hacked out a trail. "It was a

wild region, with many bears and other wild animals still in the woods," Abe wrote later, where "the panther's scream, filled night with fear" and "bears preyed on the swine." A lonesome country, settlers few, "about one human being to each square mile," families two and three miles apart.

They had toiled and hacked their way through wilderness when about 16 miles from the Ohio River they came to a rise of ground somewhat open near Little Pigeon Creek. Here the whole family pitched in and threw together a pole shed or "half-faced camp," at the open side a log fire kept burning night and day. In the next weeks of that winter Tom Lincoln, with help from neighbors and young Abe, now nearly eight, erected a cabin 18 by 20 feet, with a loft. Abe later wrote that he "though very young, was large of his age, and had an axe put into his hands at once; and was almost constantly handling that most useful instrument." The chinking of wet clay and grass ("wattle and daub") between the logs in the new cabin had not been finished in early February when something happened that a boy remembers after he is a grown man. Years later Abe wrote, "At this place A.[braham] took an early start as a hunter, which was never much improved afterwards. A few days before the completion of his eighth year, in the absence of his father, a flock of wild turkeys approached the new log-cabin, and A.[braham] with a rifle gun, standing inside, shot through a crack and killed one of them." Then came another sentence, "He has never since pulled a trigger on any larger game," making it clear that when they had deer or bear meat or other food from "larger game," it was not from his shooting. He didn't like shooting to kill and didn't care for a reputation as a hunter.

When Tom Lincoln built this cabin he didn't own the land it stood on. He was a "squatter." Not until October 15, 1817, after a 90-mile overland trip to Vincennes did he enter his claim for a quarter section of land, paying a first installment of $16 then and in December $64. The Government was selling him the land at $2.00 an acre; the $80 he had paid was one-fourth of the purchase price and he would have a clear title when he paid the other three-fourths. It had been a hard year, "pretty pinching times," as Abe put

it later. They had to chop down trees, clear away underbrush, on what few acres they planted after plowing the
hard unbroken sod. Their food was mostly game shot in
the woods nearby, deer, bear, wild turkeys, ducks, geese.
Wild pigeons in flocks sometimes darkened the sky. Their
cabin lighting at night was from fire logs, pine knots, or
hog fat. Sarah and Abe went barefoot from late spring till
autumn frosts, brought home nuts and wild fruits, watched
sometimes in the excitement of their father smoking out a
bee tree for the honey. One drawback was water supply.
Abe or Sarah had to walk nearly a mile to fetch spring
water. Tom dug several wells but they all went dry.

They were part of the American Frontier, many others
like them breaking ground never before broken, settling a
new midwest country. On wagons by thousands slipping
through the passes of the eastern mountains, or on flatboats,
scows and steamboats on the Ohio River, they were heading
west for the $2.00-an-acre Government land. Along pikes,
roads and trails heading west were broken wagon wheels
with grass growing up over the spokes and hubs, and
nearby perhaps a rusty skillet and the bones of horses and
men. They had stuck it out and lost. A saying, "The cow-
ards never started and the weak ones died by the way," was
unfair to the strong ones who died by the way of sudden
maladies or long rains, windstorms, howling blizzards.

Some of those who came were hungry, even lustful, for
land. Some were hunters, adventurers, outlaws, fugitives.
Most were hoping for a home of their own. In December
1816, when the Lincolns came to Pigeon Creek, enough
settlers had arrived in Indiana for it to be "admitted to the
Union." It could be about then little Abe asked the solemn
question, "The Union? What is the Union?"

A wagon one day late in 1817 brought into the Lincoln
clearing their good Kentucky neighbors Tom and Betsy
Sparrow and the odd quizzical 17-year-old Dennis Friend
Hanks. For some years Dennis would be a chum of Abe's
and on occasion would make free to say, "I am base born,"
explaining that his mother bore him before she married one
Levi Hall. The Sparrows were to live in the Lincoln pole
shed till they could locate land and settle. Hardly a year

had passed, however, when Tom and Betsy Sparrow were taken down with the "milk sick," beginning with a whitish coat on the tongue, resulting, it was supposed, from cows eating white snakeroot or other growths that poisoned their milk. Tom and Betsy Sparrow died and were buried in September on a little hill in a clearing in the timbers nearby.

Soon after, there came to Nancy Hanks Lincoln that white coating of the tongue; her vitals burned; the tongue turned brownish; her feet and hands grew cold and colder, her pulse slow and slower. She knew she was dying, called for her children, and spoke to them her last dim choking words. Death came October 5, 1818, the banners of autumn flaming their crimsons over tall oaks and quiet maples. On a bed of poles cleated to the corner of the cabin, the body of Nancy Hanks Lincoln lay in peace and silence, the eyelids closed down in unbroken rest. To the children who tiptoed in, stood still, cried their tears of want and longing, whispered and heard only their own whispers answering, she looked as though new secrets had come to her in place of the old secrets given up with the breath of life.

Tom Lincoln took a log left over from the building of the cabin, and he and Dennis Hanks whipsawed it into planks, planed the planks smooth, and made them of a measure for a box to bury the dead wife and mother in. Little Abe, with a jackknife, whittled pine-wood pegs. And while Dennis and Abe held the planks, Tom bored holes and stuck the whittled pegs through the holes. This was the coffin they carried next day to the little timber clearing nearby, where a few weeks before they had buried Tom and Betsy Sparrow.

So Nancy Hanks Lincoln died, 34 years old, a pioneer sacrifice, with memories of monotonous, endless everyday chores, of mystic Bible verses read over and over for their promises, of blue wistful hills and a summer when the crab-apple blossoms flamed white and she carried a boy child into the world.

A hard year followed with 12-year-old Sarah as housekeeper and cook, and Tom Lincoln with the help of Dennis and Abe trying to clear more land, plant it, and make the farm a go. It was the year Abe was driving a horse at the

mill. While he was putting a whiplash to the nag and calling, "Git up, you old hussy; git up, you old hussy," the
horse let fly a fast hind foot that knocked Abe down and
out of his senses just as he yelled, "Git up." He lay bleeding, was taken home, washed, put to bed, and lay all night
unconscious. He spoke of it afterward as a mystery of the
human mind, and later wrote of himself, "In his tenth year
he was kicked by a horse, and apparently killed for a time."
Instead of dying, as was half expected, he came to, saying,
"You old hussy," thus finishing what he started to say before he was knocked down and out.

Lonesome days came for Abe and Sarah in November
when their father went away, promising to come back. He
headed for Elizabethtown, Kentucky, through woods and
across the Ohio River, to the house of the widow Sarah
Bush Johnston. They said he argued straight-out: "I have
no wife and you no husband. I came a-purpose to marry
you. I knowed you from a gal and you knowed me from a
boy. I've no time to lose; and if you're willin' let it be done
straight off." She answered, "I got a few little debts," gave
him a list and he paid them; and they were married December 2, 1819.

He could write his name; she "made her mark." Why the
two of them took up with each other so quickly Dennis
Hanks later said, "Tom had a kind o' way with women, an'
maybe it was somethin' she took comfort in to have a man
that didn't drink an' cuss none."

Abe and Sarah had a nice surprise one morning when
four horses and a wagon came into their clearing, and their
father jumped off, then Sarah Bush Lincoln, the new wife
and mother, then her three children by her first husband,
Sarah Elizabeth (13), Matilda (10), and John D. Johnston
(9 years old). Next off the wagon came a feather mattress
and pillows, a black walnut bureau, a large clothes chest, a
table, chairs, pots and skillets, knives, forks, spoons.

"Here's your new mammy," his father told Abe as the
boy looked up at a strong, large-boned, rosy woman, with
a kindly face and eyes, a steady voice, steady ways. From
the first she was warm and friendly for Abe's hands to

touch. And his hands roved with curiosity over a feather pillow and a feather mattress.

The one-room cabin now sheltered eight people to feed and clothe. At bedtime the men and boys undressed first, the women and girls following, and by the code of decent folk no one was abashed. Dennis and Abe climbed on pegs to the loft for their sleep and liked it when later the logs were chinked against the rain or snow coming in on them. Dennis said "Aunt Sairy," the new mother, "had faculty and didn't 'pear to be hurried or worried none," that she got Tom to put in a floor and make "some good beds and cheers." Abe, like Dennis, said "cheers"; if he said "chairs" he would be taken as "uppety" and "too fine-haired."

In the earlier years he wore buckskin breeches and moccasins, a tow linen shirt and coonskin cap, "the way we all dressed them days," said Dennis Hanks. For winter snow and slush they had "birch bark, with hickory bark soles, stropped on over yarn socks." And later, "when it got so we could keep chickens, an' have salt pork an' corn dodgers, an' gyardin saas an' molasses, an' have jeans pants an' cowhide boots to wear, we felt as if we was gittin' along in the world."

Eleven-year-old Abe went to school again. Years later he wrote of where he grew up, "There were some schools, so called; but no qualification was ever required of a teacher, beyond 'readin', writin', and cipherin' ' to the Rule of Three. If a straggler supposed to understand latin, happened to sojourn in the neighborhood, he was looked upon as a wizard." School kept at Pigeon Creek when a schoolmaster happened to drift in, usually in winter, and school was out when he drifted away. Andrew Crawford taught Abe in 1820, James Swaney two years later, and after a year of no school Abe learned from Azel Dorsey. The schoolmasters were paid by the parents in venison, hams, corn, animal skins and other produce. Four miles from home to school and four miles to home again Abe walked for his learning, saying later that "all his schooling did not amount to one year."

Abe kept his school sum book sheets as though they might be worth reading again with such rhymes as:

Abraham Lincoln is my nam
And with my pen I wrote the same
I wrote in both hast and speed
and left it here for fools to read

Abraham Lincoln his hand and pen
he will be good but god knows When

Dennis Hanks made an ink of blackberry briar root and copperas, an "ornery ink," he called it. And Abe with a turkey-buzzard quill would write his name and say, "Denny, look at that, will you? *Abraham Lincoln!* That stands fur me. Don't look a blamed bit like me!" And, said Dennis, "He'd stand and study it a spell. 'Peared to mean a heap to Abe."

Having learned to read Abe read all the books he could lay his hands on. Dennis, years later, tried to remember his cousin's reading habits. "I never seen Abe after he was twelve 'at he didn't have a book some'ers 'round. He'd put a book inside his shirt an' fill his pants pockets with corn dodgers, an' go off to plow or hoe. When noon come he'd set down under a tree, an' read an' eat. In the house at night, he'd tilt a cheer by the chimbly, an' set on his backbone an' read. I've seen a feller come in an' look at him, Abe not knowin' anybody was round, an' sneak out agin like a cat, an' say, 'Well, I'll be darned.' It didn't seem natural, nohow, to see a feller read like that. Aunt Sairy's never let the children pester him. She always said Abe was goin' to be a great man some day. An' she wasn't goin' to have him hendered."

They heard Abe saying, "The things I want to know are in books; my best friend is the man who'll git me a book I ain't read." One fall afternoon he walked to see John Pitcher, a lawyer at Rockport, nearly 20 miles away, and borrowed a book he heard Pitcher had. A few days later, with his father and Dennis and John Hanks he shucked corn from early daylight till sundown. Then after supper he read the book till midnight, and next day at noon hardly knew the taste of his corn bread because of the book in front of him. So they told it.

He read many hours in the family Bible, the only book in their cabin. He borrowed and read *Aesop's Fables*, *Pilgrim's Progress*, *Robinson Crusoe*, Grimshaw's *History of the United States*, and Weems' *The Life of George Washington, with Curious Anecdotes, Equally Honorable to Himself and Exemplary to His Young Countrymen*. Books lighted lamps in the dark rooms of his gloomy hours.

When John Hanks, a cousin of Nancy Hanks, came to live with them about 1823, there were nine persons sleeping, eating, washing, mending, dressing and undressing in the one-room cabin, gathered close to the fireplace in zero weather. John Hanks and Dennis, with some neighbors, seemed to agree that while Abe wasn't "lazy" his mind was often on books to the neglect of work. A neighbor woman sized him up, "He could work when he wanted to, but he was no hand to pitch in like killing snakes." John Romine remarked, "Abe Lincoln worked for me . . . didn't love work half as much as his pay. He said to me one day that his father taught him to work, but he never taught him to love it."

When rain soaked Weems' *Life of Washington* that Josiah Crawford had loaned him, he confessed he had been careless and pulled fodder three days to pay for the book, made a clean sweep, till there wasn't an ear on a cornstalk in the field of Josiah Crawford.

Farm boys in evenings at the store in Gentryville, a mile and a half from the Lincoln cabin, talked about how Abe Lincoln was always digging into books, picking a piece of charcoal to write on the fire shovel, shaving off what he wrote, and then writing more. Dennis Hanks said, "There's suthin' peculiarsome about Abe." It seemed that Abe made books tell him more than they told other people. The other farm boys had gone to school and read *The Kentucky Preceptor*, but Abe picked out such a question as "Who has the most right to complain, the Indian or the Negro?" and would talk about it, up and down in the cornfields. When he read in a book about a boat that came near a magnetic rock, and how the magnets in the rock pulled all the nails out of the boat so it went to pieces and the people in the boat found themselves floundering in water, Abe thought it was interesting and told it to others. When he sat with the girl, Kate Roby, with their bare feet in the creek, and she spoke of the moon rising, he explained to her it was the earth moving and not the moon—the moon only seemed to rise. Kate was surprised at such knowledge.

The years pass and Abe Lincoln grows up, at 17 standing six feet, nearly four inches, long-armed with rare strength in his muscles. At 18 he could take an ax at the end of the handle and hold it out from his shoulders in a straight horizontal line, easy and steady. He could make his ax flash and bite into a sugar maple or a sycamore, one neighbor saying, "He can sink an ax deeper into wood than any man I ever saw." He learned how suddenly life can spring a surprise. One day in the woods, as he was sharpening a wedge on a log, the ax glanced, nearly took his thumb off, and the cut after healing left a white scar for life. "You never cuss a good ax," was a saying then.

Sleep came deep to him after work outdoors, clearing timberland for crops, cutting brush and burning it, splitting rails, pulling crosscut saw and whipsaw, driving the shovel-plow, harrowing, spading, planting, hoeing, cradling grain, milking cows, helping neighbors at house-raisings, logrollings, corn-huskings, hog killings. He found he was fast and strong against other boys in sports. He earned board, clothes and lodgings, sometimes, working for a neighbor farmer.

Often Abe worked alone in the timbers, daylong with only the sound of his own ax, or his own voice speaking to himself, or the crackling and swaying of branches in the wind, or the cries and whirrs of animals, of brown and silver-gray squirrels, of partridges, hawks, crows, turkeys, grouse, sparrows and the occasional wildcat. In wilderness loneliness he companioned with trees, with the faces of open sky and weather in changing seasons, with that individual one-man instrument, the ax. Silence found him for her own. In the making of him, the element of silence was immense.

On a misunderstanding one time between Lincoln and William Grigsby, Grigsby flared so mad he challenged Abe to a fight. Abe looked at Grigsby, smiled and said the fight ought to be with John D. Johnston, Abe's stepbrother. The day was set, each man with his seconds. The two fighters, stripped to the waist, mauled at each other with bare knuckles. A crowd formed a ring and stood cheering, yelling, hissing, and after a while saw Johnston getting the worst of it. The ring of the crowd was broken when Abe shouldered his way through, stepped out, took hold of Grigsby and threw him out of the center of the fight ring. Then, so they said, Abe Lincoln called out, "I'm the big buck of this lick," and his eyes sweeping the circle of the crowd he challenged, "If any of you want to try it, come on and whet your horns." Wild fist-fighting came and for months around the store in Gentryville they argued about which gang whipped the other.

Asked by Farmer James Taylor if he could kill a hog, Abe answered, "If you will risk the hog I'll risk myself." He put barefoot boys to wading in a mud puddle near the horse trough, picked them up one by one, carried them to the house upside down, and walked their muddy feet across the ceiling. The stepmother came in, laughed at the foot tracks, told Abe he ought to be spanked—and he cleaned the ceiling so it looked new.

Education came to the youth Abe by many ways outside of schools and books. As he said later, he "picked up" education. He was the letter writer for the family and for neighbors. As he wrote he read the words out loud. He asked questions, "What do you want to say in the letter? How do you want to say it? Are you sure that's the best way to say it? Or do you think we can fix up a better way to say it?" This was a kind of training in grammar and English composition.

He walked 30 miles to a courthouse to hear lawyers speak and to see how they argued and acted. He heard roaring and ranting political speakers—and mimicked them. He listened to wandering evangelists who flung their arms and tore the air with their voices—and mimicked them. He told droll stories with his face screwed up in different ways. He tried to read people as keenly as he read books. He drank enough drams of whisky to learn he didn't like the taste and it wasn't good for his mind or body. He smoked enough

tobacco to learn he wouldn't care for it. He heard rollicking
and bawdy verses and songs and kept some of them for
their earthy flavor and sometimes meaningful intentions.

His stepmother was a rich silent force in his life. The
family and the neighbors spoke of her sagacity and gump-
tion, her sewing and mending, how spick-and-span she kept
her house, her pots, pans and kettles. Her faith in God
shone in works more than words, and hard as life was, she
was thankful to be alive. She understood Abe's gloomy
spells better than anyone else and he named her as a deep
influence in him. "Abe never spoke a cross word to me,"
she said and she found him truthful. Matilda in a wild
prank hid and leaped out onto Abe's back to give him a
scare in a lonely timber. Pulling her hands against his shoulders and pressing her knees against his back, she brought
him down to the ground. His ax blade cut her ankle and
strips from his shirt and her dress had to be torn to stop
the bleeding. By then she was sobbing over what to tell her
mother; on Abe's advice she told her mother the whole
truth.

When Abe's sister Sarah, a year after marrying Aaron
Grigsby, died in childbirth in 1828, it was Sarah Bush Lincoln who spoke comfort to the nearly 19-year-old son of
Nancy Hanks at the burial of his sister. Yet somehow the
stepmother couldn't lessen the bitterness Abe held toward
Aaron Grigsby, whether he blamed Grigsby for neglect of
his sister or something else. Two brothers of Aaron, Reuben and Charles Grigsby, on the same day were marrying
Betsy Ray and Matilda Hawkins and purposely forgot to
invite Abe to the double wedding. It was then he put into
circulation a piece of writing titled "The Chronicles of
Reuben," which had many in the neighborhood tittering if
not laughing out loud at the Grigsbys. It told of what a
sumptuous affair it was, with music of harps, viols, rams'
horns, and "acclamations" at the wedding feast. "Finally
. . . the waiters took the two brides upstairs, placing one in
a bed at the right hand of the stairs and the other on the
left. The waiters came down, and Nancy the mother then
gave directions to the waiters of the bridegrooms, and they
took them upstairs but placed them in the wrong beds. The

waiters then all came downstairs. But the mother, being fearful of a mistake, made inquiry of the waiters, and learning the true facts took the light and sprang upstairs. It came to pass she ran to one of the beds and exclaimed, 'O Lord, Reuben, you are in bed with the wrong wife.' The young men, both alarmed at this, sprang out of bed and ran with such violence against each other they came near knocking each other down. The tumult gave evidence to those below that the mistake was certain. At last they all came down and had a long conversation about who made the mistake, but it could not be decided. So endeth the chapter."

A mile across the fields from the Lincoln home was the Pigeon Creek Baptist Church, a log meetinghouse put up in 1822. On June 7, 1823, William Barker, who kept the minutes and records, wrote that the church "received Brother Thomas Lincoln by letter." He was elected the next year with two neighbors to serve as a committee of visitors to the Gilead church, and served three years as church trustee. Strict watch was kept on the conduct of members and Tom served on committees to look into reported misconduct between husbands and wives, brothers and sisters, of neighbor against neighbor.

Most of the church people could read only the shortest words in the Bible, or none at all. They sat in the log meetinghouse on the split-log benches their own axes had shaped, listening to the preacher reading from the Bible. To confess, to work hard, to be saving, to be decent, were the actions most praised and pleaded for in the sermons of the preachers. Next to denying Christ, the worst sins among the men were drinking, gambling, fighting, loafing, and among the women, gossiping, backbiting, sloth and slack habits. A place named Hell where men, women and children burned everlastingly in fires was the place where sinners would go.

In a timber grove one summer Sunday afternoon, a preacher yelled, shrieked, wrung his hands in sobs of hysterics, until a row of women were laid out to rest and recover in the shade of an oak tree, after they had moaned, shaken, danced up and down, worn themselves out with "the jerks" and fainted. And young Abe Lincoln, looking on, with sober face and quiet heart, was thoughtful about what he saw before his eyes.

Some families had prayers in the morning on arising, grace at breakfast, noon prayers and grace at dinner, grace at supper and evening prayers at bedtime. In those households, the manger at Bethlehem was a white miracle, the black Friday at Golgotha and the rocks rolled away for the resurrection were nearby realities of terror and comfort, dark power and sustenance. The Sabbath day, Christmas, Easter, were days for sober thoughts and sober faces, resignation, contemplation, rest, silence.

Beyond Indiana was something else; beyond the timber and underbrush, the malaria, milk sick, blood, sweat, tears, hands hard and crooked as the roots of walnut trees, there must be something else.

After a day of plowing corn, watching crop pests, whittling bean poles, capturing strayed cattle and fixing up a hole in a snake-rail fence, while the housewife made a kettle of soap, hoed the radishes and cabbages, milked the cows, and washed the baby, there was a consolation leading to easy slumber in the beatitudes: "Blessed are the meek: for they shall inherit the earth . . . Blessed are the peacemakers: for they shall be called the children of God." It was not their business to be sure of the arguments and the invincible logic that might underlie the Bible promises of Heaven and threats of Hell; it was for this the preacher was hired and paid by the corn, wheat, whisky, pork, linen, wool and other produce brought by the members of the church.

The Sabbath was not only a day for religious meetings. After the sermon, the members, who rode horses many miles to the meetinghouse, talked about crops, weather, births and deaths, the growing settlements, letters just come, politics, Indians and land titles.

Young Abraham Lincoln saw certain of these Christians with a clean burning fire, with inner reckonings that prompted them to silence or action or speech, and they could justify themselves with a simple and final explanation that all things should be done decently and in order. Their door strings were out to sinners deep in mire, to scorners seemingly past all redemption; the Jesus who lived with law-breakers, thieves, lepers crying "Unclean!" was an instrument and a light vivifying into everyday use the abstractions behind the words "malice," "mercy," "charity."

They met understanding from the solemn young Lincoln who had refused to join his schoolmates in putting fire on a live mud turtle, and had written a paper arguing against cruelty to animals; who would bother to lug on his shoulders and save from freezing a man overloaded with whisky; who would get up before daylight and cross the fields to listen to the weird disconnected babbling of the young man, Matthew Gentry.

The footsteps of death, silent as the moving sundial of a tall sycamore, were a presence. Time and death, the partners who operate leaving no more track than mist, had to be reckoned in the scheme of life. A day is a shooting star. The young Lincoln had copied a rhyme:

> Time! what an empty vapor 'tis!
>   And days how swift they are:
> Swift as an Indian arrow—
>   Fly on like a shooting star,
> The present moment just is here,
>   Then slides away in haste,
> That we can never say they're ours,
>   But only say they're past.

His mother Nancy Hanks and her baby that didn't live, his sister Sarah and her baby that didn't live—time and the empty vapor had taken them; the rain and the snow beat on their graves. Matthew Gentry, son of the richest man in that part of Indiana, was in his right mind and then began babbling week in and week out the droolings of a disordered brain—time had done it without warning. On both man and the animals, time and death had their way. In a single week, the milk sick had taken four milk cows and 11 calves of Dennis Hanks, while Dennis too had nearly gone under.

At the Pigeon Creek settlement, while the structure of his bones, the build and hang of his torso and limbs, took shape, other elements, invisible yet permanent, traced their lines in the tissues of his head and heart.

Young Abraham had worked as a farm hand and ferry helper for James Taylor, who lived at the mouth of Anderson Creek and operated a ferry across the Ohio River. Here Abe saw steamboats, strings of flatboats loaded with farm produce, other boats with cargoes from manufacturing centers. Houseboats, arks, sleds, flatboats with small cabins in which families lived and kept house, floated toward their new homesteads; on some were women washing, children playing. Here was the life flow of a main artery of American civilization, at a vivid time of growth. Here at 18 Abe built a scow and was taking passengers from Bates Landing to steamboats in midstream. Two travelers anxious to get on a steamer came one day and he sculled them out and lifted their trunks on board. Each threw him a silver half-dollar. It gave him a new feeling; the most he had ever earned was 31 cents a day. And when one of the half-dollars slipped from him and sank in the river, that too gave him a new feeling.

One day, at a signal from the Kentucky shore, Lincoln rowed across. Two men jumped out of the brush and said they were going to "duck" him in the river. But looking him over more closely, they changed their minds. They were John and Lin Dill, brothers operating a ferry. All three went to Justice of the Peace Samuel Pate, near Lewisport, where John T. Dill swore out a warrant for the arrest of Abraham Lincoln, charged, on trial, with running a ferry without a license, in violation of Kentucky law. Lincoln testified he had carried passengers from the Indiana shore only to the middle of the river, never to the Kentucky shore. Squire Pate dismissed the warrant against Lincoln; the Dills went away sore, and Lincoln had a long talk with Squire Pate and made a friend. Afterward on days when no passengers were in sight he sometimes sculled over and watched Squire Pate on "law day" handle cases.

James Gentry, with the largest farms in the Pigeon Creek clearings, and a landing on the Ohio River, had looked Lincoln over. He believed Abe could take a cargo of produce down the Mississippi to New Orleans. Abe built a flatboat, cut oaks for a double bottom of stout planks, and a deck shelter, two pairs of long oars at bow and stern, a check post, and a setting pole for steering. In charge of the boat Mr. Gentry had placed his son Allen, the 19-year-old Lincoln, "a hired hand," as he called himself. They loaded the boat and pushed off for a thousand-mile trip on the wide, winding waterway, where flatboats were tied up at night to the riverbank, and floated and poled by day amid changing currents, strings of other flatboats, and in the paths of the proud white steamboats. The river bends ahead must be watched with ready oars and sweeps or the flatboat heads in to shore. Strong winds crook the course of the boat, sometimes blowing it ashore; one man must hustle off in a rowboat, tie a hawser to a tree or stump, while another man on the boat has a rope at the check post; and they slow her down. Warning signals must be given to other craft at night, by waving lantern or firewood. So the flatboat, the "broadhorn," went down the Father of Waters, four to six miles an hour, the crew frying their own pork and corn-meal cakes, washing their own shirts.

Below Baton Rouge, on the "Sugar Coast," they tied up at the plantation of Madame Duchesne one evening, put their boat in order, and dropped off to sleep. They woke to find seven Negroes on board trying to steal the cargo and kill the crew; the swift and long-armed Lincoln swung a crab-tree club, knocked some into the river, and with Allen Gentry chased others into the woods, both coming back to the boat bleeding. Lincoln laid a bandanna on a gash over his right eye that left a scar for life as it healed. Then they cut loose the boat and moved down the river.

At New Orleans they sold their cargo and flatboat and lingered a few days. For the first time young Lincoln saw a city of 40,000 people, a metropolis, a world port, with seagoing ships taking on cotton, sugar, tobacco and food-stuffs for Europe, a levee and wharves thick with planters, clerks, longshoremen and roustabouts loading and unloading cargoes. Sailors and deck hands from many nations and great world ports walked and straggled along, talking, shouting, roistering, their languages a fascinating jabber to the youths from Indiana. British, Yankee and French faces, Spanish, Mexican, Creole, the occasional free Negro and the frequent slave were on the streets. Gangs of chained slaves passed, headed for cotton plantations of a thousand and more acres. Women wearing bright slippers and flashy gowns; Creoles with dusks of eyes; quadroons and octoroons with soft elusive voices, streets lined with saloons and dens where men drank with men or chose from the women sipping their French wines or Jamaica rum at tables, sending signals with their eyes or fingers or openly slanging the sailors, rivermen, timber cruisers, and no lack of gamblers with dice or cards. An old city that had floated the flags of France and Britain and now of America. Here was a great and famous cathedral, here mansions of extravagant cost and upkeep, narrow streets with quaint iron grillwork fronting the second stories, live oaks drooping with Spanish moss, and many blocks of huts and hovels. The city had a feel of old times and customs, of mossy traditions, none of the raw and new as seen in Indiana.

Lincoln and Allen Gentry, heading for home after three months, rode an elegant steamboat up the Mississippi, the fare paid by James Gentry. Abe's wages at $8.00 a month, or what he hadn't spent out of $24, he paid over to his father, according to law and custom.

After a thousand miles of excitement and new sights every day, he worked a while in James Gentry's store in 1829. Then came a new excitement—Tom Lincoln was moving his family and kinfolk to Illinois where John Hanks had gone. A new outbreak of the milk sick had brought a neighborhood scare. Tom's farm wasn't paying well and John Hanks was writing letters about rich land and better crops. After buying 80 acres for $2.00 an acre and improving it 14 years, Tom sold the land to Charles Grigsby for $125 cash. Moving came natural to Tom; he could tell about the family that had moved so often their chickens knew the signs of another moving; the chickens would walk up to the mover, stretch flat on the ground, and put their feet up to be tied for the next wagon trip.

Tom and Sarah Lincoln on December 12, 1829, had been granted by the Pigeon Creek Baptist Church a "letter of Dismission" showing they were regular members in good standing, this for use in Illinois. Sister Nancy Grigsby protested she was "not satisfied with Brother and Sister Lincoln." The trustees took back the "letter of Dismission" but after investigation turned it back to Brother and Sister Lincoln and appointed Brother Lincoln on a committee to straighten out a squabble between Sister Nancy Grigsby and Sister Betsy Crawford, details of which went into the church records.

They made wagons that winter, of wood all through, pegs, cleats, hickory withes, knots of bark holding some parts together, though the wheel rims were iron. They loaded bedclothes, skillets, ovens, furniture on three wagons, ready to go early morning of March 1, 1830. Abraham Lincoln had been for some days a citizen who "had reached his majority"; he could vote at elections, was lawfully free from paying his wages to his father; he could come and go now; he was footloose.

Two of the wagons had two yoke of oxen each and one wagon had four horses. On the wagons were Tom and Sarah Bush Lincoln, her three children, John D. Johnston; Sarah, with her husband Dennis Hanks and their daughters Sarah Jane, Nancy M. and Harriet, and son John Talbot; Matilda, with her husband Squire Hall and their son John; and Abraham Lincoln on and off an ox wagon with a goad coaxing or prodding the animals and bawling at them to get along. They stopped where night found them, cooked supper, slept, and started at daybreak. What with the ground freezing at night and thawing in the day, the oxen and horses slipped and tugged, the wagon axles groaned, the wooden pegs and cleats squeaked—a journey, Lincoln said later, "slow and tiresome." They forded rivers and creeks, often breaking their way through ice; at one river, Lincoln was reported telling it, "My little dog jumped out of the wagon and the ice being thin he broke through and was struggling for life. I could not bear to lose my dog, and I jumped out of the wagon and waded waist deep in the ice and water, got hold of him and helped him out and saved him."

At the first stretch of the Grand Prairie they saw long levels of land running, with no slopes or hollows, straight to the horizon. Grass stood up six and eight feet high with roots so tough and deep that trees couldn't get rootholds. They met settlers saying the tough sod had broken many plows, but after the first year of seed corn the yield would run 50 bushels to the acre, wheat averaging 25 to 30 bushels, oats 40 to 60 bushels.

After traveling over 200 miles to Macon County, Illinois, they found John Hanks, who showed them the location he had picked for them on the north bank of the Sangamon River, about ten miles southwest of Decatur, land joining timber and prairie. John Hanks had already cut the logs for their cabin which soon was finished. They built a smokehouse and barn, cleared some 15 acres, split rails to fence it, planted corn, after which Abraham with John Hanks split 3,000 rails for two neighbors, and as "sodbusters" broke 30 acres of virgin prairie for John Hanks' brother Charles.

It was a change from the monotony of hard farm work in that summer of 1830 for Abraham to make his first political speech in Illinois. He had been delivering speeches to trees, stumps, rows of corn and potatoes, just practicing, by himself. But when two legislative candidates spoke at a campaign meeting in front of Renshaw's store in Decatur, Abraham stepped up and advocated improvement of the Sangamon River for better navigation.

Fall came and most of the Lincoln family went down with chills, fever and ague, Tom and Sarah using many doses of a quinine and whisky tonic mixture from a Decatur store. Then in December a blizzard filled the sky and piled snow two and a half feet on the ground. Soon another drive of snow made a four-foot depth of it on the level, with high drifts here and there. Rain followed, froze, and more snow covered the icy crust. Wolves took their way with deer and cattle who broke through the crust and stood helpless. Fodder crops went to ruin; cows, hogs and horses died in

the fields. Connections between houses, settlements, grain
mills, broke down; for days in 12-below-zero weather, families were cut off, living on parched corn. Some died of
cold, lacking wood to burn; some died of hunger, lacking
corn. Those who came through alive, in after years called
themselves "Snowbirds." Families like the Lincolns, with
little meat, corn and wood laid by, had it hard. Abraham
in February made a try at reaching the William Warnick
house, and crossing the Sangamon River broke through the
ice and got his feet wet. Going on the two miles to the
Warnick house, he nearly froze his feet. Mrs. Warnick put
his feet in snow to take out the frostbite, then rubbed them
with grease. For nine weeks that snow cover held the
ground. Spring thaws came and sheets of water spread in
wide miles on the prairies.

   As the roads became passable, the Lincoln family and
kin moved southeast a hundred miles to Coles County.
Abraham had other plans and didn't go with them. He had
"come of age."

Chapter 2

New Salem Days

In February 1831, John Hanks had made an agreement
with a man named Denton Offutt, a frontier hustler big
with promises and a hard drinker, that he, Abe Lincoln
and John D. Johnston would take a flatboat of cargo to
New Orleans. Offutt was to have the flatboat and cargo
ready and they were to meet him on the Sangamon River
near the village of Springfield as soon as the snow should
go off. With traveling by land made difficult by floods, they
bought a large canoe. And so, with his mother's cousin and
his stepbrother, in the spring of 1831, Abraham Lincoln,
22 years old, floated down the Sangamon River, going to a
new home, laughter and youth in his bones, in his heart a

few pennies of dreams, in his head a rag bag of thoughts he
could never expect to sell.

Leaving their canoe at Judy's Ferry and not finding Denton Offutt there, they walked to Springfield and at Andrew
Elliott's Buckhorn Tavern found Offutt lush with liquor
and promises and no flatboat. He hired them at $12 a
month and sent them to Government timberland, where
they cut down trees, got logs to Kirkpatrick's mill for
planks and gunwales. Near their shanty and camp on the
Sangamon River where the flatboat was shaping, the
Sangamon County assessor, Erastus Wright, saw Lincoln
in April with his "boots off, hat, coat and vest off. Pants
rolled up to his knees and shirt wet with sweat and comb-
ing his fuzzie hair with his fingers as he pounded away on
the boat."

In about four weeks they launched the boat, 80 feet long
and 18 feet wide, loaded the cargo of barreled pork, corn
and live hogs, and moved downstream from Sangamo
Town, steering away from snags and low water, Lincoln
on deck in blue homespun jeans, jacket, vest, rawhide boots
with pantaloons stuffed in, and a felt hat once black but
now, as the owner said, "sunburned till it was a combine of
colors." On April 19, rounding the curve of the Sangamon
at New Salem, the boat stuck on the Camron milldam, and
hung with one-third of her slanted downward over the edge
of the dam and filling slowly with water, while the cargo of
pork barrels was sliding slowly so as to overweight one end.
She hung there a day while all the people of New Salem
came down to look. Then they saw Lincoln getting part of
the cargo unloaded to the riverbank, boring a hole in the
flatboat end as it hung over the dam to let the water out,
plugging the hole, then dropping the boat over the dam and
reloading cargo. As she headed toward the Mississippi
water-course, New Salem talked about the cool head and
ready wit of the long-shanked young man.

Lincoln, Hanks and John D. Johnston floated down the
Mississippi River, meeting strings of flatboats and other
river craft. Hanks, away from home longer than expected,
left them at St. Louis. Stepping off the flatboat at New Orleans, Lincoln walked nearly a mile, on flatboats, to reach

shore. In New Orleans, Lincoln could read advertisements of traders, one giving notice: "I will at all times pay the highest cash prices for Negroes of every description, and will also attend to the sale of Negroes on commission, having a jail and yard fitted up expressly for boarding them." There were sellers advertising, "For sale—several likely girls from 10 to 18 years old, a woman 24, a very valuable woman 25, with three very likely children," while buyers indicated after the manner of one: "Wanted—I want to purchase twenty-five likely Negroes, between the ages of 18 and 25 years, male and female, for which I will pay the highest prices in cash."

Again Abraham could see the narrow cobblestoned streets and the women with rouged faces and teasing voices at the crib-house windows on side streets, Negroes shading from black to octoroon, ragged poor whites, sailors drunk and sober in a dozen different jargons, a dazzling parade of the humanly ugly and lovely in a mingling—what his eyes met again in the old strange city had him thoughtful and brooding. After a month or so, with Johnston, he took a steamboat north.

From New Orleans up the Mississippi on the steamboat and from St. Louis walking overland Lincoln must have wondered about New Salem village, the people there, his new job, the new life he was moving into. Offutt had rented the gristmill at the Sangamon River dam below the hilltop village and in St. Louis was buying a stock of goods for a new store. Lincoln was to be clerk in charge of store and mill at $15 a month and back room to sleep in. Arriving in late July Lincoln walked the village street, looked over its dozen or more cabins, searched faces he expected to see many times for many months.

On August 1, 1831, he cast his first ballot. The polls were in the home of John Camron where Lincoln was boarding and getting acquainted with Camron's 11 daughters who teased him about his long legs and arms and heard him admit he "wasn't much to look at." Voting by word of mouth, each voter spoke to the election judges his candidates' names. A judge then called out the voter's name and his

candidates, clerks recording the names "on poll sheets."
Lincoln voted for a Henry Clay Whig for Congress—and
against Joseph Duncan, then a Jackson man serving in Congress. He stayed around the polls most of the day talking
cheerily, telling stories, making friends and getting acquainted with the names and faces of nearly all the men
in the New Salem neighborhood.

The lizard story spun by the newcomer he said happened
in Indiana. In a meetinghouse deep in the tall timbers, a
preacher was delivering a sermon, wearing old-fashioned
baggy pantaloons fastened with one button and no suspenders, his shirt held at the collar by one button. In a
loud voice he announced his text, "I am the Christ, whom
I shall represent today." About then a little blue lizard ran
up under one pantaloon leg. The preacher went ahead with
his sermon, slapping his leg. After a while the lizard came
so high that the preacher was desperate, and, going on with
his sermon, unbuttoned the one button that held his pantaloons; they dropped down and with a kick were off. By
this time the lizard had changed his route and circled
around under the shirt at the back, and the preacher, repeating his text, "I am the Christ, whom I shall represent
today," loosened his one collar button and with one sweeping movement off came the shirt. The congregation sat
dazed, everything still for a minute; then a dignified elderly
lady stood up slowly and, pointing a finger toward the pulpit, called out at the top of her voice, "I just want to say
that if you represent Jesus Christ, sir, then I'm done with
the Bible."

A little later men were telling of Lincoln, Offutt and a
crew trying to load 30 large fat hogs onto a flatboat; the
hogs were slippery and stubborn and the crew couldn't
drive them on board. Offutt said, "Sew up their eyes,"
which was done, Lincoln helping, and writing it afterward,
"In their blind condition they could not be driven out of
the field they were in," so "they were tied and hauled on
carts to the boat."

Boarding in the John Camron house Lincoln could hear
at the eating table or in candlelight before bedtime how
young was the village, how it was built on hope and prom-

ise. It was only in January 1829 that Camron and his partner James Rutledge had permission from the state legislature to build the dam that Lincoln had come to know so
well. They had a survey made the following October, named
the place New Salem, and in December that year they had
sold their first lot for $12.50; on Christmas Day 1829 they
had their post office in the new store of Samuel Hill and
John McNeil. The growing village soon had three general
stores, a cooper, two carpenters, a blacksmith and wagon-
maker, a tanner, a hatter, a shoemaker, two doctors, a
carding machine, two saloons, some 25 families and about
100 people, a squire and two constables living nearby. In
easy driving distance were settlements of two to four or
more houses along creek beds or in groves—Petersburg,
Sand Ridge, Sugar Grove, Irish Grove, Clary's Grove, Indian Point, Athens, their trading center New Salem.

Far up in northern Illinois was a young village named
Chicago, also built on hope and promise, like New Salem
having about a dozen log cabins and a population of 100.
The wide stretch of prairie between New Salem and Chicago was yet to have its tall grass and tough grass roots
broken for crops from rich black soil. In southern Illinois
the pioneers chose to farm where the sod was easier to
break and near timber for firewood, fences, logs for cabins.
These pioneers came mostly from Kentucky and Tennessee
and had yet to see what crops could be raised on treeless
prairies. A young and growing country and no one more
sure and proud of New Salem's future than Denton Offutt,
promoter, booster and boomer. He saw Lincoln as honest
and able, picked him as a manager, told people, "He knows
more than any man in the United States." Somehow at this
particular time Offutt had an influence on Lincoln for good,
perhaps made Lincoln feel more sure of himself. Lincoln
never joined those who later blamed and belittled Offutt.
There was something near tenderness in the way that, years
later, Lincoln wrote, "Offutt, previously an entire stranger,
conceived a liking for A.[braham] and believing he could
turn him to account."

While waiting for Offutt in August 1831, Lincoln navigated a raft of household goods and a family, Texas bound,

from New Salem to Beardstown and walked back to New Salem, jingling good pay.

On a lot Offutt bought for $10, he and Lincoln built a cabin of logs for the new store. Offutt's goods arrived and Lincoln stacked shelves and corners. Soon stories got going about Lincoln's honesty, how he walked six miles to pay back a few cents a woman had overpaid for dry goods, and finding he had used a four-ounce weight instead of an eight, he walked miles to deliver to a woman the full order of tea she had paid for.

Offutt talked big about Lincoln as a wrestler and Bill Clary, who ran a saloon 30 steps north of the Offutt store, bet Offutt $10 that Lincoln couldn't throw Jack Armstrong, the Clary's Grove champion. Sports from miles around came to a level square next to Offutt's store to see the match; bets of money, knives, trinkets, tobacco, drinks, were put up. Armstrong, short and powerful, aimed from the first to get in close to his man and use his thick muscular strength. Lincoln held him off with long arms, wore down his strength, got him out of breath, surprised and "rattled." They pawed and clutched in many holds and twists till Lincoln threw Armstrong and had both shoulders to the grass. Armstrong's gang started toward Lincoln with cries and threats. Lincoln stepped to the Offutt store wall, braced himself, and told the gang he would fight, race or wrestle any who wanted to try him. Then Jack Armstrong broke through the gang, shook Lincoln's hand, told them Lincoln was "fair," and, "the best feller that ever broke into this settlement."

Some claimed it was a draw, and that after a long round of hard tussling and trying different holds, Lincoln said, "Jack, let's quit. I can't throw you—you can't throw me." One sure action everybody remembered was that Jack Armstrong gave Lincoln a warm handshake and they were close friends ever after. The Clary's Grove boys called on him sometimes to judge their horse races and cockfights, umpire their matches, and settle disputes. One story ran that Lincoln was on hand one day when an old man had agreed, for a gallon jug of whisky, to be rolled down a hill in a barrel. And Lincoln talked and laughed them out of doing it. He wasn't there on the day, as D. G. Burner told it, when the gang took an old man with a wooden leg, built a fire around the wooden leg, and held the man down till the wooden leg was burned off.

The Clary's Grove boys, it was told, had decided to see what stuff Abe had in him. First, he was to run a foot race with a man from Wolf. "Trot him out," said Abe. Second he was to wrestle with a man from Little Grove. "All right," said Abe. Third, he must fight a man from Sand Ridge. "Nothing wrong about that," said Abe. The foot racer from Wolf couldn't pass Abe. The man from Little Grove, short and heavy, stripped for action, ran at Abe like a battering-ram. Abe stepped aside, caught his man by the nape of the neck, threw him heels over head, and gave him a fall that nearly broke the bones. A committee from the boys came up and told him, "You have sand in your craw and we will take you into our crowd." This, perhaps half true, was beginning to be told by Henry Onstot and others.

When a small gambler tricked Bill Greene, Lincoln's helper at the store, Lincoln told Bill to bet him the best fur hat in the store that he [Lincoln] could lift a barrel of whisky from the floor and hold it while he took a drink from the bunghole. Bill hunted up the gambler and made the bet. Lincoln sat squatting on the floor, lifted the barrel off the floor, rolled it on his knees till the bunghole reached his mouth, took a mouthful, let the barrel down—and stood up and spat out the whisky. Bill won his bet. It was Bill Greene who on the witness stand once, when a lawyer asked him who were the principal citizens of New Salem, answered, "There are no principal citizens; every man in New Salem neighborhood is a principal citizen."

In spare hours Lincoln had sessions with Mentor Graham, the local schoolmaster, who told him of a grammar at John C. Vance's, six miles off; he walked the six miles, brought back the book, burned pine shavings at night in the Onstot cooper shop to light Samuel Kirkham's *English Grammar*. As he went further, he had Bill Greene hold the book and ask him questions. In the New Salem Debating Society, Lincoln in his first speech opened in a tone of apology, as though he wasn't sure of himself. He surprised both himself and those hearing him. James Rutledge, president of the society, was saying there was "more than wit and fun" in Abe's head.

In his work at the store, and in hours after work, he was meeting people, characters, faces, voices and motives, close up in a range and variety as never before in his life. James Rutledge, 50 years old, of medium height, warmhearted, square in dealings, religious, born in South Carolina, had lived in Georgia, Tennessee, Kentucky, in White County, Illinois, on Concord Creek seven miles north of New Salem. The third of his nine children, Ann Mayes Rutledge was 18, had auburn hair, blue eyes, a fair face, and Lincoln was to meet and know her. John M. Camron, Rutledge's partner and ten years younger, was a nephew of Mrs. Rutledge, had lived with or near them in White County and on Concord Creek. He was a massive, powerful man, had learned the millwright's trade, had become an ordained Cumberland Presbyterian minister, and sometimes preached in and around New Salem.

Dr. John Allen, a graduate of Dartmouth College Medical School, had left Vermont and come west for the climate, arriving in New Salem the same month as Lincoln. He was to prove himself a skilled physician and an earnest, obstinate man in his steady, quiet arguments against Negro slavery and alcoholic liquor. He went when called in all kinds of weather, sent bills for his services only to the well to do; all his fees from Sunday visits went into a fund for the church, the sick, the poor. Here was a Yankee for Lincoln to study; he had in his days met few Yankees.

There was Henry Sinco, a saloonkeeper, and Lincoln's vote August 1 had helped elect Sinco a village constable. There was James Pantier, who hunted big game, owned large tracts of land, wore a buckskin fringed shirt, sometimes had cured snake bites by rubbings and mumblings. "Uncle Jimmy" would come in from Sand Ridge to a Cumberland Presbyterian Church meeting in a schoolhouse, repeat the sermon as the preacher spoke it, nod approval or again shake a finger and in an undertone, "You are mistaken" or "Not so, brother."

Characters, men of personality and deed worth looking

at and studying, these pioneers. The father of Lincoln's good friend, James Short, was pointed at as a veteran of the Revolutionary War; he had become a wild turkey hunter, and once in blazing away at 50, had killed 16 turkeys. Another veteran, Daddy Boger, of service under George Washington, lived in Wolf, wove bushel baskets of white oak splints, and would come to the village with a basket nest under each arm, trade his baskets, rest a while, and then start home. Lincoln definitely saw history in these men; he had read about them.

Then there was Granny Spears of Clary's Grove, often helping at houses where a new baby had come; stolen by Indians when a girl and living with them she had learned how to use herbs and make salves; a little dried-up woman whose chin and nose curved out and nearly touched. Farmer Sampson, with a big family, could tell of his beef hides tanned by Philemon Morris, then taken to the cobbler Alex Ferguson who had the foot measures of the family, and, with a two-bushel sack, he was taking home a dozen pairs of shoes. Tall, erect, an impressive figure was the Reverend John M. Berry, an 1812 veteran, whose sermons and prayers touched on the liquor evil with added depth because of his acquaintance with many a hard drinker. Samuel Hill and John McNeil were the keenest traders in the village, their store doing more business than any other. Hill was hot-tempered, crafty, thrifty, often called stingy. McNeil's face and talk could puzzle people; what was going on in his head and heart he didn't report.

Young Mr. Lincoln in late 1831 and early 1832 studied a book of legal forms, signed as a witness to four deeds, wrote in his own hand several legal documents, a bill of sale and a bond, each beginning "Know all men by these presents." With the help of his good friend, Bowling Green, the justice of the peace, he was edging into law and how to write the simpler documents.

On March 9, 1832, came the boldest and most important paper he had ever written, telling the public he was stepping into politics as a candidate for the legislature of the State of Illinois. The *Sangamo Journal* at Springfield printed it and it was issued as a handbill. There was in it the tone of

a young man a little bashful about what he was doing—
and yet unafraid of his ideas and his platform, ready to debate them with any comer. A railroad for the service of
New Salem would cost too high; her one hope was steamboat traffic; therefore he favored all possible improvement
of the Sangamon River; "if elected, any measure in the legislature having this for its object, which may appear judi-
cious, will meet my approbation, and shall receive my support." He came out strong for education, books, religion,
morality. "That every man may receive at least, a moderate
education, and thereby be enabled to read the histories of
his own and other countries, by which he may duly appreciate the value of our free institutions, appears to be an
object of vital importance, even on this account alone, to
say nothing of the advantages and satisfaction to be derived
from all being able to read the scriptures and other works,
both of a religious and moral nature, for themselves." Thus,
for the benefit of any who might have heard otherwise, the
young politician showed himself as favoring books, schools,
churches, the Scriptures, religion, morality.

Touching on "the practice of loaning money at exorbitant
rates of interest," it seemed to him as though "we are never
to have an end to this baneful and corroding system." He
mentioned "a direct tax of several thousand dollars annu-
ally laid on each county, for the benefit of a few individuals
only," which might require "a law made setting a limit to
the rates of usury." In his opinion such a law could be made
"without materially injuring any class of people." He mentioned no specific cases of usury or of "cheating the law"
but seemed to assume that his readers would know who and
what he was talking about in three curious sentences: "In
cases of extreme necessity, there could always be means
found to cheat the law, while in all other cases it would
have its intended effect. I would not favor . . . a law upon
this subject, which might be very easily evaded. Let it be
such that the labor and difficulty of evading it, could only
be justified in cases of the greatest necessity."

He was young and would admit "it is probable I have
already been more presuming than becomes me." What
was his ambition? "I have no other so great as that of being

truly esteemed of my fellow men, by rendering myself worthy of their esteem." He was throwing his case "exclusively upon the independent voters of this county," making clear, "I was born and have ever remained in the most humble walks of life. I have no wealthy or popular relations to recommend me." He closed in a manner having the gray glint of his eyes and the loose hang of his long arms: "If the good people in their wisdom shall see fit to keep me in the background, I have been too familiar with disappointments to be very much chagrined." That was all. He had made his first real start in politics.

In this same March of 1832, excitement ran high in the Sangamon country over the small, light-draft steamboat *Talisman* with merchandise cargo from Cincinnati arriving at Beardstown on the Illinois River, ready, when the ice jams cleared, to make the trip upstream to New Salem and Springfield. The shipmaster had asked for help; a boatload of men, Lincoln one of them, worked with long-handled poleaxes and crowbars clearing the channel of snags and overhanging branches. The *Talisman*, puffing her smoke and blowing her whistle, moved up the Sangamon; at New Salem and other points she got cheers, laughter and waving of hands from people seeing the first steamboat making headway up that river, their river. Tying up at Portland Landing, seven miles north of Springfield, the county seat with a population of 500, merchants there advertised the arrival of goods "direct from the East per steamer *Talisman*," and celebrated with a reception and dance in the county courthouse. It was a matter aside that the shipmaster had sent a dude captain, "a vainly dressed fellow," to command the boat and this deck officer had worried the ladies of Springfield by bringing along a woman not his wife, both of them drunk and loose-tongued at the festivities.

The trip of the *Talisman* downstream was "risky business." The high waters of the spring thaw had gone down making a more narrow river and shallow channel. At the wheel, as pilot, the boat officers put Rowan Herndon, New Salem grocer and a good boatsman, with Lincoln as assistant pilot. To get past New Salem they had to tear down part of the milldam. A slow four miles a day, sometimes nearly scraping river bottom, they made it to Beardstown. Walking back to New Salem, the two pilots could jingle a nice $40 apiece, their pay as navigators of the sometimes unnavigable Sangamon.

One morning in April 1832 a rider got off his mud-spattered, sweating horse in New Salem and gave notice of Governor John Reynolds calling for 400 thirty-day volunteers from the Sangamon County state militia to report at Beardstown April 24. The Illinois frontier, like nearly every other state to the east, was to have an Indian war. The 67-year-old Black Hawk, war leader of the Sauk and Fox tribes, on April 6 had crossed the Mississippi River into Illinois, saying his people would plant corn along the Rock River. He led 368 paint-faced and eagle-feathered warriors, nearly 1,000 women and children, and 450 horses. So came reports. For a hundred years his people had hunted, fished and planted in that prairie valley until treaties with the white men sent them west of the Mississippi. Now Black Hawk claimed that "land can not be sold," that "nothing can be sold but such things as can be carried away," and that wrong was done when red men drank too deep of the firewater of the white men and signed papers selling land. In days soon to come his whooping night riders on fast ponies left cabins in ashes and white men and women killed and scalped. Also red men tumbled off their horses from the rifle shots of white men. Any high cry in the night sent white settlers to their cabins and rifles. It was held against Black Hawk that in the War of 1812 he favored the British and fought as best he could for them.

Of this April, Lincoln said later, "Offutt's business was failing—had almost failed—when the Black-Hawk war of 1832 broke out." For months it seemed the store was run by Lincoln alone, while Offutt gave his time and funds to big and risky speculations in buying and shipping produce, leaving New Salem quietly in the spring of 1832 and not being heard of for years.

Lincoln borrowed a horse and rode nine miles to Richland Creek to join a company of friends and neighbors, mostly Clary's Grove boys. Voting for a captain, each man of the company stepped out and stood by either Lincoln or one William Kirkpatrick. Three-fourths of the men at once went to Lincoln—and then one by one those standing by Kirkpatrick left him till he was almost alone. Lincoln was to write, years later, that he was "surprized" at this election and had "not since had any success in life which gave him so much satisfaction." He at once appointed Jack Armstrong first sergeant, and nine days later promoted from the ranks his rival William Kirkpatrick. They marched to Beardstown and went into camp, part of an army of 1,600 mobilizing there.

To settle a dispute over which company should have a certain campground, Lincoln wrestled with Lorenzo D. Thompson. In their first feel-outs of each other, Lincoln called, "Boys, this is the most powerful man I ever had hold of." Lincoln was thrown twice and lost the match, saying later of Thompson, "He could have thrown a grizzly bear." After Lincoln went to the ground the second time, his men swarmed in and from over their heads came Lincoln's voice, "Boys, give up your bets. If this man hasn't thrown me fairly, he could."

No easy set of men to drill into obeying orders had Lincoln, and his first military order was answered, "Go to hell." He himself was a beginner in drill regulations, and once couldn't think of the order that would get two platoons endwise, two by two, for passing through a gate. So he commanded, "This company is dismissed for two minutes, when it will fall in again on the other side of the gate."

At the brigade quartermaster's office April 25 Lincoln drew corn, pork, salt, one barrel of flour and five and a half gallons of whisky for his company. After five days there was muttering and grumbling, discipline poor; it didn't seem the kind of a war they had expected and they wrote home about it. Lincoln's company was enrolled in the state service April 28 and Lincoln drew 30 muskets and bayonets, so it looked like there might be shooting. They began marching, 25 miles one day, 20 miles another, one night camping two miles from timber or water, men sleeping on cold, damp ground. They arrived at Yellow Banks (later Oquawka), noticed the citizens there serene and satisfied, some of the men wondering what the war was about. The food wasn't good so some soldiers shot hogs and enjoyed pork chops, and the farmers were heard from.

They marched to camp near the mouth of the Rock River where on May 9 Lincoln's company, with others, was sworn into the Federal service. The next day while the U.S. Regular Army troops moved on boats, the 1,500 militia marched 26 miles in swamp muck and wilderness brush along the left bank of the river, pushing and pulling when horses and wagons bogged. When night rains came the tents didn't shed water and Lincoln heard fagged men wail and curse, along with talk of deserting.

They marched to Prophetstown, to Dixon's Ferry where they heard two days later how, without orders, troops of Major Isaiah Stillman had at dusk rushed at Indian horsemen on a rise of ground about a mile from their camp, bringing on a fight that ended in a rout and left 12 white men dead. The next day General Samuel Whiteside's army, including Lincoln's company, marched to the battle scene, arriving near sunset to witness fallen white men who lay scalped and mangled. The next day, after burials, the army was drawn up in battle line for Black Hawk's spies to see they were ready for action, after which the hungry troops marched back to Dixon's Ferry and food and a speech by Governor Reynolds promising militiamen who were eager to go home that U.S. Regulars would arrive next day.

There were farmers anxious about their crops, there was gloom over the stragglers routed and sent flying by Black Hawk's horsemen, and a lessening confidence in officers. Once, against orders, someone shot off a pistol inside the camp; the authorities found it was Captain Lincoln; he was arrested, his sword taken away, and he was held in custody one day. Another time his men opened officers' supplies of whisky; some were dead drunk and others straggled on the march; a court-martial ordered Captain Lincoln to carry a wooden sword two days. "A hard set of men," said a Regular Army officer. Bill Greene remembered Lincoln saying to officers of the U.S. Regulars that his men "must be equal in all particulars" in rations and arms to the Regular Army and "resistance will hereafter be made to unjust orders," which threat of mutiny resulted in better treatment. Greene couldn't forget either how one day an old Indian, with a safe-conduct pass from a general, rambled into camp and men rushed to kill him. Lincoln jumped to the side of the Indian and said with a hard gleam, "Men, this must not be done." Some of the mob called him a coward and his answer came like a shot, "Choose your weapons!" Hot tempers cooled off as the Clary's Grove boys began backing Lincoln and they saw he was a captain who didn't presume on his authority.

They marched up Rock River, then to Stillman's battle-field, then back along the Rock River, some men believing they were being kept busy to lessen grumbling. On May 21 came news of an Indian party near Ottawa that killed, mangled and scalped three families, 15 persons, and took away alive two girls of 17 and 15. They marched up Sycamore Creek, arrived at Pottawatomie Village where spies the day before had found a number of scalps. At this point mutiny came, troops demanding discharge. Governor Reynolds called a conference of captains, including Lincoln, and had them vote on whether to follow the enemy or go home. A tie vote was announced and General Whiteside's temper blazed in saying he would no longer lead such men except to be discharged. Four days later, after marching to Ottawa, Lincoln's company and others were mustered out of the service. Lincoln certified his muster roll, marking three men as "absent without leave."

Lincoln re-enlisted for 20 days and May 29 was mustered as a private into a company of mounted Independent Rangers under Captain Elijah Iles, a pioneer trader, land dealer, and one of the founders of Springfield. His unit had former colonels, captains, lieutenants, and one general serving as privates. About this time Colonel Zachary Taylor of the U.S. Regulars had ordered a company of militia to march to Galena, and the men refusing to go, he had reported, "The more I see of the militia the less confidence I have of their effecting anything of importance." Nevertheless Captain Iles' company marched and camped alongside the small Apple River Fort near Galena where the night before Indians had stolen 12 horses and that afternoon had shot at

and chased two men into the fort. The company slept with
guns in their arms. Arriving the next day in Galena they
found in the town of 400 so many people terrified that Captain Iles believed they would put up little or no resistance
to Indians. Three days later the company again arrived at
Dixon's Ferry, Iles reporting signs of Indians who seemed
more anxious to get horses than scalps. A 45-mile march
brought them to Fort Wilbourn on the Illinois River where
Captain Iles' company was mustered out of service.

Lincoln on June 16 enlisted for the third time, becoming
a 30-day private in the Independent Spy Corps of Captain
Jacob M. Early, a Springfield physician and Methodist
preacher who had been a private in the companies of Lincoln and Iles. On June 25 Early's Spy Corps was ordered
out on an all-night march to Kellogg's Grove where the
day before a main body of Sauks under Black Hawk, "se-
creted in a thicket," had surprised and routed the whites.
Lincoln shortly after sunrise helped bury five men. As he
told it afterward, each of the dead men "had a round, red
spot on top of his head, about as big as a dollar where the
redskins had taken his scalp." It was frightful, grotesque,
"and the red sunlight seemed to paint everything all over."
Captain Early wrote an extended report of the battle to
General Henry Atkinson of the Regular Army.

The Spy Corps made several marches and on July 1
crossed into Michigan Territory (later Wisconsin), camp-
ing and throwing up breastworks near Turtle Village (later
Beloit), sleeping on their muskets, Black Hawk being near.
Next day Early's men marched in advance of the army to
Lake Koshkonong and roundabout White Water and Burnt
Village, and for four days performed spy and scout duty for
General Atkinson's army of 450 Regulars, about 2,100
mounted volunteers, with 100 Indian allies. The general on
July 9 wrote to General Winfield Scott that the country was
so cut up with prairie, wood and swamp that it was "ex-
tremely difficult" to approach the enemy, many parts for
miles being "entirely impassable even on foot." He had de-
cided to dismiss the independent commands. On July 10
Captain Early's Spy Corps was mustered out at White
Water on Rock River, honorably discharged "with the spe-

cial thanks of Brigadier General H. Atkinson, Commander in Chief of the Army of the Illinois Frontier."

Black Hawk shaped and reshaped his army as a shadow, came and faded as a phantom, spread out false trails, set traps, lures and used the ambush. Yet the white men, though at cost, solved his style and used it to beat him. The militia under General James D. Henry and other officers proved themselves equal and at times superior to the Regulars as they drove Black Hawk north, marching in storm and night rains, performing an epic of endurance and valor, outguessing the red men who had earlier tricked them. And the end? Black Hawk, the prisoner, was taken to Washington, in the Executive Mansion facing President Jackson, the red man saying to the white, "I—am—a man—and you— are—another . . . I took up the hatchet to avenge injuries which could no longer be borne . . . I say no more of it; all is known to you."

On the night of his discharge Lincoln's horse was stolen; so was that of his comrade George Harrison. In the 200 miles to Peoria they walked and part way rode on the horses of comrades. Buying a canoe at Peoria, Lincoln and Harrison steered by turns to Havana, sold the canoe, then walked to New Salem. An army paymaster six months later in Springfield paid Lincoln some $95 for his 80 days in the war. In those days Lincoln had seen deep into the heart of the American volunteer soldier, why men go to war, march in mud, sleep in rain on cold ground, eat pork raw when it can't be boiled, and kill when the killing is good. On a later day an observer was to say he saw Lincoln's eyes misty in his mention of the American volunteer soldier.

Election was 18 days off, on August 6, and Lincoln traveled over Sangamon County, gave the arguments in his long address issued in the spring. At Pappsville, where a crowd had come to a sale, as he stepped on a box for his speech he saw fellow citizens on the edge of the crowd in a fist fight. He noticed his pilot friend Rowan Herndon getting the worst of it, stepped off the box, shouldered his way to the fight, picked a man by the scruff of the neck and the

seat of the breeches, and threw him. Back on his box, he
swept the crowd with his eyes in a cool way as though what
had happened sort of happened every day, and then made a
speech. Campaigning among farmers, he pitched hay and
cradled wheat in the fields and showed the farmers he was
one of them; at crossroads he threw the crowbar and let
the local wrestlers try to get the "crotch hoist" on him. He
closed his campaign with a speech in the county courthouse
at Springfield. On Election Day Lincoln lost, running
eighth in a field of 13 candidates. But in his own New
Salem precinct, he polled 277 of the 300 votes cast.

Later Lincoln wrote of himself after this August election,
"He was now without means and out of business, but was
anxious to remain with his friends who had treated him
with so much generosity, especially as he had nothing elsewhere to go to. He studied what he should do—thought
of learning the black-smith trade—thought of trying to
study law—rather thought he could not succeed at that
without a better education."

He bought Rowan Herndon's interest in the partnership
of Herndon and William F. Berry, merchants, giving Herndon his promissory note. Then Berry and Lincoln bought
a stock of goods under peculiar conditions. Reuben Radford at his store had spoken threats to Clary's Grove boys
and one day went away from his store telling his younger
brother that if Clary's Grove boys came in they should
have two drinks apiece and no more. The boys came, took
their two drinks, stood the young clerk on his head, helped
themselves at jugs and barrels, wrecked the store, broke
the windows and rode away yelling on their ponies. Radford looked the wreck over and on the spot sold the stock to
William G. Greene. The price was $400 which Greene
made up by paying Radford $23 in cash and giving two
notes for $188.50 each, secured by a mortgage on a New
Salem lot. Lincoln drew and witnessed the mortgage, and
on the same day he and Berry bought the stock from
Greene, paying $265 cash, assuming Greene's notes to
Radford, and throwing in a horse to boot. Thus Greene
made a profit of $242 and one horse. Across later months
there was more financing, several lawsuits and court judg-

ments. They did nothing, as Lincoln said later, "but get deeper and deeper in debt" and "the store winked out."

During the fall and winter of 1832, business didn't pick up much. Berry wasn't interested, and Lincoln was reading and dreaming. Early harvest days came; the farmers bundled grain in russet fields. From the Salem hilltop the valley of the Sangamon River loitered off in a long stretch of lazy, dreamy haze and the harvest moon came in a wash of pumpkin colors. Lincoln could sit with uninterrupted thoughts, free day after day to turn and look into himself. He was having days that might nourish by letting him sit still and get at himself. He was growing as inevitably as summer corn in Illinois loam. Leaning against the doorpost of a store to which few customers came he was growing, in silence, as corn grows. He had bought at an auction in Springfield a copy of Blackstone, the first of the law books to read. One morning he sat barefoot on a woodpile, with a book. "What are you reading?" asked Squire Godbey. "I ain't reading; I'm studying." "Studying what?" "Law." "Good God Almighty!"

Lincoln later came across an account of "the peculiar manner" of his law studies: "His favorite place of study was a wooded knoll near New Salem, where he threw himself under a wide-spreading oak, and expansively made a reading desk of the hillside. Here he would pore over Blackstone day after day, shifting his position as the sun rose and sank, so as to keep in the shade, and utterly unconscious of everything but the principles of common law. People went by, and he took no account of them; the salutations of acquaintances were returned with silence, or a vacant stare; and altogether the manner of the absorbed student was not unlike that of one distraught." This picture of himself as a law student he accepted.

Business dropped off. Berry took out a license in March 1833 for Berry and Lincoln to keep a tavern and sell retail liquors. The required bond had both names, Lincoln and Berry, but neither signature was in Lincoln's well-known handwriting. The license specified they could sell whisky at 12½ cents a pint, brandies, gins, wine and rum, at various prices.

Selling pork, salt, powder, guns, trading calico prints and bonnets for eggs and furs had only a mild interest for Lincoln, but taking the cash of men and boys for hard liquor didn't come easy—and a few weeks after the firm got its license, Lincoln, in a deal of some kind, turned his interest in the store over to Berry. It could, however, have been about this time that, as he later told it, "Lincoln did work the latter part of one winter in a little still house, up at the head of a hollow." The stills ran in many odd corners, the supply endless, corn juice priced at $1.00 and less per gallon. At gatherings, barbecues, dances, sporting events, auction sales, weddings, funerals, camp meetings, the jug and the bottle were there. Dr. Allen, in his temperance appeals, found his fiercest opponents "among church members, most of whom had their barrels of whisky at home." Even the hardshell Baptist church was not then ready to take a stand against whisky. When Mentor Graham, the schoolmaster, joined the temperance movement, the church trustees suspended him. Then, to hold a balance, the trustees suspended another member who had gone blind drunk. This action puzzled one member who stood up in meeting and, shaking a half-full quart bottle so all could see, drawled, "Brethering, you have turned one member out beca'se he would not drink, and another beca'se he got drunk, and now I wants to ask a question. How much of this 'ere critter does a man have to drink to remain in full membership in this church?"

On May 7, 1833, as Lincoln told it, he "was appointed Postmaster at New Salem—the office being too insignificant, to make his politics an objection." The pay would run about $50 a year, in commissions on receipts. He had to be in the office at Hill's store only long enough to receive and receipt for the mail which came twice a week by postrider at first and later by stage. Letters arrived written on sheets of paper folded and waxed, envelopes not yet in use. The sender of a letter paid no postage; that fell on whoever the letter was addressed to. Postage on a one-sheet letter was six cents for the first 30 miles, ten cents for 30 to 80 miles, and so on to 25 cents for more than 400 miles. Two sheets cost twice as much, three sheets three times as

much, and with every letter Lincoln had to figure how
many sheets, how far it had come, then mark the postage
in the upper right corner of the outside sheet. If anyone
didn't like his figuring as to the number of sheets the re-
ceiver could open the letter before the postmaster and settle the question.

Lincoln was free to read newspapers before delivering
them, and he read "the public prints" as never before. The
habit deepened in him of watching newspapers for political trends and issues. And he could find excitement at times
in reading the speeches made in Congress at Washington
as reported in full in the *Congressional Globe* subscribed
for by John C. Vance. It was no pleasure for him to write
later to the publishers, Blair & Rives, "Your subscriber at
this place *John C. Vance,* is dead; and no person takes the
paper from the office." It seemed he wasn't strict about
regulations, and when George Spears sent a messenger with
postage money for his newspapers and a note telling Lincoln he wanted a receipt, Lincoln replied he was "surprised"
and, "the law requires News paper postage to be paid in
advance and now that I have waited a full year you choose
to wound my feeling by intimating that unless you get a
receipt I will probably make you pay it again."

At times the post office was left unlocked for hours while
citizens who called for mail helped themselves. The postmaster could send and receive letters free but franking a
letter for someone else made him liable to a $10 fine. Not
bothering about regulations, he wrote in the upper right
corner of an outside sheet: "Free. A. Lincoln, P.M. New
Salem Ills. Sept. 22." The letter was from Matthew S.
Marsh to a brother in Portsmouth, New Hampshire, and
near its opening said: "The Post Master [Mr. Lincoln] is
very careless about leaving his office open & unlocked during the day—half the time I go in & get my papers etc. without any one being there as was the case yesterday. The letter was only marked 25 & even if he had been there &
known it was double he would not [have] charged me any
more—luckily he is a very clever fellow & a particular
friend of mine. If he is there when I carry this to the office
—I will get him to 'Frank' it . . ." As between "particular"

friends, could it have been that Marsh sometimes spoke to Lincoln as he did to his folks in his letter? Did he tell Lincoln that if no better chance offered he would teach a private school on Indian Creek, Morgan County, nearby a "sucker girl" of whom he wrote: "She possesses more qualities which assimilate with my peculiar disposition & comes nearer to the standard of what I consider essential in a wife than any girl I have ever seen. In stature middling height & slim—Light brown hair, black eyes, which suppress half their fire until she speaks, then through their soft disguise will flash an expression more of pride than ire . . . Her age 20. Such is all the description I can give of the girl who at present stands highest in my estimation. How long she will continue to do so I cannot assure even myself as I have *naturally* a *fickle* disposition . . . I have one objection to marrying in this state & that is, the women have such an everlasting number of children—twelve is the least number that can be counted on." Did Marsh say the like to young Lincoln, of whom some were saying, "He can pump a man dry on any subject he is interested in"?

Marsh was good company, a man Lincoln could learn from. So was Jack Kelso, blacksmith, fisherman, trapper, a good rifle shot, a reader of Shakespeare and Burns. He recited from those authors, Lincoln listening while Kelso talked and fished, Lincoln joining in discussions but not in the bottle Kelso usually had handy. It was said that when other men were lush from drinking they wanted to fight but Kelso would recite Shakespeare and Burns.

Lincoln signed as witness to petitions and deeds, signed honorable discharges for members of his Black Hawk War company, accepted when after the war he was elected captain of militia in Clary's Grove, drew and attested mortgages, served as clerk with $1.00 of pay at September and November elections in New Salem, received $2.50 for taking poll books 18 miles to Springfield.

For earning a living, jobs at common labor were plenty; he worked as rail splitter, mill hand, farm hand, helped out at the Hill store. Meanwhile he read or dipped into Volney's *The Ruins of Empire*, Gibbon's *Decline and Fall of the Roman Empire*, Paine's *The Age of Reason.* And his debts haunted him. They added up to more when his former partner, William F. Berry, died on short notice in January 1835, his estate practically nothing, leaving Lincoln responsible for their joint obligations. Thus his debts ran to a total of $1,100—and they wouldn't laugh away. They were little rats, a rat for every dollar, and he could hear them in the night when he wanted to sleep.

Squire Bowling Green proved a friend and counselor, explained to Lincoln what he knew of the Illinois statutes, allowed Lincoln without fee to try small cases, examine witnesses and make arguments. The squire, not yet 50, weighed 250 pounds and was nicknamed "Pot" for his paunch. He held court wearing only a shirt and pants and once when two witnesses swore a hog didn't belong to Jack Kelso and Kelso swore it did, Squire Green decided, "The two witness we have heard have sworn to a damned lie. I know this shoat, and I know he belongs to Jack Kelso."

In the fall of 1833 came Lincoln's entry into the most highly technical and responsible work he had known. Writing of it later, he said, "The Surveyor of Sangamon [County], offered to depute to A[braham] that portion of his work which was within his part of the county. He accepted, procured a compass and chain, studied Flint, and Gibson a little, and went at it. This procured bread, and kept soul and body together." There were farm sections, roads and towns needing their boundary lines marked clear and beyond doubt on maps—more than the county surveyor, John Calhoun, could handle. On the suggestion of Pollard Simmons, a farmer and Democratic politician living near New Salem, Calhoun, a Jackson Democrat, appointed Lincoln, who went 18 miles to Springfield to make sure he wasn't tied up politically and could speak as he pleased.

Then for six weeks, daytime and often all of nighttime, he had his head deep in Gibson's *Theory and Practice of Surveying* and Flint's *Treatise on Geometry, Trigonometry and Rectangular Surveying*. From decimal fractions one book ran on into logarithms, the use of mathematical instruments, operating the chain, circumferentor, surveying by intersections, changing the scale of maps, leveling, methods for mensuration of areas. Many nights, said Mentor Graham's daughter, she woke at midnight to see Lincoln and her father by the fire, figuring and explaining, her mother sometimes bringing fresh firewood for better lighting. On some nights he worked alone till daylight and it wore him down. He was fagged, and friends said he looked like a hard drinker after a two weeks' spree. Good people said, "You're killing yourself."

In six weeks, however, he had mastered his books, and Calhoun put him to work on the north end of Sangamon County. The open air and sun helped as he worked in field and timberland with compass and measurements. His pay was $2.50 for "establishing" a quarter section of land, $2.00 for a half-quarter, 25 cents to 37½ cents for small town lots. He surveyed the towns of Petersburg, Bath, New Boston, Albany, Huron, and others. He surveyed roads, school sections, pieces of farm land from four-acre plots to 160-acre farms. His surveys became known for care and accuracy and he was called on to settle boundary disputes. In Petersburg, however, he laid out one street crooked. Running it straight and regular, it would have put the house of Jemima Elmore and her family into the street. Lincoln knew her to be working a small farm with her children and she was the widow of Private Travice Elmore, honorable in service in Lincoln's company in the Black Hawk War.

For his surveying trips he had bought a horse, saddle and bridle from William Watkins for $57.86, and for nonpayment Watkins on April 26, 1834, got judgment in court and levied on Lincoln's personal possessions. It looked as though he would lose his surveying instruments. Then Bill Greene showed up and turned in a horse on the Watkins judgment—and James Short came from Sand Ridge to the auction Lincoln was too sad to attend and bid in the saddle, bridle, compass and other surveying instruments. When Short brought them to Lincoln it hit him as another surprise in his young life. Short liked Lincoln as a serious student, a pleasant joker, and said that on a farm "he husks two loads of corn to my one."

In January 1834, after a survey for Russell Godbey, Lincoln bought two buckskins from Godbey and took them to Hannah Armstrong, the wife of Jack, who "foxed his pants," sewed leather between ankles and knees for protection against briars. The Armstrongs took him in two or three weeks at a time when he needed a place to stay, Hannah saying, "Abe would drink milk, eat mush, corn-bread and butter, rock the cradle while I got him something to eat. I foxed his pants, made his shirts. He would tell stories, joke people at parties. He would nurse babies—do anything to accomodate anybody." Jack one day had a hand in an affair that A. Y. Ellis said had Lincoln "out of temper and laughing at the same time." The boys had made a large fire of shavings and hemp stalks and bet a fellow Ellis called Ike that he couldn't run his bobtail pony through the fire. Ike got a hundred-yard start, came full tilt with his hat off, and just as he reached the blazing fire his pony "flew the track and pitched poor Ike into the flames." Lincoln ran to help, crying, "You have carried this thing far enough." He was mad though he couldn't help laughing, as Ellis saw him. Jack took Ike with scorched head and face to a doctor, who shaved the head and put salve on the burn. Jack was sorry and at his house next morning gave Ike a dram, his breakfast and a skin cap and sent him home.

Lincoln worked at occasional odd jobs when there was no surveying but he made it a point to find time to keep up his political connections. On March 1, 1834, he was secretary of a public meeting at New Salem which resolved on General James D. Henry, former sheriff of Sangamon County, as their choice for governor. General Henry had become a high name in the history of the Black Hawk War, a proven strategist and a soldier of courage who shared hardships with his men. He died of tuberculosis in New Orleans four days after the New Salem meeting that favored him and Lincoln couldn't stay away from a memorial service for Henry on April 20 in the courthouse at Springfield.

In those New Salem days were some saying Lincoln would be a great man, maybe governor or senator, anyhow a great lawyer, what with his studying of law. Others saw him as an awkward, gangly giant, a homely joker who could go gloomy and show it. It was noticed he had two shifting moods, one of the rollicking, droll story, one when he lapsed silent and solemn beyond any bystander to penetrate.

He moved amid odd happenings. He mourned with others when Rowan Herndon, while cleaning a rifle, accidentally pressed the trigger, the bullet striking his wife in the neck, bringing almost instant death. One winter morning he saw young Ab Trent, chopping away at the logs of an old pulled-down stable, Ab with rags instead of shoes on his feet. He told Lincoln he was earning a dollar to buy shoes. Lincoln told him to run to the store and warm his feet. And after a while Lincoln came to the store, handed Ab Trent his ax, and told him to collect the dollar and buy shoes; the wood was chopped. Later Ab, a Democrat, told friends he was going to vote for Lincoln for the legislature. And when the poll books showed that Ab Trent had voted against Lincoln, Ab came to Lincoln with tears in his eyes and said his friends had got him drunk and had him vote against the way he intended.

In late summer or early fall of 1834 many people in New Salem, Lincoln included, wondered what had become of John McNeil. It was two years since he had left New Salem. Before leaving he had sold his interest in the Hill-McNeil store to Hill, but at 32 he was the owner of farms steadily rising in value and was rated one of the shrewdest and richest traders in New Salem. In money and looks he was considered by girls "a good catch." On December 9, 1831, Lincoln with Charles Maltby witnessed two deeds given by John Camron to John McNamar and it was then, if not earlier, that Lincoln learned John McNeil's real name was John McNamar. This also explained to Lincoln why as election clerk he didn't see McNeil's name on the poll books; the man was keeping his real name off election records. He said that he had left his family in New York State rather bad off and, setting out to make a fortune, he didn't want his family to trace and interfere with him, but he would in good time go back and help them when he had made his money.

The one person most anxious about him when he went

away from New Salem in 1832 was, in all probability, the 19-year-old Ann Rutledge. They were engaged to marry and it was understood he would straighten out affairs of his family in New York State and in not too long a time would come back to her for the marriage. He rode away on a horse that had seen service in the Black Hawk War and it was said that he wrote to Ann from Ohio of a serious three weeks' sickness there and again had written her from New York, and she had answered his letters—and that was all.

A few months after he left in September 1832, James Rutledge and John M. Camron, the two founders of New Salem, having failed in business affairs, moved with their families into the double-log house of a farm near Sand Ridge that McNamar owned through payment to Camron of $400. It could have been that McNamar was showing goodness of heart to the family of his betrothed, at the same time acquiring trusted and responsible caretakers of his property while he was away. Possibly, too, he believed Ann's feeling about him would have added assurance out of her living on his land, the same land she might live on after their marriage. McNamar was a careful and exact man, insisted on clear understandings in all bargains—and a betrothal to him was a bargain between a man and a woman and their joint properties. What they wrote to each other about motives and intentions was in letters not kept and saved.

For nearly two years no one in New Salem had heard from the man who was afraid his folks would find him and had therefore changed his name. There was guessing and byplay of the kind in a later frontier song:

Oh, what was your name in the States?
Was it Thompson or Johnson or Bates?
Did you murder your wife and fly for your life?
Say, what was your name in the States?

Sharp gossips asked, "If he hid his real name what else might he be hiding? Did he run away from a wife or from a girl he got into trouble?" This was mostly idle chatter.

For McNamar had a good name for straight dealing in business, for keeping sober, for no loose ways with girls and women. He was known for close bargains, had an eye for where values would rise; he required cash or land in payments, taking no promissory notes, one woman saying he was "cold as the multiplication table." He seemed to be the first of the early investors of New Salem to see that lack of river navigation and other conditions were to doom the village. He held off from loans to Camron and Rutledge when they began taking heavy losses on their sawmill and gristmill. He did accommodate them by paying $50 for half of Rutledge's 80 acres at Sand Ridge, seven miles from New Salem, and paying Camron $400 for one tract of 40 acres and another of 80 acres, also at Sand Ridge. He rode away from New Salem with no anxiety about promissory notes, the land he owned sure to rise in value.

And Lincoln, who called McNamar "Mack," who had surveyed the land McNamar owned, and who had lived under the same roof with Ann during the months "Mack" was a boarder at the Rutledge tavern, could hardly have been unaware of what she was going through. Her well-known betrothed had gone away saying he would be back soon; two years had gone by and except for a few weeks at the beginning no word had come from him. Did she talk over with Lincoln the questions, bitter and haunting, that harassed her? Had death taken her betrothed? Or was he alive and any day would see him riding into New Salem to claim her? And again, possibly, she kept a silence and so did Lincoln, and there was some kind of understanding beneath their joined silence.

Lincoln was to go away and stay away for months on important duties, writing her no letters that she kept and saved, she writing him no letters that he laid by as keepsakes. During the six weeks he mastered the surveying books, he could have seen her for only brief moments, if at all. And his surveying, as he said, "procured bread, and kept body and soul together." So definitely he was no man of property who like McNamar could offer her land and money, the creature comforts of life. He had arrived in New Salem "a piece of floating driftwood," as he later

wrote, and was haunted by debts that had crept high on him.
He was aware of large families, nine Rutledge children, 11
Camron daughters, Matthew Marsh writing "twelve is the
least number," and a comment that central Illinois was "a
hard country for women and cattle." His stepmother, Sarah
Bush Lincoln, said he liked people in general, children and
animals, but "he was not very fond of girls."

He was to tell T. W. S. Kidd in Springfield of his first
dream of love. When he was "a little codger" in Indiana a
wagon broke down near their place and a man, his wife and
their two girls came to the Lincoln cabin, cooking their
meals and staying till the wagon was fixed. "The woman
had books and read us stories," Kidd reported Lincoln. "I
took a great fancy to one of the girls. And when they were
gone I thought of her a great deal, and one day sitting out
in the sun by the house I wrote out a story in my mind."
On his father's horse he rode after the wagon and surprised
them. "I talked with the girl and persuaded her to elope
with me, and that night I put her on my horse, and we
started off across the prairie. After several hours we came
to a camp; and when we rode up we found it was the one
we had left a few hours before and we went in. The next
night we tried again, and the same thing happened—the
horse came back to the same place. And then we concluded
not to elope. I stayed until I had persuaded her father to
give her to me. I always meant to write that story out and
publish it. I began once, but I concluded it was not much
of a story. But I think that was the beginning of love with
me."

A. Y. Ellis, who kept a store where Lincoln had helped
out on busy days, recalled: "He always disliked to wait on
the ladies. He preferred trading with the men and boys, as
he used to say. He was a very shy man of ladies. On one
occasion, when we boarded at the same log tavern, there
came an old lady and her son and three stylish daughters,
from the state of Virginia, and stopped there for two or
three weeks; and during their stay, I do not remember of
Mr. Lincoln ever eating at the same table when they did. I
thought it was on account of his awkward appearance and
his wearing apparel."

Did he tell Ann of any dream, daydream or reverie that came to him about love in general or a particular love for her? Or did he shrink from such talk because she might be clinging to some last desperate hope that her betrothed would return? Or did she lean to a belief that McNamar was gone for all time, then shifting to another awful possibility that he would surely come back to his land and properties, perhaps bringing a wife with him? Two years of silence could be heavy and wearing. She was 21 and Lincoln 25 and in the few visits he had time for in this year when surveying and politics pressed him hard, he may have gone no further than to be a comforter. He may have touched and stroked her auburn hair once or more as he looked deep into her blue eyes and said no slightest word as to what hopes lay deep in his heart. Her mother could remember her singing a hymn he liked, with a line, "Vain man, thy fond pursuits forbear." Both were figures of fate —he caught with debts, with surveying "to keep body and soul together" while flinging himself into intense political activities, she the victim of a betrothal that had become a mysterious scandal. They were both young, with hope endless, and it could have been he had moments when the sky was to him a sheaf of blue dreams and the rise of the blood-gold red of a full moon in the evening was almost too much to live, see and remember.

Chapter 3

The Young Legislator

On April 19, 1834, Lincoln's name ran again in the *Sangamo Journal* as a candidate for the state legislature. Before that and after, he attended all sorts of political powwows, large and small, and those for whom he surveyed, and those he delivered letters to, did not fail to hear he was in the running. He had become a regular wheel horse of the Whig party backed by John T. Stuart, a Springfield lawyer and county Whig leader. This time Lincoln gave out no long address on issues as two years before. With no presidential ticket in the field, voters were freer in personal choice. Bowling Green, a local Democratic leader, out of his liking for and belief in Lincoln, offered him the support of fellow Democrats. Lincoln hesitated, talked it over with Stuart, then accepted.

Strong Jackson men, believing Stuart wanted to run for Congress, were trying to cut Stuart down. At a shooting match for a beef at Clear Lake, Lincoln told Stuart of Jackson men proposing to him "that they would drop two of their men and take him up and vote for him," for the purpose of beating Stuart. "Lincoln acted fairly and honorably about it by coming to me," said Stuart. "I had great confidence in my strength—perhaps too much. But I told Lincoln to go and tell them that he would take their votes—that I would risk it—and I believe he did so."

So Lincoln played along with the Jackson Democrats who were after Stuart's scalp and with the Bowling Green Democrats who loved him for his own sake—speaking little on issues, and showing up, when there was time, any place he could meet voters face to face, shake hands, and let them know what he was like as a man, at Mechanicsburg taking a hand where fists were flying and ending the fight.

In the election for members of the Ninth General Assembly August 4, 1834, Lincoln ran second among 13 Sangamon County candidates, John Dawson having 1,390 votes, Lincoln, 1,376. Stuart ran fourth, with 1,164 votes, nosing out the one Democrat Stuart had "concentrated" against. Now at 25, Lincoln had won his first important political office, with better pay than ever before in his life, where he would train in the tangled and, to him, fascinating games of lawmaking and parliamentary management amid political labyrinths. After election he ran the post office, made surveys and appraisals, clerked in an October election, made court appearances in connection with his debts, and November 22 was elected a delegate to the State Education Convention to be held in Vandalia December 5. He had drawn closer to Stuart, who in the Black Hawk War had been major of the battalion in which Lincoln was a company captain, later serving as a private with Lincoln in Captain Iles' and Captain Early's companies. He had served two years in the legislature, and was an able lawyer, a handsome man, six feet tall, of Kentucky ancestry, a shut-mouthed manipulator whose nickname was "Jerry Sly." He deepened Lincoln's feeling about law study and loaned him law books.

A man of faith was Coleman Smoot, a well-to-do farmer, who lent Lincoln $200, Lincoln saying it was Smoot's penalty for voting for him. Lincoln paid a small pressing debt or two, bought cloth for a suit to be made at $60, and other apparel. With other members of the legislature, in the last week of November, he made the two-day 75-mile trip to Vandalia, the state capital, by stage. When later he saw a printed statement that he had walked to Vandalia, he wrote on the same page, "No harm, if true; but, in fact, not true."

Vandalia gave some the impression it had been there a long time and was a little tired though it was only 15 years old and had been the capital only 14 years. A town of some 800 people, it overlooked the Kaskaskia River and heavy timber, and to the north and west rolling prairie. Its streets, 80 feet wide, were lined mostly with log cabins, its sidewalks worn paths in grass. Five or six large frame buildings were taverns and boardinghouses, now filling their many empty rooms with legislators and lobbyists. Two weekly newspapers, one Democratic and the other Whig, advertised bedrooms, choice liquors and rewards for fugitive slaves. Main highways crossed the town, stages rolling in regularly, their wheels dusty or mud-coated, with passengers from all directions. The new jail had a "dungeon room" for stubborn birds and a "debtors' room." Into the latter Lincoln could stray for a look at men behind bars because they couldn't pay their debts.

He roomed with Stuart whose leadership made their room a Whig center. Here and in the legislature Lincoln was to meet men, most of them young, who would become governors, Congressmen, U.S. Senators, men of influence and portent. Here he would meet a short and almost dwarf-ish man, a little giant, thick of body with a massive head,

21 years old and absolutely confident of himself—Stephen A. Douglas lobbying for his selection as state's attorney of the First Circuit. Many members had their wives and daughters along and there was a social life new to Lincoln—parties, cotillions, music and flowers, elegant food and liquor, a brilliance of silk gowns and talk that ranged from idle gabble to profound conversation about the state and nation. Around the public square in candlelighted taverns, coffee rooms and hangouts, could be heard the talk and laughter of men eating, smoking, drinking, greeting, getting acquainted, and no lack of office seekers on the hunt.

On December 1, in a two-story ramshackle brick building facing the public square, meeting on the lower floor, the House was called to order, the members sitting in movable chairs, three to a table—cork inkstands, quill pens and writing paper on each table—and on the floor a sandbox as spittoon. A fireplace and stove heated the room. Three tin dippers hung over a pail of drinking water. Evening sessions were lighted by candles in tall holders. Ceiling plaster crashed down occasionally during speeches and roll calls; members got used to it.

Among the 54 representatives Lincoln could feel that if he was a greenhorn, so were the other 35 first-term members; there were 17 second-termers, and only one veteran of three previous terms. Three-fourths of them were born in Southern states, only one member a native of Illinois. Seven members had, like Lincoln, been captains in the Black Hawk War; many had been privates. More than half were farmers, one-fourth lawyers, with a sprinkling of merchants and mechanics. A "whole-hog" Jackson man was elected speaker, Lincoln with other Whigs voting for a less than "whole-hog" Jackson Democrat. Not till the seventh ballot did the House elect a doorkeeper, several candidates being hungry to be doorkeeper. In the next few days the House heard routine reports and joined in inaugurating Governor Joseph Duncan of Jacksonville, an 1812 war veteran who at 17 enlisted in the U.S. Infantry and performed heroic service, a Democrat who had known President Jackson personally when serving in Congress and was slowly moving toward joining the Whigs. Of the 11 standing committees Lincoln was appointed to the Committee on Public Accounts and Expenditures and he was to serve on several special committees.

On December 5 Lincoln stood up, unfolded to his full height, and gave notice of a bill he would introduce. And according to the rules, three days later he laid before them a bill to limit the jurisdiction of justices of the peace. The members were interested because they had that week rejected a proposal to give the justices wider powers. Days passed into weeks and Lincoln's bill was rewritten in select committee, reported to the House where a proposed amendment was debated, and the bill referred to a special committee, Lincoln being named to the committee. When finally reported with an amendment it passed the House 39 to 7 and was sent to the Senate where it died of indefinite postponement.

On his tenth day as a member he moved that it should not be in order "to offer amendments to any bill after its third reading," and his motion was tabled as too fresh and uninformed. Better luck came with passage of his bill to authorize his friend Samuel Musick to build a toll bridge across Salt Creek in Sangamon County, and another bill for three Sangamon friends "to view, mark and permanently locate" a road from Springfield to Miller's Ferry. He offered a resolution that "our Senators be instructed, and our Representatives requested" to procure a law through which Illinois would receive not less than 20 per cent of amounts paid into the Treasury of the United States for public lands lying within Illinois. The resolution was laid on the table, without a roll call, and Lincoln let it lay.

He worked and voted for incorporation of a new state bank in Springfield, the start of an alliance that would go further. He voted for a canal to connect the Illinois River with Lake Michigan, looking toward waterway hauls from mid-Illinois to the Atlantic. His votes generally ran with those of Stuart and the Whig minority. Several times members put in bills that were in Lincoln's handwriting and it seemed his hand was in more affairs than he openly showed.

The House shook nearer storm on the National Bank issue than on any other. President Jackson had gone into open battle with the Bank, refusing to favor it with a re-charter, charging it was a "money power" that bought newspapers, politicians and Congressmen. Henry Clay, Daniel Webster and other leading Whigs clashed with Jackson, who made it an issue in 1832 when farmer and labor ballots gave Jackson 219 votes in the electoral college as against 49 for Clay. When the U.S. Senate denounced Jackson's course as lawless and unconstitutional, Jackson replied with a fierce protest which the Senate refused to print in its journal. Lincoln heard many hours of hot partisan debate on pro-Jackson and anti-National Bank resolutions. He voted with the Whigs on all such resolutions except once when he indicated he believed the U.S. Senate ought to have allowed Jackson's answer to the Senate to be printed in its journal.

Questions came up of salary raises, public roads, school funds, the public printer, the state militia, regulation of gamblers, leasing of convict labor. Lincoln worked on a committee which revived an earlier law to penalize the changing of brands on livestock with intent to steal. He served on another committee on an act "to simplify proceedings at law for the collection of debts."

Once he had the House laughing. It had nominated Samuel McHatton to be surveyor of Schuyler County and the Senate had appointed him, information then coming that there was no vacancy; the former surveyor still lived. On a motion that McHatton's nomination "be vacated" Lincoln remarked that the new surveyor could not legally oust the old one so long as the incumbent persisted in not dying. Let the matter be, he suggested, "so that if the old surveyor should hereafter conclude to die, there would be a new one ready without troubling the legislature." In the end the matter was laid on the table as Lincoln had suggested. Often there had been laughter when some member moved to lay a measure on the table "until next Fourth of July." One lobbyist noted Lincoln in this legislature as "raw-boned, angular, features deeply furrowed, ungraceful, almost uncouth . . . and yet there was a magnetism and dash about the man that made him a universal favorite."

Before midnight of February 13 the last batch of hacked

and amended bills was passed and Lincoln in two days of below-zero weather rode the stage to New Salem.

After the fixed program and schedules of Vandalia, the smoke-filled rooms and hullabaloo, Lincoln now rode lonely country roads and walked in open winter air over fields he was surveying. He had seen lawmaking and politics at a vortex and vague resolves deepened in him. And as he wrote later, he "still mixed in the surveying to pay board and clothing bills"; his law books, "dropped" when a legislature met, "were taken up again at the end of the session." The *Sangamo Journal* had announced he was its New Salem agent and would take "Meal, Buckwheat, flour, pork on newspaper accounts."

Before March was over he had completed several surveys, writing of posts, mounds, white oaks, Burr oaks, Spanish oaks, as land markers, writing scores of such meticulous sentences as: "Begining at the North East corner of the same at a White Oak 14 inches S 16 W. 78 Links White Oak 10 inches N 1 E. 66 Links." After March he seemed to have little surveying work over the rest of 1835. During that year, of whatever letters he wrote only three were kept and saved and they were scant and perfunctory, shedding no light on his personal life or love or growth. It was certain that Ann Rutledge and Lincoln knew each other and he took an interest in her; probably they formed some mutual attachment not made clear to the community; possibly they loved each other and her hand went into his long fingers whose bones told her of refuge and security. They were the only two persons who could tell what secret they shared, if any. It seemed definite that she had had letters from McNamar and probable that after a time she had once written him that she expected release from her pledge. Summer of 1835 came and in September it would be three years since McNamar had gone, more than two years since any letter had come from him.

Lincoln was reading law, hoping and expecting the next year to be admitted for practice. Later he advised a young student, "Get the books, and read and study them till you understand them in their principal features; and that is the main thing . . . Your own resolution to succeed, is more important than any other one thing." His resolution to study law drove him hard; friends worried about his health; he couldn't call on Ann often or for long. It was a seven-mile ride or walk when he called on her and her folks or at the nearby farm of "Uncle Jimmy" Short where Ann worked for a time. That she was earning wages meant the family was less well off than it had been and what money she saved could go for her expenses at the Jacksonville Female Academy 25 miles away which she "had a notion" to enter in the fall term. Her brother David was a student at Illinois College in Jacksonville and by a fellow student sent a three-in-one letter dated July 27, 1835, one to his father, another to a friend James Kittridge, and to his sister the following:

> To Anna Rutledge:
> Valued Sister. So far as I can understand Miss Graves will teach another school in the Diamond Grove. I am glad to hear that you have a notion of comeing to school, and I earnestly recommend to you that you would spare no time from improving your education and mind. Remember that Time is worth more than all gold therefore throw away none of your golden moments. I add nomore, but &c.
>   D. H. RUTLEDGE.

There seemed to have been an understanding between Ann and Lincoln, with no pledges, that they would take what luck might hand them in whatever was to happen, while they advanced their education. Lincoln had his debts, his law studies, his driving political ambitions, while she had her quandaries related to John McNamar. They would see what time might bring. August came and corn and grass stood stunted for lack of rain. Settlers came down with chills, fever, malaria, Lincoln for his aches taking spoonfuls of Peruvian bark, boneset tea, jalap and calomel.

Soon New Salem heard that Ann Rutledge lay fever-burned, her malady baffling the doctors. Many went out to the Rutledge place. Days passed. Her cousin, McGrady

Rutledge, a year younger than Ann, rode to New Salem and told Lincoln of her sickness growing worse. Lincoln rode out and they let him in for what might be his last hour with her. He saw her pale face and wasted body, the blue eyes and auburn hair perhaps the same as always. Few words were spoken, probably, and he might have gone only so far as to let his bony right hand and gnarled fingers lie softly on a small white hand while he tried for a few monosyllables of bright hope.

A few days later, on August 25, 1835, death came to Ann Rutledge and burial was in nearby Concord cemetery. Whether Lincoln went to her funeral, whether he wept in grief with others at the sight of her face in the burial box, no one later seemed to know. Her cousin, McGrady Rutledge, wrote far later, "Lincoln took her death verry hard." A letter of Matthew Marsh September 17 had a tone as though the postmaster Lincoln was in good health and cheer. But this tells us nothing of Lincoln's inner feelings. Later when Lincoln was the center of incalculable death and agony and a friend rebuked him for telling funny stories, he cried back, "Don't you see that if I didn't laugh I would have to weep?" He did no doubt take Ann's death "verry hard" yet he was ambulant and doing his work as shown by a timberland survey he completed and dated September 24, 1835.

It was to come to pass that 30 years later New Salem villagers soberly spoke and wrote that Lincoln went out of his mind, wandered in the woods mumbling and crazy, and had to be locked up, all of which was exaggeration and reckless expansion of his taking Ann's death "verry hard." Woven with the recollections of his "insanity" were also the testimonies of what a deep flaming of lyric love there had been between him and Ann. A legend of a shining, deathless, holy and pure passion arose, spread, grew by some inherent vital sheen of its own or the need of those who wanted it, of Ann Rutledge, as a poet wrote, "beloved in life of Abraham Lincoln/wedded to him,/not through union,/but through separation."

To this young raw country John McNamar returned three weeks after Ann died, bringing with him his aged mother, and reported that his father had died and he had straightened out what there was of the estate. What he said of Ann's passing and whether he visited the grave of his once-betrothed, of this there is no record. He may have gone the following December to attend at his farm the funeral services of her father who died at 54. Shortly after, he notified the Rutledge and Camron families they must move out from his place. Ann's younger sister, Sarah, lived to be 87 and at 86 an inquirer asked her where Ann had died and she answered, "I was only a little girl of six. It was not our house. The owner came back, and after father's death, we could not pay the rent. He turned mother out; and we had to move to Iowa and begin all over again. I remember how sad and how brave she was." To the question who was the owner of the house, she said, after thinking a while, "It was John McNamar! He was the man who turned mother out!"

In 1838 McNamar married and after the death of his first wife married again. Each ceremony was performed by a justice of the peace, one preacher taking note that the fees of ministers ran higher. McNamar built a commodious brick house on his farm and across the road a big barn for his fat livestock. Thirty years later when asked if he could locate the grave of Ann, he could give no help, though in one letter he wrote, "I cut the initials of Miss Ann Rutledge on a b[o]ard at the head of her grave thirty years ago." In another letter 30 years after Ann's death he wrote that there had been no rivalry between him and Lincoln and that Ann at the time she met Lincoln "attended a literary institution at Jacksonville, in company with her brother." He once intimated that Ann had died brokenhearted waiting for him and in a letter described her quaintly and with charm: "Miss Ann was a gentle Amiable Maiden without any of the airs of your city Belles but winsome and comly withal a blond in complection with golden hair, 'cherry red lips & a bonny Blue Eye.'" A Springfield lawyer in his brick farmhouse asked him where Ann had died and he pointed a trembling finger toward the west. "There, by that," he began, seeming choked with emotion, "there, by *that* currant bush, she died," giving the lawyer a first impression that he had bought the land because Ann had died on it, even though at the moment he had buried one wife and married a second. He became county assessor and proved honest and fair. He lived to be 78 unaware that in chronicles to come he would figure as an enigmatic lover.

Was there a blood strain in Lincoln that had its way in his affair with Ann Rutledge and in his entanglement with two women later? That could have been and was more than a possibility. Northwest in Hancock County were cousins and kinsmen of his, one of them, Mordecai Lincoln, a son of Lincoln's Uncle Mordecai. When living in Leitchfield, Grayson County, Kentucky, he was a tailor, a carpenter, a fiddler, but mostly a shoemaker, and at times a hard drinker. People called him a woman-hater, sworn never to marry. Yet letters showed him drawn deeply toward a girl named Patsy; they kept steady company till the evening when, under her mother's advice, it was said, she offered herself to Mordecai. And that night Mordecai had rushed from Patsy's house, didn't take time to stop in his home for his belongings, and headed for Fountain Green in Hancock County, Illinois. Patsy's father wrote a letter to Mordecai's cousin, James Lincoln, in Hancock County, of Patsy taking it hard, of the "painful circumstances of Mordecai's departure," and that Mordecai could have "stuck to the noble resolution [not to drink] he took six or seven months previous."

In Fountain Green Mordecai made wagons, cabinets, coffins, visited neighbors without telling them he was coming, talked politics, religion, gossip, played the violin, though no one could tell when he would go moody and sit brooding. His cousins, James and Abraham, a justice of the peace, and still other Lincolns, were talked about as changeable from infectious bright laughing moods to spells of gloom and silence. Though "Old Mord," as he was called before he was 40, had a name as a woman-hater, he had a secret heart. A letter he wrote to "My Favorite Girl, Elizabeth," said, "The first time I ever saw you in my life, my mind was filled with the site of your person, but such was the circumstances in my life that I thought it better for me

never to see you nor any other girl that there was any like-
lihood of my becoming so greatly attached too. But by
that means I have added fuel to the flame that is burning
in my bosom . . . Elizabeth, I naturally hone for your
company here with me, but when I look around you are not
here. All that I could do is to nourish and cherish my
strongest wishes . . ." He bought paper of robin's-egg blue
for this letter and having written it he kept and saved it and
never sent it to Elizabeth!

Still keeping a reputation as a woman-hater, when he
was 50 he wrote "Dear Catherine," a schoolteacher who
had been slandered, that he defended her good name,
wanted her "the worst of anything," and if she could not
accept him, let her think now and then of him as he always
thought of her. This he mailed to Catherine, making a copy
for himself, while he went on living alone with his dog, cat,
books, lathe and tools. He lived on, often saying hard words
of priests he didn't like, and dying in the Catholic faith in
which his mother had reared him and his brothers and sisters.

In the Lincolns of Hancock County could there be any
clues or derivations related to a wavering, hesitant love that
Lincoln might have held for Ann Rutledge, a love so deep
and strangely dazzling that it shook him with fear and
gloom? Lincoln knew of his first cousin Mordecai living in
Fountain Green and later was to go out of his way for a
visit and talk with Mordecai.

Only Mordecai of the Lincolns at Fountain Green had
the name of a woman-hater, but of the others it was said,
"It seemed as if it was because they cared so much for
women they were overwhelmed with the thought of marriage." They were known as men who could love women
but were shy of marriage. They seemed to ask whether
they loved enough and whether they had a right to marry.
Among these Hancock County Lincolns there was never a
divorce after marriage and for all their spells of gloom never
a case of insanity.

Usher F. Linder wrote of Abe Lincoln and his uncle
Mordecai being a good deal alike as storytellers. "No one
took offense at Uncle Mord's stories. I heard him tell a

bevy of fashionable girls that he knew a very large woman
who had a husband so small that in the night she often
mistook him for the baby, and that one night she picked
him up and was singing to him a soothing lullaby when he
awoke and told her that the baby was on the other side
of the bed." Lincoln remarked, "Linder, I have often said
that Uncle Mord ran off with all the talents of the family."

In a snowfall over hills and rolling prairie Lincoln rode
a stage, arriving to see Vandalia blanketed white. A special
session of the legislature opened December 7, 1835. The
senators on the upper floor were not feeling good about
fresh large cracks down the walls, the north wall bulging
out and snow sifting down on the floor which at its center
had sunk half a foot. Over the next six weeks 139 bills came
up in the House; 17 railroads chartered for Illinois towns
that wanted to see the cars and hear the whistles. Half the
bills introduced were passed, the most important the one
for the Illinois and Michigan Canal, whereby wheat selling
in Illinois at 50 cents the bushel, after the Great Lakes
haul, would bring $1.25 in Buffalo. Lincoln again put in a
bill "supplemental" to his of the previous session "for the
relief of insolvent debtors," which passed the House and
failed in the Senate. He gave special attention, writing one
amendment, to a bill that passed to incorporate the Beardstown and Sangamon Canal ending at the projected town of
Huron at Miller's Ferry northwest of New Salem. Friends
of Lincoln had invested in prospective Huron. Lincoln
the next year was to own several lots there which came to
him for surveying services, besides buying a nearby tract of
47 acres. In a speech at Petersburg, he advised people to
buy stock in the canal and probably bought some of the
stock himself, one of his few mild adventures in speculation and management toward paying his debts. The canal
never got dug, but for a time it was a high hope of its pro-
moters.

At all times national politics boiled and seethed. Under
orders from President Jackson a Democratic national convention had nominated Martin Van Buren for President,
Illinois Whigs favoring a former Jackson man, Hugh White

of Tennessee. The Whigs fought against resolutions praising Jackson and Van Buren, and most of all against approval of nominating conventions, a new way of naming
candidates. Before this a man announcing he would run for
an office was then a candidate; under the new nominating
conventions he would need the good will and the say-so of
politicians, the *Sangamo Journal*, speaking for most of the
Whigs, saying the voter now must give up private judgment and "be led up to the polls by a twine through the
gristle of the proboscis." The "whole-hog" Jackson men
were aiming to get better party loyalty from the "milk-and-
cider" Jackson men, setting forth that they would expel
from the party any man not loyal to candidates nominated
by a party convention.

Lincoln and Stuart were pleased that John Dawson,
Sangamon County Democrat, was switching to the Whigs.
On an "act to improve the breed of cattle," nicknamed
"the little bull bill," providing for inspectors in each town-
ship to keep bulls over one year of age from running at
large, Lincoln voted Nay, perhaps knowing the very names
of farmers backing him who had roving bulls. The reapportionment act, increasing the House from 55 to 91 members,
went too far, Lincoln advised, but it satisfied him that
Sangamon County was to have seven representatives instead
of four. He collected $262 as his pay for the session and
after adjournment January 18 rode the stage homeward in
that occasional fair and warmer Illinois winter weather
that whispers of spring on the way.

Again Lincoln worked away as surveyor, law student,
politician. He wrote, signed and got other signers to a petition to a county court for an increased allowance for support of Benjamin Elmore, the insane son of widow Jemima
Elmore. He wrote wills, located roads, settled boundary disputes, and on March 26 advertised a reward for return of
his horse, "a large bay horse, star in his forehead, eight
years old, shod all round, and trots and paces." On March
24 the Sangamon Circuit Court recorded him as a person
of good moral character, his first step toward admission to
the bar and law practice. He advertised that 64 persons
had uncalled-for letters which unless called for would be

sent to the dead-letter office. On May 30 he handed out mail as postmaster for the last time and told his New Salem public that their post office was moved to Petersburg.

The convention system not yet operating, he put himself in the running in June as a candidate for the legislature, writing in the *Sangamo Journal*, "I go for all sharing the privileges of the government, who assist in bearing its burthens . . . admitting all whites to the right of suffrage, who pay taxes or bear arms, (by no means excluding females.)" And next November, "if alive," he would vote for Hugh L. White, the Whig candidate for President. He stumped the county, often speaking as one of a string of Whig candidates.

In Springfield he clashed with George Forquer, a lawyer who had switched from Whig to Democrat, then being appointed by the Jackson administration as register of the land office at $3,000 a year. On his elegant new frame house Forquer had put up the first lightning rod in that part of Illinois, a sight people went out of their way to see. After a speech in the courthouse by Lincoln, Forquer took the platform saying the young man who had just spoken was sailing too high and would have to be "taken down" and he was sorry the task devolved on him, then made what was termed a "slasher-gaff speech." Lincoln stood by with folded arms, stepped to the platform, made a quiet argument in reply and then, as others recalled it, a stormy finish: "I desire to live, and I desire place and distinction; but I would rather die now than, like the gentleman, live to see the day that I could change my politics for an office worth three thousand dollars a year, and then feel compelled to erect a lightning rod to protect a guilty conscience from an offended God." Some who were there said that friends carried Lincoln from the courthouse on their shoulders.

Of one of his speeches the *Sangamo Journal* said, "A girl might be born and become a mother before the Van Buren men will forget Mr. Lincoln." In the election August 1 the county gave Lincoln the highest vote of 17 candidates for the legislature. Sangamon County was taken by the Whigs, having now seven representatives and two senators.

Soon after this sweeping victory Lincoln in stride took his bar examination before two justices of the Supreme Court, passed, gave a dinner to his examiners, and on September 9, 1836, held in his hands a license to practice law in all the courts of Illinois. On October 5 he was in a Springfield court, appearing in a case for John T. Stuart, the beginning of their partnership as a law firm. In three related suits brought by James P. Hawthorn Lincoln was defending David Wooldridge. Hawthorn claimed Wooldridge was to furnish him two yoke of oxen to break up 20 acres of prairie sod ground and was to allow him to raise a crop of corn or wheat on a certain piece of ground; and Wooldridge had failed him in both cases. Furthermore, Hawthorn claimed damages because Wooldridge struck, beat, bruised, and knocked him down; plucked, pulled, and tore large quantities of hair from his head; with a stick and his fists struck Hawthorn many violent blows on or about the face, head, breast, back, shoulders, hips, legs and divers other parts of the body, and had with violence forced, pushed, thrust and gouged his fingers into Hawthorn's eyes.

Such were the allegations, including replevin action demanding return of a black and white yoke of steers, one black cow and calf, and one prairie plow. Lincoln's first move was to bring up a board bill for eight months which Hawthorn owed Wooldridge, amounting at $1.50 a week to $45.75. Also, besides a cash loan of $100, he had used for the same eight months a wagon and team for which he should pay $90. In proceedings out of court Lincoln lost on one count, with settlement on the other two, plaintiff and defendant dividing court costs.

In October and November he made three more known surveys and said good-by to surveying.

The tall Whigs from Sangamon County averaged six feet in height, Lincoln the longest, and were nicknamed the "Long Nine." Riding the stage to Vandalia two days, they talked about schemes and strategy that would carry through the legislature the one law more important to them than any other, an act to make Springfield the capital of Illinois. Arriving, they saw that Vandalia citizens, scared by

the talk of moving the capital, had torn down the old building and were just finishing a new capitol in the center of
the public square. Lincoln looked it over, stepping around
workmen still on the job, tool sheds and piles of scaffold-
ing lumber, piles of unused sand, brick and stone, perhaps
laughing at the building hardly large enough to hold the
new legislature, with no look toward future needs.

The legislature opened December 5, 1836, old members
and 66 new ones smelling a pungent odor of fresh damp
plaster. Governor Duncan's message advised state financial
support for "all canals and railroads." On the 17 railroads
and two canals chartered at the last session not a track
had been laid nor a spade of dirt dug. The new dynamic
member, Stephen A. Douglas, brought in a huge omnibus
bill from the Committee on Internal Improvements. Nearly
every town in the state wanted a railroad or canal and this
bill would give it to them at a cost of $10,000,000, the
state to sell bonds of that amount. On the same day the
session began, this $10,000,000 program had been ap-
proved by an Internal Improvement State Convention, its
delegates businessmen of wealth and power, including
Thomas Mather, president of the State Bank in Springfield of which bank Lincoln was continuously an active
friend. As chairman of the Finance Committee Lincoln
reported that the state had balanced its budget and had a
surplus of $2,743.18, being strictly solvent.

The trading and logrolling began over the huge omnibus
bill—"You scratch my back and I'll scratch yours." Lincoln had become Whig floor leader and with the Long Nine
worked all the time at as many bargains and favors as possible for other members with an eye on the votes that would
be needed to change the capital to Springfield. Across weeks
the omnibus bill was changed, mangled, put together again,
till every town and county had something from the "grab
bag"—the railroad, track spur, canal, turnpike or other
improvement it wanted. Lincoln, though not a member,
spent so much time discussing amendments with the Internal Improvements Committee that one member later
seemed to remember Lincoln was part of the committee.
The West was young, immigrants by millions were to come,

the future was all rosy, said the pioneer stock that believed in "boom or bust." Springfield was not alone in adding a thousand of population in seven years. The reckless, over-loaded $10,000,000 Internal Improvements Bill passed by 61 to 25. There was a Council of Revision veto over which the bill was repassed by 53 to 20. Lincoln joined with a majority which voted to refuse to put the bill to a vote of the people.

On a bill to shape a new county out of Sangamon and other counties, making changes endangering the Long Nine politically, Lincoln maneuvered with amendments that defeated the bill. When Usher F. Linder put in resolutions for a sweeping investigation of the management of the State Bank of Illinois in Springfield, Lincoln made a long speech of cogent argument and pointed humor, saying Linder had "the faculty of entangling a subject, so that neither himself, or any other man, can find head or tail to it."

Back of an investigation that would cost ten or twelve thousand dollars, Lincoln saw rival interests. "These capitalists generally act harmoniously, and in concert, to fleece the people, and now, that they have got into a quarrel with themselves, we are called upon to appropriate the people's money to settle the quarrel." Lincoln denied being a special advocate of the Bank but he would stand against any politicians trying to harm the credit of the Bank. And the House heard him: "Mr. Chairman, this movement is exclusively the work of politicians; a set of men who have interests aside from the interests of the people, and who, to say the most of them, are, taken as a mass, at least one long step removed from honest men. I say this with the greater freedom because, being a politician myself, none can regard it as personal." Linder's resolution was trimmed to a limited investigation which ended in a report favorable to the Bank. On a later bill to increase by $2,000,000 the capital stock of the Bank, Lincoln voted Yea with the majority.

In three ballots for U.S. Senator, Lincoln voted for Archibald Williams of Quincy, a lawyer from Kentucky who had switched from Democrat to Whig. Election went to Richard M. Young, a circuit judge and a "milk-and-cider" Jackson man who ran ahead of a "whole-hog" Jackson man, Williams running third. In celebration fine wines and liquors flowed at a supper where dishes and goblets went flying and Stephen A. Douglas and James Shields danced on a table to the length of it amid cigar smoke, ribald songs and the laughter and follies of drinking men. Judge Young was pleased next day to pay $600 for the supper, cigars, drinks and damages.

Of Archibald Williams, Lincoln was to see more. They were tall and angular, alike in homely looks and humor. Williams' clothes were so careless that once a hotel clerk, seeing him loaf in a chair, begged pardon and asked, "Are you a guest of this hotel?" and Williams in a cool snarl, "Hell, no! I am one of its victims, paying five dollars a day!" Williams was the kind of man Lincoln could talk with about Andrew McCorkle, near Springfield, who was afraid the railroads would scare his cows so they wouldn't give milk. Or the mob that went to the house of a man and took him away and hanged him to a tree; the night was dark and in the morning they saw they had hanged the wrong man; and they went and told the widow, "The laugh is on us!" Or the revolt of the small farmers against fines to be laid on them when their "little bulls" strayed; they had roared so loud that the House on December 19 had repealed its act of the previous session by 81 to 4. And it bordered on humor of some generous kind when an omnibus bill granting divorces to a number of persons was amended to read, "and all other persons who are desirous of being divorced." Or a bill to provide a 50-cent bounty for "wolf scalps with the ears thereon."

In the House were 64 Democrats to 27 Whigs but in the Senate the roll was 22 Democrats to 18 Whigs. Through Lincoln's strategy the Senate first took up a bill to "permanently locate the seat of government of the State of Illinois." The bill passed and went to the House where maneuver and debate began to rage. A Coles County man who had "been seen" by Lincoln, moved an amendment which passed, that no less than $50,000 and two acres of land must be donated by the new capital when chosen; this would be a mean obstacle to rivals of Springfield. Other amendments, aimed at butchering the bill, came up and failed in the late afternoon as candles were lighted and members could see out of the windows a driving snow. Some members had left the hall as though there would be only more monotonous amendments. Then suddenly a motion was made to table the bill "until next Fourth of July." And the motion passed by 39 to 38! Lincoln and the seven of the Long Nine in the House voted Nay. It looked like the end for their hope of making Springfield the new capital.

That night Lincoln called his Sangamon County colleagues into conference and gave each an assignment. They went out into the driving snow and knocked on doors. They found five members who had voted to table and brought them to change their vote in the morning. They located absentees of the afternoon who favored the bill and got their word to be surely on hand in the morning. Of five members whom they had favored with votes for railroads or canals they asked for a little gratitude. To others they threatened that in the Internal Improvements Bill, not yet passed by the Senate, their two Sangamon senators and others might rub out some of the railroads and canals. To Benjamin Enloe of Johnson County they pointed out that the longest railroad in the state was to run along the west line of his county. Also it seemed they promised to make Enloe warden of the state penitentiary, which promise they kept that very month. From door to door and room to room went Lincoln's colleagues using persuasions and threats.

Next morning, February 18, Enloe moved the bill "be re-considered." A roll call demanded by Douglas showed 42 Yea and 40 Nay. One member shifting from Yea to Nay would have killed the bill. A motion to table "until the 4th of July next" lost by 37 to 46. It was hazardous and delicately shaded politics Lincoln was playing.

Over the next week came more amendments and harassing tactics, including a motion to postpone selection of a new capital till December 1839. On the third reading of the bill February 24, 1837, the House passed it by 46 to 37. The House and Senate then held a joint session on location and the fourth ballot gave Springfield 73, Vandalia 16, Jacksonville 11, Peoria 8, Alton 6, Illiopolis 3—Henry Mills of Edwards voting for Purgatory on the third ballot. The losers charged "bargain and corruption." But it was all over and Springfield put on a jubilee; citizens howled and danced around a big bonfire blazing at the old whipping post on the public square till that relic was ashes.

In the Southern States it was against the law to speak against slavery; agitators of slave revolts would be hanged and had been. The 3,000,000 Negro workers in the Southern States on the tax books were livestock valued at more than a billion dollars. In political parties and churches, in business partnerships and families, the slavery question was beginning to split the country in two. The secret "Underground Railway" ran from Slave States across Free States and over the line into Canada. An antislavery man would keep a runaway slave in his house, cellar or barn, and at night or in a load of hay in the daytime, pass him along to the next "station." Officers and slaveowners came north with warrants hunting their runaway property; Illinois was seeing them often. Also bogus slave hunters in southern Illinois kidnaped free Negroes, took them to slave soil and sold them. The governor had sent a brief note with memorials from six states notifying the House that the slavery question was becoming a burning issue.

Amid this welter, Lincoln could understand his fellow members in resolutions declaring: "We highly disapprove of the formation of abolition societies; . . . the right of property in slaves is sacred to the slave-holding States by the Federal Constitution, and . . . they cannot be deprived of that right without their consent . . ."

Lincoln voted against these resolutions, joined by only five other members, one of them Dan Stone, a Yankee graduate of Middlebury College, a lawyer and a member of the Ohio Legislature before coming to Springfield in 1833. Stone and Lincoln, three days before the legislature adjourned March 6, recorded this protest in language completely courteous but quietly unmistakable in meaning:

Resolutions upon the subject of domestic slavery having passed both branches of the General Assembly at its present session, the undersigned hereby protest against the passage of the same.

They believe that the institution of slavery is founded on both injustice and bad policy; but that the promulgation of abolition doctrines tends rather to increase than abate its evils.

They believe that the Congress of the United States has no power under the constitution, to interfere with the institution of slavery in the different States.

They believe that the Congress of the United States has the power, under the constitution, to abolish slavery in the District of Columbia; but that that power ought not to be exercised unless at the request of the people of said District.

The difference between these opinions and those contained in the said resolutions, is their reason for entering this protest.

In December of this winter, Lincoln had written a drawling, hesitant, half-bashful letter to the daughter of a rich farmer in Green County, Kentucky, Miss Mary Owens, four months older than Lincoln, plump-faced, with a head of dark curly hair, large blue eyes, five feet five inches high. On her first visit to New Salem three years before, she had interested Lincoln; her sister, Mrs. Bennett Abell, at whose house Lincoln had stayed, played matchmaker and wanted the two to get married. When starting for a visit with her sister in Kentucky, Mrs. Abell, perhaps only joking, said she would bring her sister back if Lincoln would marry her. And Lincoln said, perhaps only joking, that he accepted the proposal to become Mrs. Abell's brother-in-law.

When Miss Owens came back to New Salem with her sister in November 1836, Lincoln saw three years had worked changes, Miss Owens having lost bloom, lost teeth, and become stout. He made love to her, it seemed, in a rather easy careless way. And she held him off as one trained in Kentucky schools for refined young ladies, dressed in what one of the Greens called "the finest trimmings I ever saw." She noted Lincoln as "deficient in those little links which make up a woman's happiness." A party riding to Uncle Billy Greene's came to a creek branch with a treacherous crossing. Miss Owens noticed the other men helping their partners, Lincoln riding ahead of her without looking back. "You are a nice fellow!" heard Lincoln when she caught up with him. "I suppose you did not care whether my neck was broken or not." And he had laughed back a defense compliment; he knew she was smart enough to take care of herself. She climbed a steep hill with Lincoln and Mrs. Bowling Green, Lincoln joking and talking to her, not once offering to help carry the fat baby in Mrs. Green's arms. It seemed to Miss Owens to be "neglect" on Lincoln's part.

He puzzled her; in some things he was so softhearted. He told her he saw "a hog mired down" one day crossing a prairie and being "fixed up" in his best clothes, he said to himself he would pass on. But after he had passed on, the hog haunted him and seemed to be saying, "There, now my last hope is gone," and he had gone back and got the hog loose from the mire. Miss Owens had ideas about chivalry and wondered how a man could be so thoughtful about a mired hog and another time be so lost in his own feelings that he couldn't stay alongside his woman partner when riding across a dangerous creek. They had some vague understanding that they might marry. Lincoln had written her one letter she hadn't answered, and one cold, lonesome winter night, he wrote her a second letter:

VANDALIA, Decr. 13, 1836

MARY

I have been sick ever since my arrival here, or I should have written sooner. It is but little difference, however, as I have verry little even yet to write. And more, the longer I can avoid the mortification of looking in the Post Office for your letter and not finding it, the better. You see I am mad about that *old letter* yet I dont like verry well to risk you again. I'll try you once more any how.

The new State House is not yet finished, and consequently the legislature is doing little or nothing. The Governor delivered an inflamitory political Message, and it is expected there will be some sparring between the parties about [it as] soon as the two Houses get to business. Taylor [deliv]ered up his petitions for the *New County* to one of [our me]mbers this morning. I am told that he dispairs [of its] success on account of all the members from Morg[an C]ounty opposing it. There are names enough on the petition[,] I think, to justify the members from our county in going for it; but if the members from Morgan oppose it, which they [say] they will, the chance will be bad.

Our chance to [take th]e seat of Government to Springfield is better than I ex[pected]. An Internal-Improvement Convention was held here since we met, which recommended a loan of several mill[ions] of dollars on the faith of the State to construct Rail Roads. Some of the legislature are for it[,] and some against it; which has the majority I can not tell. There is great strife and struggling for the office of U.S. Senator here at this time. It is probable we shall ease their pains in a few days. The opposition men have no candidate of their own, and consequently they smile as complacently at the angry snarls of the contending Van Buren candidates and their respective friends, as the christian does at Satan's rage. You recollect I mentioned in the outset of this letter that I had been unwell. That is the fact, though I believe I am well about now; but that, with other things I can not account for, have conspired and have gotten my spirits so low, that I feel that I would rather be any place in the world than here. I really can not endure the thought of staying here ten weeks. Write back as soon as you get this, and if possible say something that will please me, for really I have not [been] pleased since I left you. This letter is so dry and [stupid] that I am ashamed to send it, but with my pres[ent] feelings I can not do any better.

Give my respects to M[r. and] Mrs. Abell and family.

Your friend

LINCOLN

He was as cryptic in writing to her as she was in not writing to him. It was a letter of loneliness and of hunger for love and hope running low of any answering love.

Robert L. Wilson of the village of Athens and one of the Long Nine wrote of Lincoln as having "a quaint and peculiar way" and "he frequently startled us." He seemed a "born" politician. "We followed his lead; but he followed nobody's lead. It may almost be said that he did our thinking for us. He inspired respect, although he was careless and negligent . . . He was poverty itself, but independent." They had seen much of each other in the legislature and campaigning together, Wilson writing, "He sought company, and indulged in fun without stint . . . still when by himself, he told me that he was so overcome by mental depression, that he never dared carry a knife in his pocket; and as long as I was intimately acquainted with him, he never carried a pocketknife." At a banquet in Athens, Wilson gave the toast: "Abraham Lincoln; one of Nature's Noblemen."

In Springfield, Lincoln read lavish compliments to himself in the press and sat with the Long Nine and 60 guests at a game supper where one toast ran: "Abraham Lincoln: he has fulfilled the expectations of his friends, and disappointed the hopes of his enemies."

In April he packed his saddlebags to leave New Salem where six years before he had arrived, as he said, "a piece of floating driftwood," being now a licensed lawyer, a member of the state legislature and floor leader of the Whig party. The hilltop village, now fading to become a ghost town, had been to him a nourishing mother, a neighborhood of many names and faces that would always be dear and cherished with him, a friendly place with a peculiar equality between man and man, where Bill Greene was nearly correct in saying, "In New Salem every man is a principal citizen." Bitter hours but more sweet than bitter he had had. Here he had groped in darkness and grown toward light. Here newspapers, books, mathematics, law, the ways of people and life, had taken on new and subtle meanings for him.

Chapter 4

Lawyer in Springfield

Springfield with 1,400 inhabitants in 1837 was selling to 18,000 people of the county a large part of their supplies, tools, groceries, and buying grain, pork and farm produce. There were 19 dry-goods besides other general stores, six churches, 11 lawyers and 18 doctors. Farm women coming to town wore shoes where they used to be barefoot; men had changed from moccasins to rawhide boots and shoes. Carriages held men in top boots and ruffled silk shirts, women in silks and laces. It was no wilderness that Abraham Lincoln, 28 years old, saw as he rode into Springfield April 15, 1837. Many of its people had come from Kentucky by horse, wagon and boat, across country not yet cleared of wolves, wildcats and horse thieves. A Yankee antislavery element in the Presbyterian Church had seceded to form a Second Presbyterian Church. And there were in Sangamon County 78 free Negroes, 20 registered indentured servants and six slaves.

Lincoln pulled in his horse at the general-store of Joshua Speed. He asked the price of bedclothes for a single bedstead, which Speed figured at $17. "Cheap as it is, I have not the money to pay," he told Speed. "But if you will credit me until Christmas, and my experiment here as a lawyer is a success, I will pay you then. If I fail in that I will probably never pay you at all." Speed said afterward: "The tone of his voice was so melancholy that I felt for him . . . I thought I never saw so gloomy and melancholy a face in my life." Speed offered to share his own big double bed upstairs over the store. Lincoln took his saddlebags upstairs, came down with his face lit up and said, "Well, Speed, I'm moved." A friendship, to last long, began, as with William Butler, clerk of the Sangamon Circuit Court, who told Lincoln he could take his meals at the Butler home and there would be no mention of board bills.

The circuit courtroom was in a two-story building in Hoffman's Row, and upstairs over the courtroom was the law office of the new firm of Stuart & Lincoln: a little room with a few loose boards for bookshelves, an old wood stove, a table, a chair, a bench, a buffalo robe and a small bed. Stuart was running for Congress, so Lincoln most of the time handled all of their law practice in range of his ability. Between law cases he kept up his political fences, writing many letters.

In the street could be seen farmers hauling corn, wheat, potatoes and turnips in wagons; the axles creaked; husky voices bawled at the yokes of steers while the whip thongs lashed and cracked. Droves of hogs came past, in muddy weather wallowing over their knees, the hair of their flanks spattered, their curls of tails flipping as they grunted onward to sale and slaughter. And there were horses, men riding and driving who loved roans, grays, whites, black horses with white stockings, sorrels with a sorrel forelock down a white face, bays with a white star in the forehead. To Levi Davis, Esq., of Vandalia, Lincoln wrote on April 19, "We have, generally in this country, peace, health, and plenty, and no news." Yet his own peace of mind was clouded 18 days later when again he wrote Mary Owens. She would have to be poor and show her poverty, if she married him. He was willing to marry, if she so wished. His advice would be not to marry. The letter read:

SPRINGFIELD, May 7, 1837

FRIEND MARY

I have commenced two letters to send you before this, both of which displeased me before I got half done, and so I tore them up. The first I thought was'nt serious enough, and the second was on the other extreme. I shall send this, turn out as it may.

This thing of living in Springfield is rather a dull business after all, at least it is so to me. I am quite as lonesome here as [I] ever was anywhere in my life. I have been spoken to by but one woman since I've been here, and should not have been by her, if she could have avoided it. I've never been to church yet, nor probably shall not be soon. I stay away because I am conscious I should not know how to behave myself.

I am often thinking of what we said of your coming to live at Springfield. I am afraid you would not be satisfied. There is a great deal of flourishing about in carriages here, which it would be your doom to see without shareing in it. You would have to be poor without the means of hiding your poverty. Do you believe you could bear that patiently? Whatever woman may cast her lot with mine, should any ever do so, it is my intention to do all in my power to make her happy and contented; and there is nothing I can immagine, that would make me more unhappy than to fail in the effort. I know I shall be much happier with you than the way I am, provided I saw no signs of discontent in you. What you have said to me may have been in jest, or I may have misunderstood it. If so, then let it be forgotten; if otherwise, I much wish you would think seriously before you decide. For my part I have already decided. What I have said I will most positively abide by, provided you wish it. My opinion is that you had better not do it. You have not been accustomed to hardship, and it may be more severe than you now immagine. I know you are capable of thinking correctly on any subject; and if you deliberate maturely upon this, before you decide, then I am willing to abide your decision.

You must write me a good long letter after you get this. You have nothing else to do, and though it might not seem interesting to you, after you had written it, it would be a good deal of company to me in this "busy wilderness." Tell your sister I dont want to hear any more about selling out and moving. That gives me the hypo whenever I think of it.

Yours, &c.

LINCOLN.

That summer Mary Owens and Lincoln saw each other and came to no understanding. On the day they parted, Lincoln wrote her another letter:

SPRINGFIELD, Aug. 16th, 1837

FRIEND MARY.

You will, no doubt, think it rather strange, that I should write you a letter on the same day on which we parted; and I can only account for it by supposing, that seeing you lately makes me think of you more than usual, while at our late meeting we had but few expressions of thoughts. You must know that I can not see you, or think of you, with entire indifference; and yet it may be, that you, are mistaken in regard to what my real feelings towards you are. If I knew you were not, I should not trouble you with this letter. Perhaps any other man would know enough without further information; but I consider it *my* peculiar right to plead ignorance, and your bounden duty to allow the plea. I want in all cases to do right, and most particularly so, in all cases with women. I want, at this particular time, more than any thing else, to do right with you, and if I *knew* it would be doing right, as I rather suspect it would, to let you alone, I would do it. And for the purpose of making the matter as plain as possible, I now say, that you can now drop the subject, dismiss your thoughts (if you ever had any) from me forever, and leave this letter unanswered, without calling forth one accusing murmur from me. And I will even go further, and say, that if it will add anything to your comfort, or peace of mind, to do so, it is my sincere wish that you should. Do not understand by this, that I wish to cut your acquaintance. I mean no such thing. What I do wish is, that our further acquaintance shall depend upon yourself. If such further acquaintance would contribute nothing to your happiness, I am sure it would not to mine. If you feel yourself in any degree bound to me, I am now willing to release you, provided you wish it; while, on the other hand, I am willing, and even anxious to bind you faster, if I can be convinced that it will, in any considerable degree, add to your happiness. This, indeed, is the whole question with me. Nothing would make me more miserable than to believe you miserable—nothing more happy, than to know you were so.

In what I have now said, I think I can not be misunderstood, and to make myself understood, is the only object of this letter.

If it suits you best to not answer this—farewell—a long life and a merry one attend you. But if you conclude to write back, speak as plainly as I do. There can be neither harm nor danger, in saying, to me, any thing you think, just in the manner you think it.

My respects to your sister.

Your friend

LINCOLN

He mentioned no memory of a kiss. He was her "friend" rather than lover. What they had was an "acquaintance," so definitely no affair of passion. Months passed till the first day of April 1838. And comedy and glee lighted him as he wrote to Mrs. Orville H. Browning, who lived in Quincy. The wife of a colleague in the legislature, he had found her exceptionally gracious and understanding in conversation; she had a sense of humor lacking in her husband. On this April Fool's Day he confessed he had vanity, stupidity, and had made a fool of himself:

SPRINGFIELD, April 1. 1838.

DEAR MADAM:

Without appologising for being egotistical, I shall make the history of so much of my own life, as has elapsed since I saw you, the subject of this letter. And by the way I now discover, that, in order to give you a full and inteligible account of the things I have done and suffered *since* I saw you, I shall necessarily have to relate some that happened *before*.

It was, then, in the autumn of 1836, that a married lady of my acquaintance, and who was a great friend

of mine, being about to pay a visit to her father and
other relatives residing in Kentucky, proposed to me,
that on her return she would bring a sister of hers with
her, upon condition that I would engage to become her
brother-in-law with all convenient dispach. I, of course,
accepted the proposal; for you know I could not have
done otherwise, had I really been averse to it; but privately between you and me, I was most confoundedly
well pleased with the project. I had seen the said sister
some three years before, thought her inteligent and
agreeable, and saw no good objection to plodding
life through hand in hand with her. Time passed on,
the lady took her journey, and in due time returned,
sister in company sure enough. This stomached me a
little; for it appeared to me, that her coming so readily
showed that she was a trifle too willing; but on reflection it occured to me, that she might have been prevailed on by her married sister to come, without any
thing concerning me ever having been mentioned to
her; and so I concluded that if no other objection presented itself, I would consent to wave this. All this
occured upon my *hearing* of her arrival in the neighbourhood; for, be it remembered, I had not yet *seen*
her, except about three years previous, as before mentioned.

In a few days we had an interview, and although I
had seen her before, she did not look as my immagina-
tion had pictured her. I knew she was over-size, but
she now appeared a fair match for Falstaff; I knew she
was called an "old maid", and I felt no *doubt* of the
truth of at least half of the appelation; but now, when
I beheld her, I could not for my life avoid thinking of
my mother; and this, not from withered features, for
her skin was too full of fat, to permit its contracting
in to wrinkles; but from her want of teeth, weather-
beaten appearance in general, and from a kind of notion that ran in my head, that *nothing* could have
commenced at the size of infancy, and reached her
present bulk in less than thirtyfive or forty years; and,

in short, I was not all pleased with her. But what could I do? I had told her sister that I would take her for better or for worse; and I made a point of honor and conscience in all things, to stick to my word, especially if others had been induced to act on it, which in this case, I doubted not they had, for I was now fairly convinced that no other man on earth would have her, and hence the conclusion that they were bent on holding me to my bargain. Well, thought I, I have said it, and, be consequences what they may, it shall not be my fault if I fail to do it. At once I determined to consider her my wife; and this done, all my powers of discovery were put to the rack, in search of perfections in her, which might be fairly set-off against her defects. I tried to imagine she was handsome, which, but for her unfortunate corpulency, was actually true. Exclusive of this, no woman that I have ever seen, has a finer face. I also tried to convince myself, that the mind was much more to be valued than the person; and in this, she was not inferior, as I could discover, to any with whom I had been acquainted.

Shortly after this, without attempting to come to any positive understanding with her, I set out for Vandalia, where and when you first saw me. During my stay there, I had letters from her, which did not change my opinion of either her intelect or intention; but on the contrary, confirmed it in both.

All this while, although I was fixed "firm as the surge repelling rock" in my resolution, I found I was continually repenting the rashness, which had led me to make it. Through life I have been in no bondage, either real or imaginary, from the thraldom of which I so much desired to be free.

After my return home, I saw nothing to change my opinion of her in any particular. She was the same and so was I. I now spent my time between planing how I might get along through life after my contemplated change of circumstances should have taken place; and how I might procrastinate the evil day for a time, which I really dreaded as much—perhaps more, than an irishman does the halter.

After all my suffering upon this deeply interesting subject, here I am, wholly unexpectedly, completely out of the "scrape"; and I now want to know, if you can guess how I got out of it. Out clear in every sense of the term; no violation of word, honor or conscience. I dont believe you can guess, and so I may as well tell you at once. As the lawyers say, it was done in the manner following, towit. After I had delayed the matter as long as I thought I could in honor do, which by the way had brought me round into the last fall, I concluded I might as well bring it to a consumation without further delay; and so I mustered my resolution, and made the proposal to her direct; but, shocking to relate, she answered, No. At first I supposed she did it through an affectation of modesty, which I thought but ill-become her, under the peculiar circumstances of her case; but on my renewal of the charge, I found she repeled it with greater firmness than before. I tried it again and again, but with the same success, or rather with the same want of success. I finally was forced to give it up, at which I verry unexpectedly found myself mortified almost beyond endurance. I was mortified, it seemed to me, in a hundred different ways. My vanity was deeply wounded by the reflection, that I had so long been too stupid to discover her intentions, and at the same time never doubting that I understood them perfectly; and also, that she whom I had taught myself to believe no body else would have, had actually rejected me with all my fancied greatness; and to cap the whole, I then, for the first time, began to suspect that I was really a little in love with her. But let it all go. I'll try and out live it. Others have been made fools of by the girls; but this can never be with truth said of me. I most emphatically, in this instance, made a fool of myself. I have now come to the conclusion never again to think of marrying; and for this reason; I can never be satisfied with any one who would be block-head enough to have me.

When you receive this, write me a long yarn about something to amuse me. Give my respects to Mr. Browning.

Your sincere friend

A. LINCOLN

The letter, like those to Miss Owens, was a self-portrait. He named no names but his own. Mr. and Mrs. Browning took it as the queer prank of a mind of fantasy and humor. The Rabelaisian streak in it was one well known to those who had heard Lincoln's storytelling. Had he named the woman he could have had credit as a vicious gossip. He rollicked on in the fun of having gotten out of a scrape. And yet in this period of his life he let himself go in sarcasm and satire that was to bring him shame and humiliation. He would change. He was to learn, at cost, how to use the qualities of pity and compassion that lay deeply and naturally in his heart, toward wiser reading and keener understanding of all men and women he met.

Later when Mrs. Abell visited her sister in Kentucky, Miss Owens told neighbors that Abe Lincoln said to Mrs. Abell, in Springfield, "Tell your sister that I think she was a great fool because she did not stay here and marry me." If true, he was as baffling to them as to himself in heart affairs.

The 1837 business panic had come, banks failing, depositors out of luck, loans called and money tight, the *Sangamo Journal* saying the "groan of hard times is echoed from one end of the country to the other." The State Bank in Springfield had "suspended specie payments"; you could have folding paper money but no coin, no hard money. Governor Duncan had called a special session of the legislature which met July 10 in Vandalia, voted against repeal of the $10,000,000 Internal Improvements scheme which the governor said was "fraught with evil." Approval of banks suspending specie payments was voted, Lincoln continuously defending the Springfield bank. On watch and swift, he was against repeated resolutions to repeal the bill making Springfield the state capital. After two weeks he was back in Springfield joining in the dirtiest mud-slinging campaign that Springfield politics had ever seen, "no holds barred," many old friendships to go on the rocks.

The Whigs were running for probate judge Dr. Anson G. Henry, egotist, orator, gadfly, peppery fighter who welcomed enemies. Against him was General James Adams, a lawyer, a veteran of the War of 1812 and a minor Indian war, 54 years old, and one of the old settlers of Springfield. The Adams men published insinuations that Henry, as a commissioner in the building of the new capitol, was a wild spender of the people's money. The Whigs called public meetings, appointed a bipartisan committee and whitewashed Henry. The Whig sheriff Garret Elkin canceled his subscription to the new Democratic paper, the *Illinois Republican*, because of a mean article about Dr. Henry; that paper printed another mean article and Sheriff Elkin went to the office of the paper and horsewhipped the editor, George R. Weber. A brother of Weber got himself a knife, found Elkin and a friend Daniel Cutright and managed to sink the knife into both of them; the three involved were arrested.

Meantime, Mrs. Joseph Anderson, a widow, had come to Springfield to sell ten acres of land left her by her husband, only to find General Adams claimed that the ten acres had been signed over to him by her husband for a legal debt he owed Adams. Stuart and Lincoln took her case. Lincoln searched records and wrote six anonymous letters printed weekly in the *Sangamo Journal* which questioned "Gen. Adams's titles to certain tracts of land, and the manner in which he acquired them," and how Adams got a ten-year lease to two city lots for $10. Two days before the August 7 election a handbill, written but not signed by Lincoln, was given out over the town. It recited a series of alleged facts about the ten acres claimed by Mrs. Anderson and an assignment of judgment by Anderson to Adams being freshly handwritten in what appeared to be the handwriting of Adams. In effect, Lincoln was publicly accusing Adams of being a forger and swindler, this without a trial, with no evidence heard from the accused, and witnesses cited from only one side. It seemed Lincoln expected this handbill to blast Adams out of politics. He guessed wrong. In the August 7 election Adams won by 1,025 votes against 792 for Henry.

Adams now gave in the *Republican* a six-column reply to Lincoln and Lincoln in a one-column reply said affidavits offered by Adams were "all false as hell" and "I have a character to defend as well as Gen. Adams, but I disdain to *whine* about it as he does." Two weeks after election the *Sangamo Journal* reprinted the pre-election handbill. Instead of suing Lincoln and the *Journal* for libel Adams wrote another six columns for the *Republican*. Lincoln seemed to have played for a libel suit, hoping he could lay his evidence before a jury. As a final challenge to a libel suit, the *Sangamo Journal* in November reprinted the pre-election handbill with its unmistakable implication that Adams was a forger and swindler, Adams making no answer. Nor did Adams take action when an editorial supposed to have been written by Lincoln was published in the *Sangamo Journal*, giving a copy of an indictment found against Adams in Oswego County, New York, in 1818, the crime charged being forgery of a deed. "A person of evil name and fame and of wicked disposition," was the *Journal*'s allusion to Adams.

In the course of replying to Lincoln, Adams had included Stephen T. Logan, an able and respected lawyer, as connected with Lincoln in forgery. Logan sued Adams for libel at $10,000 damages; the case was finally dismissed on Adams' payment of costs with a statement for the record that he "never intended" to charge Logan with forgery. In the courts the Stuart and Lincoln case of Mrs. Anderson for ten acres of land never came to trial, was dropped when Adams died; his widow and heirs got the ten acres. Through the entire affair Lincoln showed none of the management sagacity he had at Vandalia and little of the cool persuasive logic, mixed with good humor, of which he was capable at his best.

In law office routine Lincoln took depositions, drew deeds, filed declarations, bills of complaint, praecipes, perhaps taking an afternoon off when the famous Whig, Dan-

iel Webster, made an hour and a half speech at a barbecue
in a grove west of town. An official of the Post Office Department came one day to Springfield and asked about a
certain amount of dollars and cents that had come into the
hands of Lincoln as postmaster at New Salem. Lincoln
brought out a sack and counted the money in it, the exact
amount asked for by the inspector, who took the money,
gave a receipt, and went away satisfied. People in trouble
over land or money or love, witnesses, murderers, scandal-
mongers and slanderers, came to pour out their stories
within the walls of the Stuart and Lincoln law office. In
one of his first murder cases, Lincoln failed to save William Fraim, a 20-year-old, who in a drunken brawl killed
a fellow laborer; he was convicted and hanged.

On a hot summer day Harvey Ross came to prove ownership of his farm at Macomb, needing the testimony of a
witness near Springfield. Court had closed, Lincoln explained, but they would go out to Judge Thomas' farm.
With a bundle of papers in one hand and in the other a red
handkerchief for wiping sweat, Lincoln with Ross and the
witness walked to the farm. The judge had gone to a tenant
house on the north part of the farm, to help his men put up
a corncrib and hog pen, said Mrs. Thomas; the main road
would be a half-mile but cutting across the cornfield from
the barn would be only a quarter-mile. They struck out
Indian file, Lincoln still with papers in one hand and red
handkerchief in the other. Arriving where the judge and
his men were raising logs, Lincoln put the case to the judge,
who looked over the papers, swore in the witness, and, with
pen and ink from the tenant house, signed the documents.
All were in shirt sleeves, and Lincoln remarked it was a
kind of shirt-sleeve court they were holding. "Yes," laughed
the judge, "a shirt-sleeve court in a cornfield." On Lincoln
offering to roll up logs the judge guessed he could stand a
little help, so they pitched in and when Ross asked the judge
his fee the judge said he guessed their help was pay enough.

Lawyer Lincoln studied the face of Eliza Lloyd as she
told of her husband, Peter, leaving her with a newborn
baby, never furnishing support, becoming a habitual drunkard and, jailed for larceny, having broken jail. Lincoln

wrote a bill of complaint "that the bonds of matrimony heretofore and now existing between the said Peter Lloyd and your oratrix be dissolved."

In a sensational murder case Stuart and Lincoln had their hands full in many weeks of 1838. Their last captain in the Black Hawk War, Jacob M. Early, a Democrat, had tangled with Henry B. Truett, another Democrat, over a political office. In the parlor of the Spottswood Hotel in Springfield they came to hot words and wild threats. On Truett drawing a pistol, Early picked up a chair to defend himself or to attack Truett. Truett shot Early dead. After indictment of Truett, Stephen A. Douglas was appointed prosecuting attorney, the regular prosecutor being a witness in the case. Assisting Stuart and Lincoln for the defense were attorneys, all Whig, Stephen T. Logan, Edward D. Baker and Cyrus Walker, who managed to get delays from March 14 till trial began October 9, when public feeling against Truett had simmered down. So many people had read or heard about the case, and formed opinions, that not till the third day was a twelfth juror agreed on.

Logan contended that Early, a larger man than Truett, with an upraised chair in his hands, carried a deadly weapon, Truett believing the chair would come crashing on his head and kill him. Prosecutor Douglas insisted Truett came to the Spottswood Hotel with a gun, meaning to pick a fight with Early. Lincoln's plea to the jury was considered very effective and partly responsible for the verdict of acquittal for Truett. Before moving actively into the case in March, Stuart and Lincoln each accepted from Truett a note for $250 secured by a mortgage on two sections of land. That Truett was a man of violence who liked gunplay was a comment some years later when Truett, then in San Francisco, fought a duel and sank a bullet in his opponent.

In October 1837 the Reverend Jeremiah Porter was to speak against slavery in a church. A crowd gathered, some swearing they would mob him. Edward D. Baker cooled the crowd down, Porter made his address, but it took more wise handling of the crowd to get Porter out of town with no marks on him. At a citizens meeting in the courthouse a few days later, Judge Thomas C. Browne in the chair, resolutions were passed that "The doctrine of immediate emancipation . . . is at variance with christianity," and "abolitionists . . . are . . . dangerous members of society, and should be shunned by all good citizens." In nearby St. Louis a free mulatto named McIntosh resisting arrest had stabbed a deputy sheriff to death; a mob seized him in the street, took him to a suburb, chained him to a tree, burned him to death and the next morning boys threw stones at the skull as a target.

Into nearby Alton had moved a 35-year-old abolitionist Presbyterian minister, after editing a paper in St. Louis. His printing press arrived on a Sunday and that night was dumped into the Mississippi River by unknown persons. Friendly citizens bought him another printing press which a mob took and threw into the river, as they did a third printing press after he had helped organize an Illinois anti-slavery society. Word came that Ohio abolitionists were sending him another printing press. It arrived and was moved into a warehouse where a guard was kept. A night mob stormed the warehouse November 7, 1837, and failing to get in, tried to set the warehouse on fire. Elijah Parish Lovejoy rushed out to stop the attempt at arson and fell dead from a mob bullet. His brother, Owen Lovejoy, a Congregational minister, knelt at the grave and vowed "never to forsake the cause that had been sprinkled with my brother's blood." Lincoln over at Springfield could not know that in years to come, amid inscrutable political labyrinths, he and Owen Lovejoy would understand and cling to each other, Lincoln to write, "To the day of his death, it would scarcely wrong any other to say, he was my most generous friend."

In a carefully written address, "The Perpetuation of Our Political Institutions," before the Young Men's Lyceum of Springfield in January 1838, Lincoln's theme was the spirit of violence in men overriding law and legal procedure. He pointed to the men of the Revolution who, at cost of death and mutilation, had won the liberties of men now being violated, saying, "whenever the vicious portion of population shall be permitted to gather . . . and burn churches, ravage and rob provision stores, throw printing presses into rivers, shoot editors, and hang and burn obnoxious persons at pleasure, and with impunity; depend on it, this Government cannot last." It was Lincoln's masterpiece of thought and speech up to this, his 29th year. No quotes from it could indicate the main closely woven fabric of the address. He dealt with momentous sacred ideas, basic in love of the American Dream, of personal liberty and individual responsibility. They were seeds in his mind foreshadowing growth. He spoke a toleration of free discussion; even abolitionists, keeping within the law, could have their say, a viewpoint not agreeable to the dominant southern element of Sangamon County who, if not in the listening audience, could read the printed text in the *Sangamo Journal*.

Again running for the legislature in the summer of 1838, Lincoln spent most of the campaign speaking for Stuart who was running for Congress against Douglas. Once when Stuart took sick, Lincoln went to Bloomington and debated with Douglas. Once in Archer G. Herndon's store, over a sloppy wet floor, Stuart and Douglas tussled and mauled each other, "fought like wildcats." And three days before election a Douglas speech in front of the Market House riled the tall, supple Stuart, who got a neck hold on the short, thick Douglas and dragged him around the Market House. Stuart came out of it with a scar for life where Douglas put a deep bite in his thumb. In the August 6 election Lincoln led in a field of 17 candidates. In a total of 36,495 votes, Stuart won over Douglas by the slim majority of 36 votes. Douglas cried for a recount but couldn't get it.

In Vandalia in December the Whigs nominated Lincoln for speaker of the House, and failing of election he worked as Whig floor leader. Again his maneuvers and votes favored the Internal Improvements spending, partly because he with others had so earnestly promised the funds for improvements to members who voted for Springfield as the new capital. Vandalia still had able members trying to keep her as the capital. Again Lincoln toiled on county reorganizations, on state reapportionment, and supported the Illinois and Michigan Canal. His main proposal, for the state to buy from the Federal Government public lands of about 20,000,000 acres at 25 cents an acre to be resold for $1.25 an acre, was approved, but came to no later results. Up till this time state tax money had come only from land owned by outsiders in Illinois and Lincoln voted for a new tax of 25 cents per $100 of assessed valuation on *all* real property in Illinois. To one member worried about property owners crying against the new law Lincoln said it took from the *"wealthy few"* rather than the *"many poor"* and definitely the wealthy few were "not sufficiently numerous to carry the elections."

He wrote William Butler and cleared up bad feeling between Butler and Ned Baker. "Your . . . letter to him was written while you were in a state of high excitement . . . it reached Baker while he was writhing under a severe toothache." As to Butler writing of Lincoln's bad conduct in some piece of legislation, he wrote Butler, "I am willing to pledge myself in black and white to cut my own throat from ear to ear, if, when I meet you, you shall *seriously* say, that you believe me capable of betraying my friends for any price."

He wrote to Stuart as to some business or legislative matter, "Ewing wont do any thing. He is not worth a damn. Your friend A. Lincoln." At his suggestion that the House membership should be limited to 99 or less, another member spoke of the Long Nine *"and old women"* seeming to favor the number 9. "Now," said Lincoln, "if any woman, old or young, ever thought there was any peculiar charm in this distinguished specimen of number 9, I have, as yet, been so unfortunate as not to have discovered it." After adjournment March 4 he rode out of Vandalia with perhaps a last backward look at the city he had helped rub off the map as the state capital.

Back in Springfield at law practice, Lincoln wrote his partner in Washington the news and for information wanted, as in one letter, "a d——d hawk billed yankee is here, besetting me at every turn I take, saying that Robt Kinzie never received the $80. to which he was entitled. Can you tell me any thing about the matter?" On payment of a fee, he would wrap "Stuart's half" in a piece of paper so marked.

He had seen the convention system working well for the Democrats and helped organize the first state Whig convention. It met in Springfield, named him one of five presidential electors for Illinois and a member of the State Central Committee. In December he made a speech of nearly two hours, an elaborate, intricate financial discussion of President Van Buren's scheme to replace the National Bank by a sub-treasury. He named high Democratic officials as making fortunes out of their stealings from the Government. "Look at Swartwout with his $1,200,000, Price with his $75,000, Harris with his $109,000." They and others had gone "scampering away with the public money to Texas, to Europe," and other spots of refuge. A *"running* itch" was their malady, operating "very much like the cork-leg, in the comic song, did on its owner; which, when he had once got started on it, the more he tried to stop it, the more it would run away." In closing he registered an oath: "Before High Heaven, and in the face of the world, I swear eternal fidelity to the just cause, as I deem it, of the land of my life, my liberty and my love." In a letter to Stuart he wrote, "Well, I made a big speech, which is in progress of printing in pamphlet form. I shall send you a copy."

In this December, the new capitol unfinished, the Senate met in the Methodist Church, the House in the Second Presbyterian Church. The Whigs had a majority of one in the House, each party 18 members in the Senate. Lincoln served on a committee to investigate the State Bank and signed a report which found, in the main, little mismanagement, though it was rated not good banking for the directors to allow Samuel Wiggins of Cincinnati to borrow $108,000 to pay installments on his $200,000 of bank stock, nor for the directors to make large loans to themselves and to favored individuals. Lincoln voted against forfeiture of the bank's charter, which passed, and then for a new law to revive the charter, which passed. He guided through passage a bill to incorporate the town of Springfield into a city. His amendment to the bill would make more than 12 per cent interest on loans illegal; it passed the House and died in the Senate, which pleased all loan sharks.

He voted against repeal of the big Internal Improvements Bill. This jungle of finance had by now brought the state into debt $17,000,000 and in less than two years the state was to stop payment of interest. Little was saved out of the vast wreck except the Illinois and Michigan Canal which Lincoln helped to save, and in time by able refinancing it was made a paying project. Lincoln and others kept the main colossal but crumbling scheme alive and Lincoln wrote to Stuart, to no avail, asking him to try to get action on Lincoln's plan of a previous session for the state to buy and sell public lands at a profit.

In that session the *Sangamo Journal* reported that Wickliff Kitchell in effect accused Lincoln of being drunkenly extravagant in favoring a bond issue of $1,500,000 to complete the Illinois and Michigan Canal. "Already prostrated by debt," said Kitchell, "that gentleman thinks it would be for the interest of the State to go still deeper." Kitchell told of a drunkard in Arkansas who "lost his reason" and lay in a dumb stupor from liquor. His wife couldn't bring him to. A neighbor came in and said "brandy toddy" might help. The drunk sat up at the word "toddy," saying, "That is the stuff!" Kitchell remarked, "It is so with the gentleman from Sangamon—more debt would be for the better."

Mr. Lincoln replied, "I beg leave to tell an anecdote. The gentleman's course the past winter reminds me of an eccentric old bachelor who lived in the Hoosier State. Like the gentleman from Montgomery [County], he was very famous for seeing *big bugaboos* in everything. He lived with an older brother, and one day he went out hunting. His brother heard him firing back of the field, and went out to see what was the matter. He found him loading and firing into the top of a tree. Not being able to discover anything in the tree, he asked him what he was firing at. He replied a squirrel—and kept on firing. His brother believing there was some humbug about the matter, examined his person, and found on one of his eyelashes a *big louse* crawling about. It is so with the gentleman from Montgomery. He imagines he can see squirrels every day, when they are nothing but *lice.*" "The House," said the *Sangamo Journal*, "was convulsed with laughter."

The national Whig convention in December 1839 nominated for President William Henry Harrison of Ohio, former Congressman and U.S. Senator, an 1812 war veteran and above all the commander and victor in the Battle of Tippecanoe defeating Chief Tecumseh. Nor did the Whigs fail to tell the country, howsoever true it might be, that Harrison lived in a plain log cabin and his drink was cider. Little mention was made that Harrison had lost his seat in Congress by voting against Missouri's admission to the Union unless as a Free and not a Slave State, which had its appeal to Lincoln as an early boomer of Harrison. Lincoln joined in the debating tournament in Springfield that ran eight straight evenings in December, Springfield learning, in a way, where Whig and Democrat stood. Lincoln as a four-time candidate for the legislature stumped his own district, and down into southern Illinois and over into Kentucky for the national ticket, often making two-hour speeches, at times debating with Douglas.

To a Whig conclave in Springfield in June 1840, came 15,000 people in wagons, carriages, horseback and afoot, in log cabins hauled by oxen. Thirty yoke of oxen drew one log cabin on wheels with live coons climbing a hickory tree and hard cider on tap by the cabin door. Lincoln's speech from a wagon was homely, familiar and natural, one man who heard it saying, "One story he told well illustrated the argument he was making. It was not an impure story, yet it was not one it would be seemly to publish." The *Illinois Register* said that on the platform he had too much of "an assumed clownishness" and should improve his manners.

The campaign raged around the 1837 panic, Democratic administration failures, hard times, and the Whig cry that the Democrats had been in office too long and it was time for a change. Feeling ran high and hot. Lincoln in March wrote to Stuart: "Yesterday Douglas, having chosen to consider himself insulted by something in the 'Journal,' undertook to cane Francis [the editor] in the street. Francis caught him by the hair and jammed him back against a market-cart, where the matter ended by Francis being pulled away from him. The whole affair was so ludicrous that Francis and everybody else (Douglas excepted) have been laughing about it ever since." Lincoln and Francis were two of five editors of a Whig paper, *The Old Soldier*. A "confidential" circular in stilted language tried to warm up every Whig party worker into personal activity, especially to see that all Whigs went to the polls. The wild campaign ended with Harrison as winner, with 234 electoral votes against Van Buren's 60, Harrison the first northern and western man to be sent to the White House. It was a famous campaign proving that sometimes the American democracy goes on a rampage and shows it has swift and terrific power, even though it is not sure what to do with that power.

Among Illinois Whigs were regrets. They carried their national ticket, but lost the state to the Democrats. This put a new color on a case they were interested in. Months earlier they had charged the Democrats with fraud in voting; thousands of Irish workmen in the canal zone had started a test action before a circuit judge who ruled that foreign-born inhabitants must be naturalized before they could vote. The Democrats took the case to the Supreme Court, knowing that if they lost the case they would lose thousands of votes.

Then came the newly elected legislature into session, with a Democratic majority. Douglas wrote a bill which became law. It set up five new supreme court judgeships; these with the four old judges would be the supreme court of the state besides doing the work of the circuit court judges, who were thrown out. The bill passed the Senate by a vote of 22 to 17, and the House by a vote of 45 to 43. By this move the Democrats saved the canal zone vote for their party, appointed Democrats as clerks in half the counties of the state as provided in the bill. Stephen A. Douglas, no longer register of the land office under a Whig national administration, was appointed a Supreme Court judge. The reply of the Whig party was a calm address issued by a committee of which Lincoln was a member, declaring "that the independence of the Judiciary has been destroyed—that hereafter our courts will be independent of the people, and entirely dependent upon the Legislature—that our rights of property and liberty of conscience can no longer be regarded as safe from the encroachments of unconstitutional legislation."

During one session the voting was often close; when the Democrats wanted a quorum and the Whigs didn't one day, the Democrats locked the door of the House to keep the quorum in. Lincoln, Joe Gillespie and another Whig raised a window and jumped out and hid. They were laughed at loud and long because they forgot they had voted on a motion to adjourn and by so voting had made a quorum that counted before they had vamoosed.

Lincoln joined with Whigs and Democrats and by 70 to 11 votes killed a bill to give the Territory of Wisconsin the 14 northern counties of Illinois. Thus Illinois kept in its border the vital and growing Great Lakes port of Chicago. The bright little prairie town of Galesburg in Knox County won incorporation by 52 to 31, Lincoln voting Aye. The session ended. An eastern visitor wrote, "The Assembly appeared to be composed all of young men, some of them mere boys; it forcibly reminded me of a debating school of boy students. I was more amused than instructed." Plainly he had missed some of the wild howling hours, and some of the "mere boys" he saw were beginning their ride to high place and power in the nation. In his Whig circular and in certain long speeches Lincoln let go with overcolored passages of a style that he later referred to as "fizzlegigs and fireworks." He was learning.

Several days in January 1841 Lincoln was in his seat only part of the day's session, on January 12 answering only two of the four roll calls; then for five straight days he was absent from the legislature. A letter of January 22 to a Whig member who had gone home had the current gossip: "We have been very much distressed, on Mr. Lincoln's account; hearing he had two Cat fits, and a Duck fit since we left. Is it true?" On January 24 the lawyer James Conkling was writing to a woman, "Poor L! how are the mighty fallen!

He was confined about a week, but though he now appears again he is reduced and emaciated in appearance and seems scarcely to possess strength enough to speak above a whisper . . . he has experienced 'That surely 'tis the worst of pain To love and not be loved again.' " On January 20 Lincoln had written to Stuart in Washington, "I have, within the last few days, been making a most discreditable exhibition of myself in the way of hypochondriaism and thereby got an impression that Dr. Henry [Lincoln's physician] is necessary to my existence. Unless he gets that place [as Springfield postmaster] he leaves Springfield." The letter closed, "Pardon me for not writing more; I have not sufficient composure to write a long letter." He had met a woman and found his heart and mind in storm after storm.

Ninian W. Edwards of the Long Nine, a polished aristocrat and son of a former governor of Illinois, was the same age as Lincoln, and they had campaigned together and joined in Whig conferences. The Edwards' house, built of brick, stood two stories high and could have held a dozen prairie-farmer cabins. To this house in 1839 came a young woman from Lexington, Kentucky. She had been there two years before on a short visit. Now she had come to stay, Miss Mary Todd, a younger sister of Elizabeth, the wife of Ninian W. Edwards. Granddaughters of Todds who had fought through the American Revolution, their father, Robert Smith Todd, had been a captain in the War of 1812, had been clerk of the House and a state Senator, and was president of the Bank of Kentucky in Lexington.

Miss Mary Todd was 21, plump, swift, beaming. With her somewhat short figure sheathed in a gown of white with black stripes, low at the neck and giving free play to her swift neck muscles, the skirt fluffed out in a balloonish hoop, shod in modish ballroom slippers, she was a center of likes and dislikes among those who came to the house of her sister. For Lincoln, as he came to know her, she was lighted with magnets, the first aggressively brilliant feminine creature who had crossed his path so that he lost his head. One woman remarked that he didn't go as much as other young men for "ladies company." He saw in Mary Todd, with her pink-rose smooth soft skin, light brown hair hinting of bronze, ample bosom, flying glimpses of slippers, a triumph of some kind; she had finished schools where "the accomplishments" were taught; she spoke and read French. She had left her home in Kentucky because of a dispute with her stepmother. She was impetuous, picked the ridiculous angle, the weak point of anyone she disliked and spoke it with thrust of phrase. Her temper colored her; she could shine with radiance at a gift, a word, an arrival, a surprise, an achievement of a little cherished design, at winning a withheld consent. A shaft of wanted happiness could strike deep in her. Mary Todd was read, informed and versed in apparel and appearance. She hummed gay little ditties putting on a flowered bonnet and tying a double bowknot under her chin. A satisfying rose or ostrich plume in her hair was a psalm.

Her laughter could dimple in wreaths running to the core of her; she was born to impulses that rode her before she could ride them. After excesses of temper had worn her to exhaustion, she could rise and stand up to battle again for a purpose definitely formed. In the Edwards' circle they believed there were clues to her character in a remark she passed at a fireside party one evening. A young woman married to a rich man along in years was asked, "Why did you marry such a withered-up old buck?" and answered, "He had lots of houses and gold." And the quick-tongued Mary Todd in surprise: "Is that true? I would rather marry a good man, a man of mind, with a hope and bright prospects ahead for position, fame, and power than to marry all the houses, gold, and bones in the world."

In 1840 Lincoln and Mary Todd were engaged to be married. Ninian W. Edwards and his wife had argued she was throwing herself away; it wasn't a match; she and Lincoln came from different classes of society. Her stubborn Covenanter blood rose; she knew her own mind and spoke it; Lincoln had a future; he was her man more than any other she had met.

The months passed. Lincoln, the solitary, the melancholy, was busy, lost, abstracted; he couldn't go to all the parties, dances, concerts Mary Todd was going to. She flared with jealousy and went with other men; she accused him; tears;

misunderstandings. They made up, fell out, made up again. The wedding was set for New Year's Day, 1841.

And then something happened. The bride or the groom, or both, broke the engagement. It was a phantom wedding, mentioned in hushes. There was gossip and dispute about whether the wedding had been set for that date at all. Lincoln was a haunted man. Was he sure he didn't love her? He walked the streets of Springfield; he brooded, went to Dr. Henry's office, took Dr. Henry's advice and wrote a long statement of his case for a doctor in Louisville. And the doctor answered that in this kind of case he could do nothing without first a personal interview. Lincoln wrote his partner Stuart: "I am now the most miserable man living. If what I feel were equally distributed to the whole human family, there would not be one cheerful face on the earth."

He was seeing Dr. Henry often, and wrote Stuart, "Whether I shall ever be better I can not tell; I awfully forbode I shall not. To remain as I am is impossible; I must die or be better, it appears to me. The matter you speak of on my account, you may attend to as you say, unless you shall hear of my condition forbidding it. I say this, because I fear I shall be unable to attend to any business here, and a change of scene might help me. If I could be myself, I would rather remain at home with Judge Logan. I can write no more." He begged Stuart to go the limit in Washington toward the appointment of Dr. Henry as postmaster in Springfield. "You know I desired Dr. Henry to have that place when you left; I now desire it more than ever." He added that nearly all the Whig members of the legislature besides other Whigs favored the doctor for postmaster. On Lincoln asking it, Stuart requested the new Secretary of State at Washington, Daniel Webster, to appoint Lincoln chargé d'affaires at Bogotá, far from Springfield, but nothing came of it.

The legislature adjourned. Josh Speed was selling his store and going back to his folks in Kentucky. Lincoln in a struggle to come back traveled to Louisville in August and staying with Speed some three weeks shared talk and counsel with that rare friend. Speed recalled Lincoln saying he had done nothing to make any human being remember that he had lived; he wished to live to connect his name with events of his day and generation and to the interest of his fellow men. Slowly, he came back. A sweet and serene old woman, Joshua Speed's mother, talked with him, gave him a mother's care, and made him a present of an Oxford Bible.

In mid-September he was in Illinois again, writing to Speed's sister Mary about his tooth that failed of extraction when he was in Kentucky, "Well, that same old tooth got to paining me so much, that about a week since I had it torn out, bringing with it a bit of the jawbone . . . my mouth is now so sore that I can neither talk, nor eat."

Chapter 5

"I Am Going to Be Married"

Joshua Speed, deep-chested, broad between the ears, had spots soft as May violets. And he and Abraham Lincoln told each other their secrets about women. "I do not feel my own sorrows much more keenly than I do yours," Lincoln wrote Speed in one letter. And again: "You know my desire to befriend you is everlasting."

The wedding day of Speed and Fanny Henning had been set; and Speed was afraid he didn't love her; it was wearing him down; the date of the wedding loomed as the hour for a sickly affair. He wrote Lincoln he was sick. And Lincoln wrote what was wrong with Speed's physical and mental system, a letter tender as loving hands swathing a feverish forehead, yet direct in its facing of immediate facts. It was a letter showing that Lincoln in unlucky endings of love affairs must have known deep-rooted, tangled, and baffling misery.

"You are *naturally of a nervous temperament,*" he wrote. "And this I say from what I have seen of you personally, and what you have told me concerning your mother at various times, and concerning your brother William at the time his wife died." Besides this general cause, he gave three special reasons for Speed's condition—first, exposure to bad weather on his journey; second, *"the absence of all business and conversation of friends*, which might divert your mind, give it occasional rest from *that intensity* of thought, which will some times wear the sweetest idea thread-bare, and turn it to the bitterness of death. The third is, *the rapid and near approach of that crisis on which all your thoughts and feelings concentrate."*

Lincoln's broodings over the mysteries of personality, man's behavior, the baffling currents of body and mind, his ideas about his own shattered physical system were indicated in his telling Speed: "If . . . as I expect you will at some time, be agonized and distressed, let me, who have some reason to speak with judgement on such a subject, beseech you, to ascribe it to the causes I have mentioned; and not to some false and ruinous suggestion of the Devil . . . The *general one*, nervous debility, which is the key and conductor of all the particular ones, and without which *they* would be utterly harmless, though it *does* pertain to you, *does not* pertain to one in a thousand. It is out of this, that the painful difference between you and the mass of the world springs." That is, Lincoln believed that he and his friend had exceptional and sensitive personalities.

Lincoln was writing in part a personal confession in telling Speed: "I know what the painful point with you is, at all times when you are unhappy. It is an apprehension that you do not love her as you should. What nonsense!—How came you to court her? Was it because you thought she deserved it; and that you had given her reason to expect it? If it was for that, why did not the same reason make you court . . . at least twenty others of whom you can think, & to whom it would apply with greater force than to *her?* Did you court her for her wealth? Why, you knew she had none. But you say you *reasoned* yourself *into* it. What do you mean by that? Was it not, that you found yourself unable to *reason* yourself *out* of it? Did you not think, and partly form the purpose, of courting her the first time you ever saw or heard of her? . . . There was nothing *at that time* for reason to work upon. Whether she was moral, amiable, sensible, or even of good character, you did not, nor could not then know; except perhaps you might infer the last from the company you found her in. All you then did or could know of her, was her *personal appearance and deportment;* and these, if they impress at all, impress the *heart* and not the head.

"Say candidly, were not those heavenly *black eyes,* the whole basis of all your early *reasoning* on the subject? . . . Did you not go and take me all the way to Lexington and back, for no other purpose but to get to see her again . . . What earthly consideration would you take to find her scouting and despising you, and giving herself up to another? But of this you have no apprehension; and therefore you can not bring it home to your feelings. I shall be so anxious about you, that I want you to write me every mail."

Thus ended a letter which had begun, "My Dear Speed: Feeling, as you know I do, the deepest solicitude for the success of the enterprize you are engaged in, I adopt this as the last method I can invent to aid you, in case (which God forbid) you shall need any aid."

A few days before Speed's wedding, Lincoln wrote to the bridegroom. "I assure you I was not much hurt by what you wrote me of your excessively bad feeling at the time you wrote. Not that I am less capable of sympathising with you now than ever; . . . but because I hope and believe, that your present anxiety and distress about *her* health and *her* life, must and will forever banish those horid doubts, which I know you sometimes felt, as to the truth of your affection for her. If they can be once and forever removed, (and I almost feel a presentiment that the Almighty has sent your present affliction expressly for that object) surely, nothing can come in their stead, to fill their immeasurable measure of misery. The death scenes of those we love, are surely painful enough; but these we are prepared to, and expect to see. They happen to all, and all know they must happen . . . Should she, as you fear, be destined to an early grave, it is indeed, a great consolation to know that she is so well prepared to meet it. Her religion, which you once disliked so much, I will venture you now prize most highly."

Lincoln hoped Speed's melancholy forebodings as to

Fanny's early death were not well founded. "I even hope, that ere this reaches you, she will have returned with improved and still improving health; and that you will have met her, and forgotten the sorrows of the past, in the enjoyment of the present. I would say more if I could; but it seems I have said enough. It really appears to me that you yourself ought to rejoice, and not sorrow, at this indubitable evidence of your undying affection for her. Why Speed, if you do not love her, although you might not wish her death, you would most calmly be resigned to it. Perhaps this point is no longer a question with you, and my pertenacious dwelling upon it, is a rude intrusion upon your feelings . . . You know the Hell I have suffered on that point, and how tender I am upon it. You know I do not mean wrong. I have been quite clear of hypo [hypochondria] since you left,—even better than I was along in the fall. I have seen Sarah [Rickard] but once. She seemed verry cheerful, and so, I said nothing to her about what we spoke of." Speed had "kept company" with Sarah and hoped she wasn't taking it hard that he was going to marry.

Speed's wedding day came; the knot was tied. And soon he read lines from Lincoln at Springfield: "When this shall reach you, you will have been Fanny's husband several days . . . But you will always hereafter, be on ground that I have never occupied, and consequently, if advice were needed, I might advise wrong. I do fondly hope, however, that you will never again need any comfort from abroad. But should I be mistaken in this—should excessive pleasure still be accompanied with a painful counterpart at times, still let me urge you, as I have ever done, to remember in the dep[t]h and even the agony of despondency, that verry shortly you are to feel well again. I am now fully convinced, that you love her as ardently as you are capable of loving. Your ever being happy in her presence, and your intense anxiety about her health . . . would place this beyond all dispute in my mind.

"I incline to think it probable, that your nerves will fail you occasionally for a while; but once you get them fairly graded now, that trouble is over forever. I think if I were you, in case my mind were not exactly right, I would avoid being *idle* . . . If you went through the ceremony *calmly* . . . or even with sufficient composure not to excite alarm in any present, you are safe, beyond question." A postscript to one letter read, "I have been quite a man ever since you left."

The single man received a letter from his just-married friend, and wrote: "Yours of the 16th Inst. announcing that Miss Fanny and you 'are no more twain, but one flesh,' reached me this morning. I have no way of telling how much happiness I wish you both; tho' I believe you both can conceive it. I feel somwhat jealous of both of you now; you will be so exclusively concerned for one another, that I shall be forgotten entirely . . . I regret to learn that you have resolved to not return to Illinois. I shall be verry lonesome without you. How miserably things seem to be arranged in this world! If we have no friends, we have no pleasure; and if we have them, we are sure to lose them, and be doubly pained by the loss . . ."

The Washingtonian Temperance Society was so named because General George Washington had been a mild drinking man who knew when to stop. Lincoln on February 22, 1842, at a large gathering of Washingtonians, after riding in a carriage as "the orator of the day," gave an address on "Charity in Temperance Reform." He pictured the reformed drunkard as the best of temperance crusaders. Men selling liquor, and men drinking it, were blamed too much. Denunciation of them was both *"impolitic"* and "unjust." And why? "Because, it is not much in the nature of man to be driven to any thing; still less to be driven about that which is exclusively his own business . . . If you would win a man to your cause, *first* convince him that you are his sincere friend . . . Assume to dictate to his judgment, or to command his action, or to mark him as one to be shunned and despised, and he will retreat within himself . . . you shall no more be able to pierce him, than to penetrate the hard shell of a tortoise with a rye straw."

He sketched history, the practice of drinking "old as the world itself." The sideboard of the parson and the ragged pocket of the houseless loafer both held whisky. "Physicians prescribed it in this, that, and the other disease. Government provided it for its soldiers and sailors; and to have a rolling or raising, a husking or hoe-down, any where without it, was *positively insufferable.*" The making of it was regarded as honorable.

Were the benefits of temperance to be only for the next generation, for posterity? "There is something so ludicrous in *promises* of good, or *threats* of evil, a great way off . . . 'Better lay down that spade you're stealing, Paddy,—if you don't you'll pay for it at the day of judgment.' 'Be the powers, if ye'll credit me so long, I'll take another, jist.'" And proud would be the title of that land in which "there shall be neither a slave nor a drunkard."

In the audience were reformed drunkards. Lincoln was keyed to these men. He didn't drink, but he did wish to say, "In my judgment, such of us as have never fallen victims, have been spared more from the absence of appetite, than from any mental or moral superiority over those who have."

And one young lawyer who liked his whisky stood at the door of the Second Presbyterian Church, as the people walked out, and reported he heard persons not pleased with the address, catching one remark, "It's a shame that he should be permitted to abuse us so in the house of the Lord." The *Illinois State Register* inquired whether Lincoln and other politicians had "joined the Washingtonian Society from any other than political motives," and "Would they have joined it if it had been exceedingly unpopular?"

Bowling Green died in this February and Lincoln went to the funeral at New Salem. The widow, Nancy Green, who had nursed Lincoln in sickness and fed him hot biscuits smothered in honey, asked him to speak. He stood at the side of the burial box, looked down at the still, white face of his old friend, teacher and companion, turned toward the mourners, the New Salem faces he knew so well. He may have been composed and spoken words of comfort and light. But one version had it that only a few broken and choked words came from him, tears ran down his face and he couldn't go on.

A few days after Joshua Speed's wedding, the newly married man wrote to Lincoln that he was still haunted by "something indescribably horrible and alarming." Lincoln's reply February 25, 1842, gave light on his own experience and methods of overcoming melancholy, "hypo," torment of mind and nerves. He wrote that he opened Speed's letter "with intense anxiety and trepidation—so much, that although it turned out better than I expected, I have hardly yet, at the distance of ten hours, become calm," and then, "I tell you, Speed, our *forebodings,* for which you and I are rather peculiar, are all the worst sort of nonsense." Lincoln believed he could see that since Speed's last letter, Speed had grown *"less miserable"* and not worse, writing: "You say that 'something indescribably horrible and alarming still haunts you.['] You will not say *that* three months from now, I will venture. When your nerves once get steady now, the whole trouble will be over forever. Nor should you become impatient at their being very slow, in becoming steady. Again; you say you much fear that that Elysium of which you have dreamed so much, is never to be realized. Well, if it shall not, I dare swear, it will not be the fault of her who is now your wife. I now have no doubt that it is the peculiar misfortune of both you and me, to dream dreams of Elysium far exceeding all that any thing earthly can realize. Far short of your dreams as you may be, no woman could do more to realize them, than that same black eyed Fanny. If you could but contemplate her through my imagination, it would appear ridiculous to you, that any one should for a moment think of being unhappy with her. My old Father used to have a saying that 'If you make a bad bargain, *hug* it the tighter.' "

This letter was confidential and for Speed only. "I write another letter enclosing this, which you can show her, if she desires it. I do this . . . because, she would think strangely perhaps should you tell her that you receive no letters from me; or, telling her you do, should refuse to let her see them." For Speed in an earlier year, Lincoln had recited:

Whatever spiteful fools may say,
Each jealous, ranting yelper,
 No woman ever went astray
Without a man to help her.

A month passed and Lincoln had news from Speed that the marriage was a complete success and bells rang merrily, Speed far happier than he ever expected to be. To which Lincoln replied: "I know you too well to suppose your expectations were not, at least sometimes, extravagant; and if the reality exceeds them all, I say, enough, dear Lord. I am not going beyond the truth, when I tell you, that the short space it took me to read your last letter, gave me more pleasure, than the total sum of all I have enjoyed since that fatal first of Jany. '41."

He referred to Mary Todd for the first time in his letters to Speed. ". . . it seems to me, I should have been entirely happy, but for the never-absent idea, that there is *one* still unhappy whom I have contributed to make so. That still kills my soul. I can not but reproach myself, for even wishing to be happy while she is otherwise. She accompanied a large party on the Rail Road cars, to Jacksonville last monday; and on her return, spoke, so that I heard of it, of having enjoyed the trip exceedingly. God be praised for that."

Three months later there came to Lincoln thanks and thanks from Speed for what he had done to bring and to keep Speed and Fanny Henning together. He wrote to Speed: "I am not sure there was any merit, with me, in the part I took in your difficulty; I was drawn to it as by fate . . . I could not have done less than I did. I always was superstitious; and as part of my superstition, I believe God made me one of the instruments of bringing your Fanny and you together, which union, I have no doubt He had foreordained. Whatever he designs, he will do for *me* yet . . . If, as you say, you have told Fanny *all*, I should have no objection to her seeing this letter, but for it's reference to our friend here. Let her seeing it, depend upon whether she has ever known any thing of my affair; and if she has not, do not let her."

"Our friend here" meant Mary Todd. Lincoln was now sure he had made a mistake, first of all in not taking Speed's advice to break off his engagement with Mary Todd, and then in not going through and keeping his resolve to marry her. "As to my having been displeased with your advice, surely you know better than that. I know you do; and therefore I will not labour to convince you. True, that subject is painfull to me; but it is not your silence, or the silence of all the world that can make me forget it. I acknowledge the correctness of your advice too; but before I resolve to do the one thing or the other, I must regain my confidence in my own ability to keep my resolves when they are made.

"In that ability, you know, I once prided myself as the only, or at least the chief, gem of my character; that gem I lost—how, and when, you too well know. I have not yet regained it; and until I do, I can not trust myself in any matter of much importance. I believe now that, had you understood my case at the time, as well as I understood yours afterwards, by the aid you would have given me, I should have sailed through clear; but that does not now afford me sufficient confidence, to begin that, or the like of that, again."

Such was the frank and pitiless self-revelation he did not wish Fanny Henning Speed to see unless she knew everything else. He closed his letter, "My respect and esteem to all your friends there; and, by your permission, my love to your Fanny." In one sentence he had sketched himself, "I am so poor, and make so little headway in the world, that I drop back in a month of idleness, as much as I gain in a year's rowing."

Mrs. Simeon Francis, wife of the editor of the *Sangamo Journal*, invited Lincoln to a party in her parlor, brought Lincoln and Miss Todd together and said, "Be friends again." Whatever of fate or woman-wit was at work, and whatever hesitations and broodings went on in Lincoln's heart, they were friends again. But they didn't tell the world so.

Joining the quiet little parties in the Francis house was Julia Jayne, who with Mary Todd, concocted articles printed in the *Sangamo Journal*, Whig satires on the state auditor of accounts, James Shields, his ways, manners and clothes. Of four letters signed "Rebecca" Lincoln wrote one, and it was in part overly gabby and mean, edging on malice —and yet often comic, as in reference to a gathering: "They wouldn't let no democrats in, for fear they'd disgust the ladies, or scare the little galls, or dirty the floor. I looked in at the window, and there was this same fellow Shields floatin about on the air, without heft or earthly substance, just like a lock of cat-fur where cats had been fightin . . . and the sweet distress he seemed to be in,—his very features in the exstatic agony of his soul, spoke audibly and distinctly—'Dear Girls, *it is so distressing*, but I cannot marry you all . . . it is not my fault that I am *so* handsome and *so* interesting." This anonymous letter of Lincoln's signed only "Rebecca," ended, "If some change for the better is not made, its not long that neither Peggy, or I, or any of us, will have a cow left to milk, or a calf's tail to wring."

One "Rebecca" article written by Miss Todd and Miss Jayne read in part: "Now I want you to tell Mr. S. that rather than fight I'll make any apology, and if he wants *personal* satisfaction, let him only come here and he may squeeze my hand . . . Jeff tells me the way these fireeaters do is to give the challenged party choice of weapons, &c. which bein the case I'll tell you in confidence that I never fights with any thing but broom-sticks or hot water, or a shovel full of coals, or some such thing . . ."

Shields, a bachelor of 32, had been a lawyer ten years and a member of the legislature with Lincoln. He was a fighting Irishman born in Dungannon, County Tyrone, Ireland. He asked the *Sangamo Journal* editor who wrote the articles and was told Lincoln took all responsibility for them. Then Shields challenged Lincoln to a duel. Lincoln's seconds notified Shields' seconds that Lincoln chose to fight with cavalry broadswords, across a plank ten feet long and nine to twelve inches broad. The two parties traveled by horse and buggy, and by an old horse-ferry, and September 22 met on a sand bar in the Mississippi River, within three miles of Alton but located in the State of Missouri beyond reach of the Illinois laws against dueling.

Lincoln, seated on a log, practiced swings and swishes in the air with his cavalry broadsword, while friends, lawyers, seconds on both sides, held a long conference. After the main long one came shorter conferences with Lincoln and with Shields. Then a statement was issued declaring that although Mr. Lincoln was the writer of the article signed "Rebecca" in the *Sangamo Journal* of September 2, he had no intention of injuring the personal or private character or standing of Mr. Shields as a gentleman or a man, that he did not think that said article could produce such an effect; and had he anticipated such an effect, he would have foreborne to write it; said article was written solely for political effect, and not to gratify any personal pique against Mr. Shields, for he had none and knew of no cause for any. The duel had become a joke but Lincoln never afterward mentioned it and his friends saw it was a sore point that shouldn't be spoken of to him. A story arose and lived on that when first, as the challenged party, he had his choice of weapons, he said, "How about cow dung at five paces?"

At the meetings of Lincoln and Mary Todd in the Francis home, Miss Todd made it clear to him that if another date should be fixed for a wedding, it should not be set so far in the future as it was the time before. Lincoln agreed and early in October wrote to Speed: "You have now been the husband of a lovely woman nearly eight months. That you are happier now than you were the day you married her I well know . . . and the returning elasticity of spirits which is manifested in your letters. But I want to ask a closer question—'Are you now, in *feeling* as well as *judgement*, glad you are married as you are?' From any body but me, this would be an impudent question not to be tolerated; but I know you will pardon it in me. Please answer it quickly as I am impatient to know." Speed answered yes and yes, his marriage had brought happiness. A few weeks later, Lincoln came to the room of James Matheny, before Matheny was out of bed, telling his friend, "I am going to be married today."

On the street Lincoln met Ninian W. Edwards and told Edwards that he and Mary were to be married that evening. Edwards gave notice, "Mary is my ward, and she must be married at my house." When Edwards asked Mary Todd if what he had heard was true, she told him it was true and they made the big Edwards house ready.

Lincoln took all care of a plain gold ring, the inside engraved: "Love is eternal." At the Edwards house on the evening of November 4, 1842, the Reverend Charles Dresser in canonical robes performed the ring ceremony of the Episcopal church for the groom, 33, and the bride, soon to be 24.

Afterward in talk about the wedding, Jim Matheny said Lincoln had "looked as if he was going to slaughter." Gossip at the Butler house where Lincoln roomed had it that, as he was dressing, Bill Butler's boy came in and asked, "Where are you going?" Lincoln answering, "To hell, I suppose." However dubious such gossip, Lincoln, seven days after his wedding, wrote to Sam Marshall at Shawneetown, discussed two law cases, and ended the letter: "Nothing new here, except my marrying, which to me, is matter of profound wonder."

The Lincoln couple boarded and roomed at $4.00 per week in the plain Globe Tavern, where their first baby came August 1, 1843, and was named Robert Todd. Soon after, they moved into their own home, bought for $1,500, a story-and-a-half frame house a few blocks from the city center. The framework and floors were oak, the laths hand-split hickory, the doors, door frames and weatherboarding black walnut. The house was painted, wrote one visitor, "a Quaker tint of light brown." In the back lot were a cistern, well and pump, a barn 30 by 13 feet, a carriage house 18 by 20. Three blocks east the cornfields began and farms mile after mile.

In the nine, and later, 15 counties of the Eighth Judicial District or "Eighth Circuit," Lincoln traveled and tried cases in most of the counties, though his largest practice was in Logan, Menard, Tazewell and Woodford, which were part of the Seventh Congressional District. He rode a horse or drove in a buggy, at times riding on rough roads an hour or two without passing a farmhouse on the open prairie. Mean was the journey in the mud of spring thaws, in the blowing sleet or snow and icy winds of winter. Heavy clothing, blankets or buffalo robes over knees and body, with shawl over shoulders, couldn't help the face and eyes that had to watch the horse and the road ahead. When pelting showers or steady rain came, he might stop at a farm-house but if court was meeting next day, there was nothing to do but plod on in wet clothes.

The tavern bedrooms had usually only a bed, a spittoon, two split-bottom chairs, a washstand with a bowl and a pitcher of water, the guest in colder weather breaking the ice to wash his face. Some taverns had big rooms where a dozen or more lawyers slept of a night. In most of the sleepy little towns "court day" whetted excitement over trials to decide who would have to pay damages or go to jail. Among the lawyers was fellowship with men of rare brains and ability who would be heard from nationally, some of them to be close associates of Lincoln for years. Over the Eighth Circuit area, 120 miles long and 160 miles wide at its limit, ranging from Springfield to the Indiana line, Lincoln met pioneer frontier humanity at its best and worst, from the good and wise to the silly and aimless.

With Stuart away months in Congress, and busy with politics when at home, the heavy routine work fell on Lincoln, who had learned about all he could of law from Stuart. They parted cordially and Lincoln went into partnership with Stephen T. Logan, acknowledged leader of the Springfield bar. Nine years older than Lincoln, he was a former circuit judge, Scotch-Irish and Kentucky-born—a short sliver of a man with tight lips and a thin voice that could rasp, his hair frowsy and red. He wore linsey-woolsey shirts, heavy shoes, and never a necktie, yet he was known as one of the most neat, careful, scrupulous, particular,

exact and profoundly learned lawyers in Illinois in preparing cases and analyzing principles involved. From him Lincoln was to learn more than he had known of the word
"thorough" in law practice. Perhaps slight yet definite was
the influence of Logan in Lincoln's writing later:

> The true rule, in determining to embrace, or reject
> any thing, is not whether it have *any* evil in it; but
> whether it have more of evil, than of good. There are
> few things *wholly* evil, or *wholly* good. Almost every
> thing . . . is an inseparable compound of the two; so
> that our best judgment of the preponderance between
> them is continually demanded.

Lincoln argued in the Supreme Court the famous case
of Bailey *vs.* Cromwell. Cromwell had sold Bailey a Negro
girl, saying the girl was a slave. Bailey had given a note
promising to pay cash for the slave. Lincoln argued, in
part, that the girl was a free person until proven to be a
slave, and, if not proven a slave, then she could not be
sold nor bought and no cash could be exchanged between
two men buying and selling her. The Supreme Court decided that the "girl being free" therefore "could not be the
subject of a sale" and Bailey's promissory note was "illegal."

For Miss Eliza Cabot, a Menard County schoolteacher
suing for slander, Lincoln won a verdict for $1,600. In one
damage suit the best Lincoln could get for his client was
one cent. In June 1842 Logan and Lincoln had eight bank-
ruptcy cases in the U.S. District Court. They defended one
bankrupt client, Charles H. Chapman, charged with per-
jury, Chapman getting five years in the penitentiary, though
pardoned five months later. In such a case, it was generally
understood among fellow attorneys that if Lincoln believed
a client guilty, he made a poor showing before judge and
jury.

Since 1839 Lincoln had traveled the circuit a few months
each year. In DeWitt County he and Douglas were joint
counsel in the defense of Spencer Turner indicted "for not
having the fear of God before his eyes but being moved and
seduced by the instigation of the Devil." Turner had as-

saulted one Matthew K. Martin with "a wooden stick of the value of ten cents" inflicting on the right temple of the said Martin "one mortal wound." The plea was not guilty and the jury was convinced of Turner's innocence.

Since joining Logan, Lincoln had more cases in the higher courts in Springfield. In December 1841 he argued 14 cases in the Supreme Court, losing only four. Of 24 cases in that court during 1842 and 1843 he lost only seven. But Logan was taking a son into partnership, and he saw, too, that Lincoln was about ready to head his own law firm. And Logan, a Whig, elected a member of the legislature in 1842, had an eye on going to Congress, as did Lincoln. The firm had, on Lincoln's advice, taken in as a law student a young man, William H. Herndon, nine years younger than Lincoln, who had clerked in the Speed store and slept upstairs. Shortly after Herndon's admittance to law practice in December 1844, Lincoln and he formed a partnership and opened their office. The younger man had spoken amazement at Lincoln's offer to take him on, Lincoln saying only, "Billy, I can trust you and you can trust me." From then on for years he was "Billy" and called the other man "Mr. Lincoln."

Herndon was intense, sensitive, had hair-trigger emotions. His grandfather in Virginia had given slaves their freedom; his father, a former store and tavern keeper, in politics had fought to make Illinois a Slave State. The son knew tavern life, and was near vanity about how he could read men by their eyes. He was of medium height, rawboned, with high cheekbones, dark eyes set far back, his shock of hair blue-black. He knew rough country boy talk and stories, tavern lingo, names of drinks, the slang of men about cards, horse races, chicken fights, women. Yet he was full of book learning, of torches and bonfires, had a flamboyance about freedom, justice, humanity. He was close to an element in Sangamon County that Lincoln termed "the shrewd wild boys." He liked his liquor, the bars and the topers and tipplers of the town. He was a Whig, was plain himself and was loved by many plain people. Lincoln, in a political letter, had referred to his own arrival in Sangamon "twelve years ago" as "a strange[r], friendless, uneducated, penniless boy, working on a flat boat—at ten dollars per month" and was now astonished "to learn that I have been put down here as the candidate of pride, wealth, and arristocratic family distinction." There was a factor of politics as well as law in his choosing for a partner the money-honest, highfalutin, whimsical, corn-on-the-cob, temperamental, convivial Bill Herndon.

Chapter 6

Running for Congress

"Now if you should hear any one say that Lincoln don't want to go to Congress, I wish you as a personal friend of mine, would tell him you have reason to believe he is mistaken." Thus Lincoln was writing in mid-February 1843 to an active Whig, Richard S. Thomas. As a state party leader, with other Whigs, he wrote in March a campaign circular, an "Address to the People of Illinois," analyzing national issues, favoring a tariff for revenue rather than direct taxation, the National Bank opposed by the Democrats, a state income by sale of public lands; he warned hesitant Whigs they must use the convention system for nominations or go on losing to "the common enemy"; he pleaded for party unity, writing that "he whose wisdom surpasses that of all philosophers, has declared 'a house divided against itself cannot stand.'"

He tried to get the Sangamon County delegates to a district convention to endorse him for Congress, but the convention had pledged them to Edward D. Baker. Born in London, England, a Black Hawk War private, a lawyer certified in Carrollton, Illinois, once a state senator, Baker was one of the inner circle of Springfield Whigs, a brilliant and dramatic speaker who could shift modulations from hard ringing steel to rose and rainbow, a stubborn fighter moving with dash and gallantry. When "Ned" Baker loved a

man or a cause, he could pour it out in lavish speech. And
Lincoln's heart went out in admiration and affection for
Ned Baker as perhaps to no other man in Springfield.
Named a delegate to the district convention, pledged to
support Baker, Lincoln wrote to Speed, "I shall be 'fixed'
a good deal like a fellow who is made groomsman to the
man what has cut him out, and is marrying his own dear
'gal'."

At the district convention in Pekin, a third rival, John
J. Hardin, had a majority at hand for the nomination. Lincoln, for the sake of party unity, moved the nomination be
made unanimous. Tall, well-tailored, having an air of command, a Transylvania University graduate, Hardin had
been Lincoln's rival for Whig floor leadership in the legislature. In speech he stammered but had an ease and grace
about it so no one minded. The Kentucky son of a distinguished U.S. Senator, a Black Hawk War veteran, a brigadier general of state militia, he had a paying law practice
in Jacksonville and an ever-keen eye for a seat in Congress.

Lincoln engineered passage of a resolution by 18 votes to
14, whereby the convention, as individuals, recommended
E. D. Baker as the Whig party nominee for Congress in
1844, subject to the decision of the convention then. It
seemed that Lincoln, with Baker and Hardin, had made
an arrangement that Baker would follow Hardin in 1844 as
the nominee and Lincoln would follow Baker in 1846. Lincoln was later to remind Hardin of "the proposition made
by me to you and Baker, that we should take a turn a
piece." Hardin would claim the purpose of the resolution
was "to soothe Baker's mortified feelings," Lincoln being
certain that was not "*the sole*" object. Some delegates came
away understanding that three Whig leaders had agreed on
a rotation, "a turn a piece" in Congress.

Lincoln pledged himself to party harmony and when
Hardin won his seat in Congress at the August election,
Sangamon County gave him three times the majority of his
own Morgan County. Nevertheless, when Lincoln voted
August 7 he spoke out the names of only two candidates,
constable and justice of the peace. Why he didn't vote for
Hardin for Congress, nor for, nor against, any Whig can-

didates for the county offices, had no explanation from him. It was the more odd because in Whig circulars he had strictly urged all Whigs to go to the polls and vote for all Whigs. Possibly the election clerks were slovenly incomplete in recording what they heard. If he failed to vote for Hardin, it went unnoticed by opponents or rivals who could have used it against him. Hardin went to Congress, followed the Whig party line, and in 1844 stepped aside and let Baker have nomination and election.

Early in the 1844 presidential campaign, after bloody riots in Philadelphia, and Democratic forces blaming Whigs as wishing hate and violence toward "foreigners and Catholics," Lincoln at a public meeting in Springfield moved passage of resolutions he had written, "That the guarantee of the rights of conscience, as found in our Constitution, is most sacred and inviolable, and one that belongs no less to the Catholic, than to the Protestant; and that all attempts to abridge or interfere with these rights, either of Catholic or Protestant, directly or indirectly . . . shall ever have our most effective opposition." In late October he spoke in Indiana for the national ticket and Henry Clay, the third-time Whig candidate for President. Election Day found him in Gentryville, Indiana. In this November, James K. Polk of Tennessee won by 170 electoral votes over 105 for Clay, his Illinois majority 12,000.

When Baker came back from Washington, he hesitated about telling Lincoln he wouldn't run again, because of the chance Hardin might run and they both might lose out. Soon after, however, he told Lincoln that he would decline nomination—and when the next year another baby boy arrived at the Lincoln home, he was named Edward Baker Lincoln.

As Lincoln had feared and foreseen, Hardin wanted to run again. On January 7, 1846, Lincoln wrote Dr. Robert Boal, a party worker in Marshall County, "Since I saw you last fall . . . All has happenned as I then told you I expected it would—Baker's declining, Hardin's taking the track, and so on. If Hardin and I stood precisely equal— that is, if *neither* of us had been to congress, or if we *both* had—it would only accord with what I have always done, for the sake of peace, to give way to him; and I expect I should do it . . . But to yield to Hardin under present circumstances, seems to me as nothing else than yielding to one who would gladly sacrifice me altogether. This, I would rather not submit to. That Hardin is talented, energetic, usually generous and magnanimous, I have, before this, affirmed to you, and do not now deny. You know that my only argument is that 'turn about is fair play.' This he, practically at least, denies." When Hardin later saw county delegations moving toward Lincoln, he proposed that instead of nominating by convention the Whigs should poll the counties of the district, with no candidate allowed to electioneer outside his own county. Lincoln wrote to Hardin, "I am entirely satisfied with the old system under which you and Baker were successively nominated and elected to congress; and because the whigs of the District are well acquainted with that system."

At his office desk Lincoln dipped his goose-quill pen into an inkstand and wrote to editors, politicians, voters, precinct workers, saying in one letter, "I have . . . written to three or four of the most active whigs in each precinct of the county." He reckoned, in one letter, the counties for or against his nomination. A movement against him on foot in a town, he wrote the editor of the paper there, "I want you to let nothing prevent your getting an article in your paper, of *this week*." He could appeal frankly, "If your feelings towards me are the same as when I saw you (which I have no reason to doubt) I wish you would let nothing appear in your paper which may opperate against me. You understand. Matters stand just as they did when I saw you."

The blunt little sentence crept in often, "You understand." Some letters ended, "Confidential of course," or "Dont speak of this, lest they hear of it," or "For your eye only." There were times to travel in soft shoes. "It is my intention to take a quiet trip through the towns and neighbourhoods of Logan county, Delevan, Tremont, and on to & through the upper counties. Dont speak of this, or let it relax any of your vigilance. When I shall reach Tremont, we will talk every thing over at large." A direct personal appeal was phrased, "I now wish to say to you that if it be consistent with your feelings, you would set a few stakes for me." No personal feelings against Hardin must be permitted. "I do not certainly know, but I strongly suspect, that Genl. Hardin wishes to run again. I know of no argument to give me a preference over him, unless it be 'Turn about is fair play.' " And again, to another: "It is my intention to give him [Hardin] the trial, unless clouds should rise, which are not yet discernable. This determination you need not however, as yet, announce in your paper—at least not as coming from me . . . In doing this, let nothing be said against Hardin—nothing deserves to be said against him. Let the pith of the whole argument be *'Turn about is fair play.'* "

Hardin began to feel outguessed and outplayed and wrote to Lincoln complaining. Lincoln, on February 7, 1846, answered with the longest political letter he had ever written, a masterpiece of merciless logic. Point by point he cornered Hardin, writing at its close, "In my letter to you, I reminded you that you had first at Washington, and afterwards at Pekin, said to me that if Baker succeeded he would most likely hang on as long as possible, while with you it would be different." Hardin's letter to him imputed "management," "manoevering," "combination" and had the reproach, "It is mortifying to discover that those with whom I have long acted & from whom I expected a different course, have considered it all fair to prevent my nomination to congress." Under such imputations, wrote Lincoln, "It is somewhat difficult to be patient." He ended, "I believe you do not mean to be unjust, or ungenerous; and I, therefore am slow to believe that you will not yet think *better* and think *differently* of this matter." Nine days later Hardin drew out of the contest, and the district convention at Petersburg, May 1, by acclamation nominated Lincoln for Congress in the one district in Illinois more certain than any other of Whig victory.

Against Lincoln the Democrats put up Peter Cartwright, a famous and rugged old-fashioned circuit rider, a storming evangelist, exhorter and Jackson Democrat. He had carried his Bible and rifle over wilderness, had more than once personally thrown out of church a drunk interrupting his sermon. He was thick-set, round-faced, and liked to refer to his wickedness at horse racing, card playing and dancing before he was converted. He was 61 and Lincoln 37, both of them very human. He had lived near New Salem, held camp meetings near there, and Lincoln had seen him and heard of his ways. A deacon spoke a cold, precise, correct prayer and Cartwright had to say, "Brother, three prayers like that would freeze hell over." When a presiding elder at a church meeting in Tennessee whispered to Cartwright, pointing out a visitor, "That's Andrew Jackson," the reply was: "And who's Andrew Jackson? If he's a sinner God'll damn him the same as he would a Guinea nigger."

Cartwright's men kept reports going: Lincoln's wife was a high-toned Episcopalian; Lincoln held drunkards as good as Christians and church members; Lincoln was a "deist" who believed in God but did not accept Christ nor the doctrines of atonement and punishment; Lincoln said, "Christ was a bastard." Lincoln put out a handbill giving the most complete and specific statement he had ever made publicly regarding his religion. It read:

> A charge having got into circulation in some of the neighborhoods of this District, in substance that I am an open scoffer at Christianity, I have by the advice of some friends concluded to notice the subject in this form. That I am not a member of any Christian Church, is true; but I have never denied the truth of the Scriptures; and I have never spoken with intentional disrespect of religion in general, or of any denomination of Christians in particular. It is true that in early life I was inclined to believe in what I understand is called the "Doctrine of Necessity"—that is, that the human mind is impelled to action, or held in rest by some power, over which the mind itself has no control; and I have sometimes (with one, two or three, but never publicly) tried to maintain this opinion in argument. The habit of arguing thus however, I have, entirely left off for more than five years. And I add here,

I have always understood this same opinion to be held by several of the Christian denominations. The foregoing, is the whole truth, briefly stated, in relation to myself, upon this subject.

I do not think I could myself, be brought to support a man for office, whom I knew to be an open enemy of, and scoffer at, religion. Leaving the higher matter of eternal consequences, between him and his Maker, I still do not think any man has the right thus to insult the feelings, and injure the morals, of the community in which he may live. If, then, I was guilty of such conduct, I should blame no man who should condemn me for it; but I do blame those, whoever they may be, who falsely put such a charge in circulation against me.

He went to a religious meeting where Cartwright in due time said, "All who desire to give their hearts to God, and go to heaven, will stand." A sprinkling of men, women and children stood up. The preacher exhorted, "All who do not wish to go to hell will stand." All stood up—except Lincoln. Then Cartwright in his gravest voice: "I observe that many responded to the first invitation to give their hearts to God and go to heaven. And I further observe that all of you save one indicated that you did not desire to go to hell. The sole exception is Mr. Lincoln, who did not respond to either invitation. May I inquire of you, Mr. Lincoln, where you are going?"

Lincoln slowly rose: "I came here as a respectful listener. I did not know that I was to be singled out by Brother Cartwright. I believe in treating religious matters with due solemnity. I admit that the questions propounded by Brother Cartwright are of great importance. I did not feel called upon to answer as the rest did. Brother Cartwright asks me directly where I am going. I desire to reply with equal directness: I am going to Congress." Thus it was told.

Whig friends raised $200 for his personal campaign expenses. After the election he handed them back $199.25, saying he had spent only 75 cents in the campaign. The count of ballots gave Lincoln 6,340 votes, Cartwright

4,829, Walcott (Abolitionist) 249. He wrote to Speed, "Being elected to Congress, though I am very grateful to our friends, for having done it, has not pleased me as much as I expected."

Eleven days after Lincoln's nomination in May, Congress had declared a state of war between the United States and Mexico, authorizing an army of 50,000 volunteers and a war fund of $10,000,000 to be raised. In speeches Lincoln seemed briefly to advise all citizens to stand by the flag of the nation, supply all needs of the brave men at the fighting fronts, till an honorable peace could be secured. Trained rifle companies of young men offered service; of 8,370 volunteers in Illinois only 3,720 could be taken; they went down the Mississippi, across the Gulf to Texas, and on into baking hot deserts of Mexico.

Hardin enlisted and was appointed a colonel; he was to die a soldier of valor leading his men in the Battle of Buena Vista. James Shields was appointed brigadier general to command the Illinois troops and was to fall with a bullet through his lungs, leading a charge in the Battle of Cerro Gordo. Many of the young men wild to enlist had heard since 1836 of the Alamo, of San Jacinto, of almost incredibly heroic Texans against heavy odds overwhelming Mexican armies and winning independence for the Republic of Texas. The war now declared was, in part, for the boundary claimed by Texas, the Rio Grande.

Lincoln "never was much interested in the Texas question," as he wrote in October 1845, seemed only dimly aware of a variety of irrresistible American forces acting by fact and dream. The fact was that Texas, New Mexico and California were passionately wanted in the domain of the United States because of the immense land and wealth foreseen in them. The dream was of "an ocean-bound republic," and America "from sea to sea." A Democratic editor saw this surge as Manifest Destiny; nothing could stop it. When Congress in March 1845 had passed resolutions to annex Texas, and a Texas convention in June was unanimous for joining the Union of States, the Mexican government warned that Texas was still a Mexican province. The Mexican Congress had voted $4,000,000 for war against

Texas. President Polk ordered American troops in "protective occupation" on a strip of land in dispute at the Rio Grande. The inevitable clashes came—and the all-out war was on. Though the Americans were outnumbered four to one in nearly all actions, they had better cannon, riflemen and strategy. The battles ended September 14, 1847, when Mexico City was taken. The two outstanding generals, Winfield S. Scott and Zachary Taylor, were both Whigs. Texas, New Mexico and California came into the U.S. domain. The long and bitter dispute with Great Britain over the Oregon boundary, bringing war threats on both sides, was settled by Polk backing down from the cry of "54° 40' or fight" to 49°. So there was Manifest Destiny, "America from sea to sea"—the cost high in money and lives.

Lincoln saw more shame than glory in the political steps and procedures involved. In June 1846 he had seen Ned Baker return from Washington to raise an Illinois regiment, and start for Mexico, where he led Shields' brigade when Shields fell wounded. He had heard of Baker going to Washington the following December and ending a speech to Congress two days before he resigned his seat: "There are in the American Army many who strongly doubt the propriety of the war, and especially the manner of its commencement; who yet are ready to pour out their hearts' best blood, and their lives with it, on a foreign shore, in defense of the American flag and American glory." This, for Lincoln, was the Whig party policy and the music of the hour. He studied the passionate words of Senator Thomas Corwin, "If I were a Mexican, I would tell you, 'Have you not room in your own country to bury your dead men? If you come into mine, we will greet you with bloody hands and welcome you to hospitable graves.' "

Chicago was a four-day stage trip and Lincoln arrived in that city of 16,000 in July 1847, one of hundreds of delegates to the River and Harbor Convention, run by Whigs, and aimed to promote internal improvements and to rebuke laxity of the Polk administration. Thousands of out-of-town spectators, finding hotels and rooming houses overcrowded, slept on lake ships or camped in the streets, to be

on hand in the morning in the big tent to see and hear
famous men from all over the country. Here Lincoln met
Tom Corwin of Ohio, Edward Bates and Thomas Hart
Benton of Missouri, and Thurlow Weed, a Whig party boss
in New York State. The notable New York lawyer David
Dudley Field, spoke against certain internal improvements
as unconstitutional; Horace Greeley wrote to his New
York *Tribune* that "Hon. Abraham Lincoln, a tall specimen
of an Illinoisan . . . was called out, and spoke briefly and
happily." Some delegates remembered Lincoln answered
Field's objection to federal improvement of the Illinois
River because it ran through only one state, by asking
through how many states the federally improved Hudson
River ran.

Lincoln had his first look at mighty Lake Michigan, blue
water moving on to meet the sky, a path for ship transport
of wheat to New York and Europe. Farmers and wheat-
buyers were hauling wheat to Chicago from 250 miles away;
lines of 10 to 20 wagons headed for Chicago were common.
Lincoln had no regrets over his long efforts for the canal to
connect the Illinois River and Lake Michigan.

Lincoln's term in Congress was to start in December
1847; he went on riding the Eighth Circuit, driving a rattletrap buggy or on horseback, sometimes perhaps as he
tied his horse to a hitching post, hearing a voice across the
street, "That's the new Congressman Lincoln." It was a
horsey country of horsey men. They spoke of one-horse
towns, lawyers, doctors. They tied their horses to hitching
posts half-chewed away by horse teeth. They brushed horse
hair from their clothes after a drive. They carried feed bags
of oats and spliced broken tugs with rope to last till they
reached a harness shop.

His yearly income ranged from $1,200 to $1,500, com-
paring nicely with the governor's yearly $1,200 and a cir-
cuit judge's $750. By now he had probably paid the last
of his personal "National Debt." An incomplete fee book
of Lincoln and Herndon for 1845-47 showed fees from
$3.00 to $100, most entries $10. Sometimes groceries and
farm produce were accepted for fees. Lincoln was known to

say he had no money sense, and never had money enough
to fret him.

At Petersburg, he and Herndon, defending James Dor-
man charged with manslaughter, won the case. Another
client, Ammai Merill, charged with payments in counterfeit
coin, got three years at hard labor in the penitentiary. Lincoln's friend, Samuel D. Marshall of Shawneetown, had
taken the damage suit of Thomas Margrave against William
G. Grable for the seduction of Margrave's daughter. Lincoln argued the case in Supreme Court, which affirmed
the damages awarded by the lower court, and wrote Marshall his fee would be $5.00 and two years subscription to
Marshall's paper, the *Illinois Republican*. In a divorce suit
Lincoln penned his comment, "A pitiful story of marital
discord."

"Feeling a little poetic this evening," Lincoln wrote in
early 1846 to Andrew Johnston at Quincy, and he would
send on "a piece of poetry of my own making," though
"I find a deal of trouble to finish it." On a speaking trip
that took him to Gentryville, old memories flooded in on
him and he wrote "My Childhood Home I See Again," including verses about the insane son of James Gentry:

> Poor Matthew! I have ne'er forgot
>   When first with maddened will,
> Yourself you maimed, your father fought,
>   And mother strove to kill;
>
> And terror spread, and neighbours ran,
>   Your dang'rous strength to bind;
> And soon a howling crazy man,
>   Your limbs were fast confined.
>
> How then you writhed and shrieked aloud,
>   Your bones and sinews bared;
> And fiendish on the gaping crowd,
>   With burning eye-balls glared.

And begged, and swore, and wept, and prayed,
  With maniac laughter joined—
How fearful are the signs displayed,
  By pangs that kill the mind!

And when at length, tho' drear and long,
  Time soothed your fiercer woes—
How plaintively your mournful song,
  Upon the still night rose.

I've heard it oft, as if I dreamed,
  Far-distant, sweet, and lone;
The funeral dirge it ever seemed
  Of reason dead and gone.

To drink it's strains, I've stole away,
  All silently and still,
Ere yet the rising god of day
  Had streaked the Eastern hill.

But this is past and nought remains
  That raised you o'er the brute.
Your mad'ning shrieks and soothing strains
  Are like forever mute.

Now fare thee well: more thou the cause
  Than subject now of woe.
All mental pangs, but time's kind laws,
  Hast lost the power to know.

On his visit to Gentryville, Lincoln had seen Matthew
Gentry, still alive, drooling, gentle, harmless, reminding
Lincoln of

The very spot where grew the bread
  That formed my bones, I see.
How strange, old field, on thee to tread,
  And feel I'm part of thee!

This was not imagination: it was autobiographical confession. Later that year he sent Andrew Johnston another version of the poem, along with doggerel titled "The Bear Hunt." Published in the Quincy *Whig*, his verses did not carry Lincoln's name.

The mind of Lincoln enjoyed roving and questioning. He wrote at different times his independent thinking about the protective tariff which the Whigs favored. "In the early days of the world, the Almighty said to the first of our race 'In the sweat of thy face shalt thou eat bread'; and since then, if we except the *light* and the *air* of heaven, no good thing has been, or can be enjoyed by us, without having first cost labour. And, inasmuch [as] most good things are produced by labour, it follows that [all] such things of right belong to those whose labour has produced them. But it has so happened in all ages of the world, that *some* have laboured, and *others* have, without labour, enjoyed a large proportion of the fruits. This is wrong, and should not continue. To [secure] to each labourer the whole product of his labour, or as nearly as possible, is a most worthy object of any good government." How could a government effect this? One remedy would be to, "as far as possible, drive *useless* labour and *idleness* out of existence." For example, "Iron & every thing made of iron, can be produced, in sufficient abundance, [and] with as little labour, in the United States, as any where else in the world; therefore, all labour done in bringing iron & it's fabrics from a foreign country to the United States, is useless labour." As to cotton, "Why should it not be spun, wove &c. in the very neighbourhood where it both grows and is consumed, and the carrying thereby dispensed with?" He speculated on naked first principles: "If at any time all *labour* should cease, and all existing provisions be equally divided among the people, at the end of a single year there could scarcely be one human being left alive—all would have perished by want of subsistence . . . Universal *idleness* would speedily result in universal *ruin;* and . . . *useless labour* is, in this respect, the same as *idleness*." Therefore, reasoned Lincoln, to abandon the protective tariff "must result in the increase of both useless labour, and idleness."

In a long unsigned article in the Quincy *Whig*, April 15, 1846, Lincoln wrote of a case that had haunted him for five years. In June 1841 the three Trailor brothers, Archibald, William and Henry, had been seen with Archibald Fisher, who was known to carry considerable money on him. And Fisher had disappeared. Henry Trailor in a two-day examination denied and denied, finally confessing that his brothers had killed Fisher in woods northwest of Springfield and had brought the body back to where they had left Henry to stand watch at a buggy in a dense brush thicket. The two brothers then drove toward Hickox's millpond and returned in a half-hour saying they had put "him" in a safe place. The news spread like a prairie fire; wild talk ran of lynching. Hundreds of people seeking Fisher's body raked, fished, drained the millpond and tore down the dam to lower the water; cellars, wells, pits, were searched, fresh graves pried into, dead horses and dogs dug up, to no result.

A letter was published from the postmaster nearest William Trailor's home in Warren County, stating that William had returned home and was saying boastfully that Fisher was dead and had willed him $1,500. William and Archibald were arrested and put on trial, with Lincoln, Logan and Ned Baker in defense. Besides Henry Trailor's testimony, which cross-examination couldn't shake, a respectable lady testified to seeing William and Archibald with Fisher enter the timber northwest of town and return without Fisher. It was proved that since Fisher vanished, William and Archibald had passed an unusual number of gold pieces. Many witnesses testified to signs of a struggle in a thicket and a trail to buggy tracks that led in the direction of the millpond.

It looked as though the noose waited for the two defendants till a star witness arrived, Dr. Robert Gilmore from Warren County, who swore that Fisher was not only alive, but living in Gilmore's home, and only because of Fisher's low physical condition the doctor had not brought Fisher with him. "Gilmore also stated," wrote Lincoln, "that he had known Fisher for several years, and that he had understood he was subject to temporary derangement of mind, owing to an injury about his head received in early life. There was about Dr. Gilmore so much of the air and manner of truth, that his statement prevailed in the minds of the audience and of the court, and the Trailors were discharged; although they attempted no explanation of the circumstances proven by the other witnesses. On the next Monday, Myers [an officer] arrived in Springfield, bringing with him the now famed Fisher, in full life and proper person . . . it may well be doubted, whether a stranger affair ever really occurred. Much of the matter remains in mystery to this day. The going into the woods with Fisher, and returning without him, by the Trailors; their going into the woods at the same place the next day, after they professed to have given up the search, the signs of a struggle in the thicket, the buggy tracks at the edge of it; and the location of the thicket and the signs about it, corresponding precisely with Henry's story, are circumstances that have never been explained. William and Archibald have both died since—William in less than a year, and Archibald in about two years after the supposed murder. Henry is still living but never speaks of the subject."

Thus wrote Lincoln five years after the trial. In the week of the trial he wrote Speed an exciting, quizzical, 2,000-word account, ending, "Hart, the little drayman that hauled Molly [Mary Todd] home once, said it was too *damned* bad, to have so much trouble, and no hanging after all." Archibald Trailor, a 30-year-old carpenter, had always borne so good a name in Springfield that a few days after the trial a big public meeting passed resolutions of regret that he should ever have been accused of a crime. Also five years after the trial, a court awarded Logan and Lincoln $100 defense fees but the sheriff of Warren County reported he could find no property in the hands of James Smith, executor of the estate of William Trailor.

A few weeks before Lincoln's start to Washington he took the case of Robert Matson at Charleston. Matson, a

young bachelor of a respectable Kentucky family, worked
his large farm with slaves brought from Kentucky for the
spring planting and sent back to Kentucky after the fall
harvest, thus keeping within the Illinois law that no Negro
or mulatto could stay in the state year after year "without
a lawful certificate of freedom." But one slave Matson had
kept year after year as foreman and overseer, Anthony Bryant, who could read his Bible and preach Methodist sermons. Among slaves brought to the farm in the summer of
1845 was Bryant's wife, Jane, a shining mulatto said to be
the daughter of a brother of Matson. Of her six children,
three were plainly of mingled Negro and white blood, one
girl having blue eyes and long red hair.

Matson's housekeeper, Mary Corbin, in jealous anger one
day shrieked to Jane Bryant, "You're going back to Kentucky and you're going to be sold way down South in the
cotton field." The terrorized Anthony Bryant rode at midnight two miles on horseback with his wife and one child,
his other children afoot, to the inn of the antislavery Gideon M. Ashmore. A young doctor from Pennsylvania, Hi-
ram Rutherford, sent word to other antislavery men to be
ready for any chase and search by Matson. By a justice of
peace action Matson got Jane Bryant and her children
locked up in the county jail for 58 days. Next Matson was
arrested and convicted of living unlawfully with Mary Corbin, a woman not his wife.

The main action came when Matson went into circuit
court, calling for damages from Rutherford of $2,500 at
slave property valuations. Rutherford found Lincoln tilted
in a chair on the tavern veranda, having finished one story
and about to start another, and they went to one side for a
talk.

As Rutherford told his troubles, he noticed Lincoln
growing sober, sad, looking far off, shaking his head in a
sorry way. "At length, and with apparent reluctance, Lincoln answered that he could not defend me, because he had
already been counselled with in Matson's interest," said
Rutherford later. "This irritated me into expressions more
or less bitter. He seemed to feel this, and endeavored in his

plausible way to reconcile me to the proposition that, as a lawyer, he must represent and be faithful to those who counsel with and employ him. Although thoroughly in earnest I presume I was a little hasty. The interview and my quick temper made a deep impression on Mr. Lincoln, I am sure, because he dispatched a messenger to me followed by another message, that he could now easily and consistently free himself from Matson and was, therefore, in a position if I employed him to conduct my defense. But it was too late; my pride was up. Instead, I employed Charles H. Constable."

Before Judges Wilson and Treat, of the Supreme Court of the state, Lincoln and Usher F. Linder, as Matson's lawyers, seemed to expect to win by showing that Matson had no plans for permanently locating slaves in Illinois. And yet, Lincoln's statements sounded like a searching inquiry into the facts and elemental justice of the case, rather than an argument for a plaintiff. A Coles County lawyer, D. F. McIntyre, saw Lincoln as clumsy at favoring his client. He made no attempt to batter down the points of the opposition, and practically gave his case away by outright admission that if the Kentucky slaveowner had brought his slaves to Illinois for the purpose of working them and using them as slaves on the Coles County farm, the Negroes were thereby entitled to freedom. McIntyre noted that Lincoln said the whole case turned on one point. "Were these negroes passing over and crossing the State, and thus, as the law contemplates, *in transitu*, or were they actually located by consent of their master? If only crossing the State, that act did not free them, but if located, even indefinitely, by the consent of their owner and master, their emancipation logically followed." McIntyre noted further: "When Mr. Lincoln arose to make the closing argument, all eyes were fixed upon him to hear what reasons he could or would assign, in behalf of this slave holder, to induce the court to send this mother and her children back into lives of slavery. But strange to say Lincoln did not once touch upon the question of the right of Matson to take the negroes back to Kentucky. His main contention was

that the question of the right of the negroes to their freedom could only be determined by a regular habeas corpus
proceeding."

Judge Wilson leaned forward and asked: "Mr. Lincoln,
your objection is simply to the form of the action by which,
or in which this question should be tried, is it not?" "Yes,
sir." Then came the high point of the day for Lincoln.
Judge Wilson asked: "Now, if this case was being tried on
issue joined in a habeas corpus, and it appeared there, as
it does here, that this slave owner had brought this mother
and her children, voluntarily, from the State of Kentucky,
and had settled them down on his farm in this State, do
you think, as a matter of law, that they did not thereby
become free?" And Lincoln answered, "No, sir, I am not
prepared to deny that they did."

Linder then argued, for Matson, that the Federal Constitution protected slaves as chattel property which could not
lawfully be taken from Matson. But the court decree October 16, 1847, declared Jane Bryant and her children "are
discharged from the custody as well of the Sheriff as of
Robert Matson and all persons claiming them as slaves, and
they shall be and remain free from all servitude whatever
to any person or persons from henceforward and forever."

Matson that night slipped away, quit the county, and
paid Lincoln no fee, Lincoln rather sure he had earned
no fee. Rutherford saw Lincoln on leaving for Springfield
and, "He gave no sign of regret because, as a lawyer, he
had upheld the cause of the strong against the weak," Rutherford forgetting his own proud words when Lincoln twice
went the limit trying to break into the case on the side he
preferred.

Lincoln had begun wearing broadcloth, white shirts with
white collar and black silk cravat, sideburns down three-
fourths the length of his ears. Yet he was still known as
carelessly groomed, his trousers mentioned as creeping to
the ankles and higher, his hair rumpled, vest wrinkled, and
at the end of a story putting his arms around his knees,
raising his knees to his chin and rocking to and fro. Standing he loomed six feet four inches; seated he looked no

Upper: The older Sarah Bush Lincoln. Only known photograph of Lincoln's beloved stepmother (Meserve). *Lower:* Traditionally the one-room log cabin in which Lincoln was born. Now part of the Lincoln Memorial at Hodgenville, Kentucky (CS).

Upper right: Photograph of a daguerreotype. Earliest known portrait, possibly made in Washington about 1848, of Congressman Lincoln (Meserve). *Upper left:* Joshua Speed, bosom friend with whom Lincoln shared confidences about women and marriage (Meserve). *Center left:* Joseph Medill, probably 1858, from a photograph loaned by Alicia Patterson. *Lower left:* William H. Herndon, 16 years the law partner of Lincoln (Huntington Library).

Upper right: Photograph made in Chicago in 1854 at 12 North Wells Street. Original presented to Chicago Historical Society by George Schneider. *Lower left:* Early photograph of Mary Todd Lincoln (CS). *Lower right:* Stephen Arnold Douglas, powerful, dramatic political opponent of Lincoln for many years (Meserve).

Upper left: Brady photograph of President Lincoln with his cherished youngest son and companion Thomas Todd ("Tad") (Meserve). *Upper right:* Mrs. Abraham Lincoln in party gown, flowers, and jewels (Meserve). *Lower left:* Tad in his uniform of "Colonel" in the U.S. Army (National Archives). *Lower center:* William Wallace Lincoln, third son (CS). *Lower right:* Robert Todd Lincoln, first-born of the four Lincoln sons (Meserve).

Upper: The Lincoln House in Springfield during 1860 campaign, Lincoln in white coat or linen duster at right of door (Meserve). *Lower left:* William H. Seward, U.S. Senator from New York and titular leader of Republican party until Lincoln's nomination (CS). *Lower right:* Thurlow Weed, editor of Albany *Evening Journal,* friend of Seward and his intensely active political manager (Meserve).

THE RAIL,
THAT OLD ABE SPLIT.

This is THE RAIL
That Old Abe split.

This is THE FENCE
That was made with
   The Rail that Old Abe split.

This is THE FIELD
Enclosed by the Fence,
That was made with
   The Rail that Old Abe split.

This is THE ROAD
That passed through the Field,
Enclosed by the Fence,
That was made with
   The Rail that Old Abe split.

This is THE TEAM
That traveled the Road,
That passed through the Field,
Enclosed by the Fence,
That was made with
   The Rail that Old Abe split.

This was THE BOY
That drove the Team,
That traveled the Road,
That passed through the Field,
Enclosed by the Fence,
That was made with
   The Rail that Old Abe split.

This is THE HOUSE
To be filled by the Boy,
That drove the Team,
That traveled the Road,
That passed through the Field,
Enclosed by the Fence,
That was made with
   The Rail that Old Abe split.

PITTSBURGH FLAG MANUFACTORY, 45 FIFTH STREET.
Flags from 3 inches to 50 feet.   J. PITTOCK, Agent for Co.

A republican broadside, campaign of 1860.

Upper left: Brady photograph made in Washington nine days before inauguration, 1861 (Meserve). *Upper right:* Inauguration crowd before the unfinished Capitol, March 4, 1861 (Meserve). *Lower, left to right:* Edwin McMasters Stanton of Ohio, second Secretary of War (CS), Simon Cameron of Pennsylvania, first Secretary of War (CS), Gideon Welles of Connecticut, Secretary of the Navy, diarist extraordinary (USASC), Salmon Portland Chase of Ohio, Secretary of the Treasury, constant Presidential aspirant (CS).

CONFEDERATE GENERALS. *Upper left:* Robert Edward Lee (Library of Congress). *Upper right:* Early photograph of Thomas J. ("Stonewall") Jackson (CS). *Lower, left to right:* Joseph E. Johnston (Meserve). Nathan Bedford Forrest (Meserve). J.E.B. ("Jeb") Stuart (Meserve). James Longstreet (Meserve).

UNION GENERALS. *Upper left:* William Tecumseh Sherman (Meserve). *Upper right:* Ulysses Simpson Grant (Meserve). *Lower, left to right:* George Gordon Meade (CS), Joseph Hooker (CS), Ambrose E. Burnside (Meserve), Henry W. Halleck (Meserve).

Upper left: Jefferson Davis, President of the Confederate States of America, former Senator from Mississippi and Mexican War veteran (McClees). *Upper center:* Alexander Stephens of Georgia, Vice-President of the CSA, intimate with Lincoln when they were members of Congress (USASC). *Upper right:* William Lowndes Yancey, "fire-eater" orator who led Alabama into secession (Meserve). *Center:* Christopher Gustavus Memminger of South Carolina, Wurttemburg born, Secretary of the Treasury of the CSA (Meserve). *Lower left:* John C. Breckinridge, resigned U.S. Senator from Kentucky, Confederate general, later Secretary of War of the CSA (Meserve).

Upper: Photograph by Alexander Gardner, November 15, 1863, four days before the Gettysburg speech. Stern, austere, one of the most popular portraits of Lincoln (Meserve). *Lower:* Lincoln, troubled about McClellan's "slows," pays a surprise visit to the Army of the Potomac Commander in October, 1862 (Meserve).

Lincoln facing McClellan in Antietam camp after the battle, October, 1862. The best photograph of Lincoln, the tall man in the tall hat. Detail from photograph in Gardner Album No. 1 (Museum of Modern Art).

Upper left: Horace Greeley, editor of the New York *Tribune* (CS). *Upper right:* Harriet Beecher Stowe of *Uncle Tom's Cabin* (CS). *Center:* Julia Ward Howe of "The Battle Hymn of the Republic" (CS). *Lower:* Kate Chase Sprague, "society" leader and politician (Meserve).

Upper left: Union infantry
rank and file (USASC). *Upper right:* Confederate rank
and file troopers captured at
Gettysburg (CS). *Center:* Escaped slaves, "contrabands,"
outfitted for Labor inside Union lines (CS). *Lower:* Union
officers and privates (CS).

Upper: Lincoln's private secretaries, John Hay (left) and John G. Nicolay (right), who accompanied the President-elect to Washington and were White House residents (Meserve). *Upper right:* Andrew Johnson of Tennessee, elected Vice-President 1864 (USASC).

Lower, left to right: Charles Sumner, Boston antislavery aristocrat, U.S. Senator from Massachusetts (CS); John C. Fremont, explorer, California millionaire rancher, Major General, politician constantly at odds with Lincoln (Meserve); Clement L. Vallandigham of Ohio, Congressman and violent opponent of Lincoln (McClees).

The Last Photographs of Lincoln By Alexander Gardner, April 10, 1865, the day after Lee's surrender at Appomattox. Tad is shown with his father, upper left (Meserve).

taller than average, except for his knees rising above the chair's seat level.

When at home in Springfield, he cut wood, tended to the house stoves, curried his horse, milked the cow. Lincoln's words might have a wilderness air and log-cabin smack, the word "idea" more like "idee," and "really" a drawled Kentucky "ra-a-ly." He sang hardly at all but his voice had clear and appealing modulations in his speeches; in rare moments it rose to a startling and unforgettable high treble giving every syllable unmistakable meaning. In stoop of shoulders and a forward bend of his head there was a grace and familiarity making it easy for shorter people to look up into his face and talk with him.

In a criminal case Lincoln agreed with Usher F. Linder that each should make the longest speech he could, talking till he was used up. And, as Linder told it, Lincoln "ran out of wind" at the end of an hour, while he, Linder, rambled on three hours to the jury.

When Martin Van Buren stopped overnight in Rochester, friends took along Lincoln to entertain the former President. Van Buren said of the evening that his sides were sore from laughing. Lincoln might have told of the man selling a horse he guaranteed "sound of skin and skeleton and free from faults and faculties." Or the judge who, trying to be kindly, asked a convicted murderer, politically allied to him, "When would you like to be hung?" Or the lawyer jabbing at a hostile witness who had one large ear: "If he bit off the other ear he would look more like a man than a jackass." Or of the old man with whiskers so long it was said of him when he traveled, "His whiskers arrive a day in advance." Or of Abram Bale, the tall and powerful-voiced preacher from Kentucky, who, baptizing new converts in the Sangamon River, was leading a sister into the water, when her husband, watching from the bank, cried out: "Hold on, Bale! Hold on, Bale! Don't you drown her. I wouldn't take the best cow and calf in Menard County for her."

Once in a courthouse, Lincoln rattled off a lingo changing letters of words, so that "cotton patch" became "potten catch" and "jackass" became "jassack," giving tricky twists to barnyard and tavern words. The court clerk asked Lincoln to write it out and took special care for years of the paper on which Lincoln scribbled verbal nonsense. The *Illinois State Register* termed him a "long-legged varmint" and "our jester and mountebank." A client seeing Lincoln with one leg on the office desk, said, "That's the longest leg I've ever seen in this country." Lincoln lifted the other leg to the desk, and, "Here's another one just like it." Or so it was told.

In the small clique of Springfield Whigs who had come to wield party controls, the opposition dubbed Lincoln the "Goliath of the Junto." On streets, in crowds or gatherings, Lincoln's tall frame stood out. He was noticed, pointed out, questions asked about him. He couldn't slide into any group of standing people without all eyes finding he was there. His head surmounting a group was gaunt and strange, onlookers remembering the high cheekbones, deep eye sockets, the coarse black hair bushy and tangled, the nose large and well shaped, the wide full-lipped mouth of many subtle changes from straight face to wide beaming smile. He was loose-jointed and comic with appeals in street-corner slang and dialect from the public square hitching posts; yet at moments he was as strange and far-off as the last dark sands of a red sunset, solemn as naked facts of death and hunger. He was a seeker. Among others and deep in his own inner self, he was a seeker.

Leasing his Springfield house for a yearly rental of $90, "the North-upstairs room" reserved for furniture storage, Lincoln on October 25, 1847, with wife, four-year-old Robert and 19-month-old Eddie, took stage for St. Louis, and after a week of steamboat and rail travel, arrived in Lexington, Kentucky. There relatives and friends could see Mary Todd Lincoln and her Congressman husband she took pride in showing. They stayed three weeks. Lincoln saw the cotton mills of Oldham, Todd & Company, worked by slave labor, driving out with his brother-in-law, Levi Todd, assistant manager.

He got the feel of a steadily growing antislavery movement in Kentucky. He saw slaves auctioned, saw them chained in gangs heading south to cotton fields, heard ominous news like that of "Cassily," a slave girl, under indictment for "mixing an ounce of pounded glass with gravy" and giving it to her master, John Hamilton, and his wife Martha. He had heard of the auction sale in Lexington of Eliza, a beautiful girl with dark lustrous eyes, straight black hair, rich olive complexion, only one sixty-fourth African, white yet a slave. A young Methodist minister, Calvin Fairbank, bid higher and higher against a thick-necked Frenchman from New Orleans. Reaching $1,200, the Frenchman asked, "How high are you going?" and Fairbank, "Higher than you, Monsieur." The bids rose to where Fairbank said slowly, "One thousand, four hundred and fifty dollars." Seeing the Frenchman hesitating, the sweating auctioneer pulled Eliza's dress back from her shoulders, showing her neck and breasts, and cried, "Who is going to lose a chance like this?" To the Frenchman's bid of $1,465, the minister bid $1,475. Hearing no more bids, the auctioneer shocked the crowd by "lifting her skirts" to "bare her body from feet to waist," and slapping her thigh as he called, "Who is going to be the winner of this prize?" Over the mutter and tumult of the crowd came the Frenchman's slow bid of "One thousand, five hundred and eighty dollars." The auctioneer lifted his gavel, called "one-two-three." Eliza turned a pained and piteous face toward Fairbank, who now bid "One thousand, five hundred and eighty-five." The auctioneer: "I'm going to sell this girl. Are you going to bid?" The Frenchman shook his head. Eliza fell in a faint. The auctioneer to Fairbank: "You've got her damned cheap, sir. What are you going to do with her?" And Fairbank cried, "Free her!" Most of the crowd shouted and yelled in glee. Fairbank was there by arrangement with Salmon P. Chase and Nicholas Longworth of Cincinnati, who had authorized him to bid as high as $25,000. Fairbank had since gone to the penitentiary for other antislavery activity and in his life was to serve 17 years behind bars.

Lincoln saw in the Todd and other homes the Negro house servants, their need to be clean, their handling of food and linen, the chasm between them and Negro field hands who lived in "quarters." He read books in the big library of Robert Todd, went to many parties and in the capital city of Kentucky met leading figures of the state and nation. He heard Henry Clay on November 13 before an immense audience: "Autumn has come, and the season of flowers has passed away . . . I too am in the autumn of life, and feel the frost of age," terming the Mexican War one of "unnecessary and offensive aggression," holding, "It is Mexico that is defending her firesides, her castles and her altars, not we." For the United States to take over Mexico and govern it, as some were urging, Clay saw as impossible, and there would be danger in acquiring a new area into which slavery could move.

Chapter 7

Congressman Lincoln

By stage and rail the Lincoln family traveled seven days to arrive in Washington December 2, staying at Brown's Hotel, then moving to Mrs. Sprigg's boardinghouse on ground where later the Library of Congress was built. They saw a planned city with wide intersecting streets, squares, parks, a few noble buildings on spacious lawns, yet nearly everywhere a look of the unfinished, particularly the Capitol with its dark wooden dome, its two wings yet to be built. Cobblestoned Pennsylvania Avenue ran wide from the Capitol to the White House yet a heavy rain on Polk's inauguration day brought mudholes where parading soldiers slipped and sprawled.

Here lived 40,000 people, among them 8,000 free Negroes and 2,000 slaves. Here were mansions and slums; cowsheds, hog pens and privies in back yards; hogs, geese and chickens roving streets and alleys. Sidewalks were mostly of gravel or ashes. Thirty-seven churches of varied faiths, competed with out-numbering saloons, card and dice joints, houses where women and girls aimed to please male customers. Ragged slaves drove produce wagons; gangs of slaves sold or to be sold at times moved in chains along streets. Lincoln saw a jail near the Capitol which he was to term "a sort of negro livery-stable," where Negroes were kept to be taken south "precisely like a drove of horses." Yet here too were libraries, museums, fountains, gardens, halls and offices where historic and momentous decisions were made, ceremonials, receptions, balls, occasions of state and grandeur, and all the dialects of America from Louisiana to Maine, the Southern drawl, the Yankee nasal twang, the differing western slang.

Lincoln liked Mrs. Sprigg's place, the lodgings and meals, the Whig anti-slavery members of Congress who ate there, especially the abolitionist war horse from Ohio, Joshua R. Giddings. When Lincoln couldn't referee a table dispute, he could usually break it up with an odd story that had point. But Mrs. Lincoln couldn't find company, attractions, women, social events of interest to her, and with her husband one of the busiest men in Congress, missing only seven roll calls in the long session that was opening, after three months of it she traveled with the two boys to her father's home in Lexington.

In the Hall of Representatives, after the oath of office, Lincoln drew a seat in the back row of the Whig side. Many faces and names in the House and over in the Senate became part of him, part of his life then and in years after. George Ashmun, John G. Palfrey and Robert Winthrop of Massachusetts, John Minor Botts of Virginia, Howell Cobb and Alexander Stephens of Georgia, Andrew Johnson of Tennessee, Robert C. Schenck of Ohio, Caleb B. Smith of Indiana, Jacob Thompson of Mississippi, David Wilmot of Pennsylvania—Lincoln could have no dim forevision of the events and tumults where those men would be joined or tangled with him.

He could see at one desk a little man with delicate sideburns, a mouth both sweet and severe. Eighty years old, this man had been professor of rhetoric at Harvard, U.S. Senator from Massachusetts, President of the United States from 1825 to 1829, after which he was in Congress for 17 years. In the foreign service in Paris he had seen Napoleon return from Elba. This was John Quincy Adams, one of the foremost and fiery Whigs to cry that the war with Mexico was instigated by slaveholders for the extension of slave territory. Over in the Senate Lincoln could see the Illinois wonder boy who had had two terms in the House, had been elected to a third, but resigned before taking his seat to start his first term in the upper chamber. Stephen A. Douglas quoted Frederick the Great, "Take possession first and negotiate afterward," and declared, "That is precisely what President Polk has done."

American armies in Mexico were clinching their hold on that country, which had cost the Government $27,000,000 and the people the lives of 27,000 soldiers. With Mexico beaten, questions rose: "What shall we force Mexico to pay us? Since she has no money, how much of her land shall we take? Or shall we take over all of Mexico?"

Lincoln on December 22 introduced resolutions respectfully requesting the President to inform the House as to the exact "spot of soil" where first "the blood of our *citizens* was so shed." He directly implied that the President had ordered American troops into land not established as American soil. The President, Lincoln said later, was attempting "to prove, by telling the *truth*, what he could not prove by telling the *whole truth*."

In the House January 12, 1848, Lincoln defended the vote of his party a few days before in declaring "that the war with Mexico was unnecessarily and unconstitutionally commenced by the President." He spoke of the course he and others followed. "When the war began, it was my opinion that all those who, because of knowing too *little*, or because of knowing too *much*, could not conscientiously approve the conduct of the President, in the beginning of it, should, nevertheless, as good citizens and patriots, remain silent on that point, at least till the war should be ended."

Since Mexico by revolution had overthrown the government of Spain, and Texas by revolution had thrown off the government of Mexico, Lincoln discussed the rights of peoples to revolutionize. "Any people anywhere, being inclined and having the power, have the *right* to rise up, and shake off the existing government, and form a new one that suits them better . . . Any portion of such people that *can, may* revolutionize, and make their *own*, of so much of the territory as they inhabit. More than this, a *majority* of any portion of such people may revolutionize, putting down a *minority*, intermingled with, or near about them, who may oppose their movement. Such minority, was precisely the case, of the tories of our own revolution. It is a quality of revolutions not to go by *old* lines, or *old* laws; but to break up both, and make new ones."

The President's justifications of himself reminded Lincoln that "I have sometimes seen a good lawyer, struggling for his client's neck, in a desperate case, employing every artifice to work round, befog, and cover up, with many words, some point arising in the case, which he *dared* not admit, and yet *could* not deny." He rehearsed the intricate Whig arguments that American troops invaded Mexican soil, and, "I more than suspect," as to the President, "that he is deeply conscious of being in the wrong,—that he feels the blood of this war, like the blood of Abel, is crying to Heaven against him . . . His mind, tasked beyond it's power, is running hither and thither, like some tortured creature, on a burning surface, finding no position, on which it can settle down, and be at peace . . . He knows not where he is. He is a bewildered, confounded, and miserably perplexed man. God grant he may be able to show, there is not something about his conscience, more painful than all his mental perplexity!"

It was a fiercely partisan speech, in a style Lincoln would in time abandon. He knew little or nothing of the pressure on Polk and misread Polk. For months the President hesitated; he *was* a miserably perplexed man. Of Robert Walker, his Secretary of the Treasury, the President noted in his diary, "He was for taking all of Mexico"; of Buchanan, his Secretary of State, the notation was similar. Finally, he wrote in his diary, after endless advice to seize the whole territory of the Mexican nation: "I replied that I was not prepared to go to that extent, and furthermore, that I did not desire that anything I said should be so obscure as to give rise to doubt or discussion as to what my true meaning was; that I had in my last message declared that I did not contemplate the conquest of Mexico."

Lincoln voted for all supplies and aid to soldiers in the field, and for every measure laying blame on Polk and the administration. He hoped the folks back home would understand his conduct. But many of the folks back home couldn't see it, not even Bill Herndon. The Belleville *Advocate* of March 2 reported a meeting in Clark County of "patriotic Whigs and Democrats" which resolved "That Abe Lincoln, the author of the 'Spotty' resolutions in Congress against his own country, may they be long remembered by his constituents, but may they cease to remember him, except to rebuke him." The *Illinois State Register* told of newspapers and public meetings that declared Lincoln to be "a second Benedict Arnold." The *Register* favored taking over all of Mexico and making it part of the United States.

In an emotion-drenched speech February 2, Alexander Stephens voiced the depths of Whig scorn of the President, in somewhat the vein of parts of Lincoln's speech some three weeks earlier. "The principle of waging war against a neighboring people to compel them to sell their country, is not only dishonorable, but disgraceful and infamous. What! shall it be said that American honor aims at nothing higher than land? . . . Never did I expect to see the day when the Executive of this country should announce that our honor was such a loathsome, beastly thing, that it could not be satisfied with any achievements in arms, however brilliant and glorious, but must feed on earth—gross, vile dirt!—and require even a prostrate foe to be robbed of mountain rocks and desert plains!"

Lincoln wrote to Herndon: "I just take up my pen to say, that Mr. Stephens of Georgia, a little slim, pale-faced, consumptive man, with a voice like Logan's, has just concluded the very best speech, of an hour's length, I ever heard. My old, withered, dry eyes, are full of tears yet. If he writes it out any thing like he delivered it, our people shall see a good many copies of it."

A new Senator from Mississippi, who at Buena Vista had stayed in his saddle with a bleeding foot till the battle was won, a cotton planter, Jefferson Davis, was saying Mexico was held by "title of conquest," that Yucatan should be annexed or England would take it, and if the American advance to the Isthmus was resisted, he favored war with Britain. His bill for ten regiments to garrison Mexico passed the Senate by 29 to 19 but was pigeon-holed in the House, where Whigs controlled. The need of the South for new areas into which slavery could spread, and by which the South would have political representation to match that of the growing North, had brought splits and factions in both parties north and south.

Senator John C. Calhoun of South Carolina believed, "People do not understand liberty or majorities. The will of the majority is the will of a rabble. Progressive democracy is incompatible with liberty." His mantle of leadership seemed to be falling on Jefferson Davis who in this year of 1848 told the Senate that if folly, fanaticism, hate and corruption were to destroy the peace and prosperity of the Union, then "let the sections part . . . and let peace and good will subsist." With this readiness to break up the Union, the Southern Whigs, Toombs, Stephens, and above all Henry Clay, could not agree. In the North the Democrats were losing unity in several states on the issue of whether slavery should be extended into the new vast territories acquired and being settled. Among New York Democrats had come the "Hunkers," who were said to hanker after office on any principle, and the "Barnburners," so named after the Dutchman who burned down his barn to get rid of the rats. Also in New York were the elder Silver-Gray Whigs and the Radicals.

Over the country those having ears had heard of the Wilmot Proviso cutting across party lines, setting Southern Whigs against Northern, Southern Democrats angry with the Northern. Thirty-four-year-old David Wilmot of Pennsylvania, a Jacksonian Democrat who had fought for the rights of labor and against imprisonment for debt, had in 1846 offered a rider to the appropriations bill, a proviso that slavery would be shut out from all lands acquired by the Mexican War. Since then, over and over, this proviso had been moved as an amendment to this and that bill before Congress. Lincoln voted for the proviso, so he wrote, "at least" 40 times, he was sure. This hammering away at no further spread of slavery brought movements, outcries of injustice and interference, and threats of secession from Southern leaders.

Incidents constantly arose as one in February 1848 at Mrs. Sprigg's boardinghouse. The Negro servant in the house had been buying his freedom at a price of $300; he had paid all but $60 when, one day, two white men came to the house, knocked him down, tied and gagged him, took him to a slave jail, and had him sent to New Orleans for sale. Joshua Giddings asked for a hearing by the House and was voted down by 98 to 88.

One February morning John Quincy Adams stood up to speak, suddenly clutched his desk with groping fingers, then slumped to his chair, was carried out to linger and die, saying, "This is the last of earth, but I am content." In a final hour Henry Clay in tears had held the old man's hand. Lincoln served with a committee on arrangements; there was a funeral of state, many saying Mr. Adams could have no fear of the Recording Angel.

In the House post office was a storyteller's corner and fellowship. Stephens of Georgia could say, "I was as intimate with Mr. Lincoln as with any other man except perhaps Mr. Toombs." Lincoln could tell of Stuart and Douglas campaigning; arriving late one night at a tavern, the landlord showed them two beds, each with a man sleeping in it. Douglas asked their politics and the landlord pointed to one a Whig and the other a Democrat, Douglas saying, "Stuart, you sleep with the Whig and I'll sleep with the Democrat." Or the Kentucky justice of the peace, tired of two lawyers wrangling after his decision, speaking out: "If the court is right—and she think she air—why, then you air wrong, and she knows you is—shet up!"

Lincoln wrote to Herndon that "by way of getting the hang of the House," he had spoken on a post office question, and, "I was about as badly scared, and no worse, as I am when I speak in court." His House record showed him working hard and faithfully on petitions, appointments, pensions, documents for constituents, routine measures

such as internal improvements, public roads, canals, rivers
and harbors. He found the wrangling and quibbling much
the same as in the Illinois Legislature. Once he counseled
that to pay for canals with canal tolls and tonnage duties,
before the canals were dug, was like the Irishman and his
new boots: "I shall niver git 'em on till I wear 'em a day
or two, and stretch 'em a little."

One evening at the library of the Supreme Court, after
digging in many books and documents, Lincoln drew out
volumes to read in his room at Mrs. Sprigg's. The library
was going to close for the night, so he tied a large bandanna around the books, ran a stick through the knots,
slung the stick over his shoulder, and walked out of the library. Wearing a short circular blue cloak he had bought
since coming to Washington, he walked to his Capitol Hill
lodging, where he read in his books, then took a brass
key from his vest pocket and wound his watch, put his boot
heels into a bootjack and pulled off his boots, blew out the
candlelights and crept into a warm yellow flannel night-
shirt that came down halfway between his knees and ankles.

In April he had written his wife, "Dear Mary: In this
troublesome world, we are never quite satisfied. When you
were here, I thought you hindered me some in attending
to business; but now, having nothing but business—no variety—it has grown exceedingly tasteless to me. I hate to
sit down and direct documents, and I hate to stay in this old
room by myself." He wrote of shopping, as she wished,
for "the little plaid stockings" to fit "Eddy's dear little feet,"
and "I wish you to enjoy yourself in every possible way
. . . Very soon after you went away, I got what I think a
very pretty set of shirt-bosom studs—modest little ones,
jet, set in gold, only costing 50 cents a piece, or 1.50 for
the whole. Suppose you do not prefix the 'Hon' to the address on your letters to me any more . . . and you are entirely free from head-ache? That is good—good—consid-
ering it is the first spring you have been free from it since
we were acquainted. I am afraid you will get so well, and
fat, and young, as to be wanting to marry again . . . I did
not get rid of the impression of that foolish dream about

dear Bobby till I got your letter written the same day. What did he and Eddy think of the little letters father sent them? Dont let the blessed fellows forget father." Their children were a common and warm bond.

In June he wrote to her at Lexington, "The leading matter in your letter, is your wish to return to this side of the Mountains. Will you be a *good girl* in all things, if I consent? Then come along, and that as *soon* as possible. Having got the idea in my head, I shall be impatient till I see you . . . Come on just as soon as you can. I want to see you, and our dear—*dear* boys very much. Every body here wants to see our dear Bobby." Her letter to him had said, "How much, I wish instead of writing, we were together this evening. I feel very sad away from you." But campaign duties pressed him and her visit to Washington couldn't be managed.

He wrote to her July 2 a long newsy letter ending, "By the way, you do not intend to do without a girl, because the one you had has left you? Get another as soon as you can to take charge of the dear codgers. Father expected to see you all sooner; but let it pass; stay as long as you please, and come when you please. Kiss and love the dear rascals." He signed his letters to her "Affectionately A. Lincoln," and hers to him were signed "Truly yours M.L."

It seemed byplay and banter in his ending a July letter to Herndon, "As to kissing a pretty girl, [I] know one very pretty one, but I guess she wont let me kiss her."

In a dignified speech June 20 Lincoln questioned intentions to amend the Constitution indicated in the Democratic platform. He advised, "No slight occasion should tempt us to touch it. Better not take the first step, which may lead to a habit of altering it . . . New provisions, would introduce new difficulties, and thus create, and increase appetite for still further change. No sir, let it stand as it is." On July 27 he told the House that "on the prominent questions . . . Gen: Taylor's course is at least as well defined as is Gen: Cass' " (the Democratic nominee), adding later, "I hope and *believe*, Gen: Taylor, if elected, would not veto the [Wilmot] Proviso. *But* I do not *know* it.

Yet, if I knew he would, I still would vote for him. I should do so, because, in my judgment, his election alone, can defeat Gen: Cass; and because, *should* slavery thereby go to the territory we now have, just so much will certainly happen by the election of Cass."

After this candid presentation he swung into the comic vein of a stump speech before a rough-and-tumble crowd. He pointed to General Cass during nine years drawing ten rations a day from the Government at $730 a year. "At eating too, his capacities are shown to be quite as wonderful. From October 1821 to May 1822 he ate ten rations a day in Michigan, ten rations a day here in Washington, and near five dollars worth a day on the road between the two places! And then there is an important discovery in his example—the art of being paid for what one eats, instead of having to pay for it . . . Mr. Speaker, we have all heard of the animal standing in doubt between two stacks of hay, and starving to death. The like of that would never happen to Gen: Cass; place the stacks a thousand miles apart, he would stand stock still midway between them, and eat them both at once, and the green grass along the line would be apt to suffer some too at the same time . . . I have heard some things from New-York; and if they are true, one might well say of your party there, as a drunken fellow once said when he heard the reading of an indictment for hog-stealing. The clerk read on till he got to, and through the words 'did steal, take, and carry away, ten boars, ten sows, ten shoats, and ten pigs' at which he exclaimed 'Well, by golly, that is the most equally divided gang of hogs, I ever did hear of.' If there is any *other* gang of hogs more equally divided than the democrats of New-York are about this time, I have not heard of it." The Baltimore *American* said the speaker kept the House roaring.

Distinct, irrevocable events of 1848 were throwing shadows pointing to events lurking in farther shadows dark beyond reading. In February the Mexican War ended with a treaty; New Mexico and Upper California were ceded to the United States; the lower Rio Grande from its mouth to El Paso became the boundary of Texas; for territory acquired the United States was to pay Mexico $15,000,000.

Calhoun, Davis, Rhett and others of the South were openly trying to organize secession of the Southern States from the Union. In the North was explosive force in the Free-Soil party which nominated the former Democratic President Martin Van Buren for President and Charles Francis Adams, son of John Quincy Adams, for Vice-President. Their platform called for "the rights of free labor against the aggressions of the slave power," cheap postage, "free grants" of land to actual settlers, with the slogan "Free Soil, Free Speech, Free Labor, and Free Men." Names that counted were in the new party, Salmon P. Chase of Ohio, Charles Sumner of Massachusetts, William Cullen Bryant, Longfellow, Lowell, Whittier, David Wilmot and others. Antislavery Whigs and Democrats were pouring into the new party in some states saying here was a cause to fight for, whereas the Whig and Democratic party platforms straddled, weaseled and stood for nothing on any issue of the hour.

The great Whig hero, Daniel Webster, had a certain majesty but "lacked popular appeal." The other idolized veteran Whig hero, Henry Clay, had run three times and lost. And Lincoln, with Stephens and others, in a clique calling themselves "The Young Indians," served in the forefront of those who saw Zachary Taylor as the one candidate to win in the coming campaign. True enough, Taylor was owner on his Louisiana plantation of more than a hundred slaves, was naïve and somewhat ignorant of politics; he had never voted for President but said that had he voted for President in 1844 it would have been for Clay; he saw the Wilmot Proviso as "a mere bugbare" of agitators and it would disappear; he cautioned, "I am not an ultra Whig." But the name of "Old Zach" at 64 carried magic; he was honest, rugged, plain; against terrific odds his armies, by his keen strategy and dogged courage, had won for him the beloved nickname of "Old Rough and Ready." He had spoken of the war as uncalled-for and had moved his troops into action only under direct orders which he obeyed as a trained and loyal soldier.

In the Philadelphia convention in June the first ballot gave Taylor 111, Henry Clay 97, General Winfield Scott

43, Daniel Webster 22. As a delegate, Lincoln voted for Taylor on all ballots, cheered the nomination of Taylor on the fourth, and wrote to Illinois that Taylor's nomination took the Democrats "on the blind side" and "It turns the war thunder against them. The war is now to them, the gallows of Haman, which they built for us, and on which they are doomed to be hanged themselves." He could see a variety of factions, "all the odds and ends are with us"; all was high hope and confidence.

A letter of Herndon June 15 was "heart-sickening," "discouraging," Lincoln wrote, advising his young partner, "You must not wait to be brought forward by the older men. For instance do you suppose that I should ever have got into notice if I had waited to be hunted up and pushed forward by older men. You young men get together and form a Rough & Ready club . . . as you go along, gather up all the shrewd wild boys about town, whether just of age, or a little under age." Herndon had asked him to send along all speeches made about Taylor and Lincoln wrote that he had sent on the *Congressional Globe* containing "every speech made by every man" in both Houses, and, "Can I send any more? Can I send speeches that nobody has made?" Another Herndon letter questioned the motives of "the old men," and Lincoln wrote, "I suppose I am now one of the old men . . . I was young once, and I am sure I was never ungenerously thrust back . . . Allow me to assure you, that suspicion and jealousy never did help any man in any situation . . . You have been a laborious, studious young man" and he shouldn't allow his mind "to be improperly directed."

Because of the Whig party's "turn about is fair play" policy, Lincoln was not running for re-election to Congress. When news came to him of the August 7 election in Illinois, Stephen T. Logan, running for Lincoln's seat, had lost by 106 votes to a Mexican War veteran. Lincoln at headquarters of the national Whig committee was busy franking documents, helping edit a Whig paper *The Battery*, getting out campaign literature, writing political letters. He was assigned to speak in New England where the Free-Soilers had a threatening strength. By "steam cars" to New

York and probably boat to Norwich he made the three-day trip that had him September 12 in Worcester, Massachusetts, where he declared that Taylor was "just the man to whom the interests, principles and prosperity of the country might be safely intrusted." The Free-Soil platform in general was like the pantaloons the Yankee peddler offered for sale, "large enough for any man, small enough for any boy." He spoke in New Bedford, Boston, Chelsea, Cambridge, and in a day speech at Dedham, a young Whig took note, "He wore a black alpaca sack coat, turned up the sleeves of this, and then the cuffs of his shirt. Next he loosened his necktie and soon after took it off altogether. He soon had his audience as by a spell. I never saw men more delighted. His style was the most familiar and offhand possible."

At Taunton a reporter wrote, "His awkward gesticulations, the ludicrous management of his voice and the comical expression of his countenance, all conspired to make his hearers laugh at the mere anticipation of the joke before it appeared." He quoted a sarcastic Free-Soiler, "General Taylor is a slaveholder, therefore we go for him to prevent the extension of slavery," and said the correct form of the syllogism should be: "General Taylor is a slaveholder, but he will do more to prevent the extension of slavery than any other man whom it is possible to elect, therefore we go for Taylor." At Tremont Temple in Boston he spoke after Governor William H. Seward of New York who was soon to be elected U.S. Senator. At their hotel Lincoln told Seward he had been thinking about Seward's speech, and, "I reckon you are right. We have got to deal with this slavery question, and got to give much more attention to it hereafter."

Traveling west Lincoln at Albany talked with Thurlow Weed and together they visited Millard Fillmore, Whig candidate for Vice-President. Next Lincoln saw Niagara Falls. He left Buffalo September 26 on the steamer *Globe* for a 1,047-mile cruise that had him in Chicago October 5. He wrote deep meditations on Niagara Falls, its "wonder" and "great charm," and how, "When Columbus first sought this continent—when Christ suffered on the cross—when

Moses led Israel through the Red-Sea—nay, even, when Adam first came from the hand of his Maker—then as now, Niagara was roaring here . . . The Mammoth and Mastodon —now so long dead, that fragments of their monstrous bones, alone testify, that they ever lived, have gazed on Niagara." Lincoln's sense of history and the past, for all his incessant newspaper reading, came from books that became part of his mind.

In Chicago he spoke for the Whig ticket two hours to a crowd so large it had to adjourn from the courthouse to the public square. With Mrs. Lincoln and the children he traveled to Springfield. Of his two-hour speech in a Peoria stopover, the *Democratic Press* said, "Mr. Lincoln blew his nose, bobbed his head, threw up his coat tail, and delivered an immense amount of sound and fury." Before Election Day he spoke in eight or ten Illinois towns for the Whig ticket, always advising that a vote for the Free-Soil ticket might turn out to be a vote for Cass. As to the United States reaching out for more territory, he quoted the farmer about land, "I ain't greedy; I only want what jines mine."

Election returns (exclusive of South Carolina, where the legislature chose electors) gave a popular vote for Taylor 1,360,752; Cass 1,219,962; Van Buren 291,342. Ohio elected six Free-Soilers to Congress, other states six more, which forebode the slavery issue would blaze on. Cass had carried Illinois but there was comfort that Ned Baker, who had moved to Galena, was elected to Congress. Lincoln had written of him, "He is a good hand to raise a breeze." It counted a little, too, that his congressional district had given a whopping majority of more than 1,500 for Taylor. And the new legislature elected a new U.S. Senator, James Shields, a Democrat, with whom Lincoln had more than a slight acquaintance.

In a corner of his Springfield office Lincoln whittled and shaped a wooden model of a steamboat with "adjustable buoyant air chambers," "sliding spars," ropes and pulleys. On the Detroit River he had seen a steamboat stuck on a sand bar; barrels, boxes and empty casks forced under the vessel lifted it off. Lincoln finished a model, wrote a description of its workings, and the next year had it patented.

In late November 1848 Lincoln left Springfield for St. Louis and by steamboat up the Ohio River and then by rail reached Washington and took his seat in the House December 7, three days after the Thirtieth Congress had convened. While traveling, he wrote that he took "very extra care" of a letter containing money. "To make it more secure than it would be in my hat, where I carry most all my packages, I put it in my trunk."

He spoke briefly and moderately for river and harbor improvements by Federal aid and a more liberal policy in public lands for settlers, voting regularly for measures aimed at free governments in California and New Mexico, voting again for the Wilmot Proviso whenever it came up. He voted often against sweeping, straight-out abolitionist measures to prohibit slavery immediately and without reservations in the District of Columbia.

He loved his fellow boarder Joshua Giddings, a big, hearty, earnest, honest, rugged Buckeye of a man, but he couldn't vote for Giddings' bill to make a clean sweep-out of slavery in the District. Those who later saw Lincoln's growth beginning with his humiliations of this period gave him too little credit for the early sagacity of his resolution before the House January 10, 1849; on seeing no chance for its adoption he didn't introduce it as a bill. What he offered was the keenest solution then possible of the slavery problem in the District. In it was the foretokening that he could umpire between the North and the South, that he understood both sections without prejudice, that he could relate the tangled past to the uncertain future by offering only what might be workable in the immediate present.

He proposed that no new slaves, could be brought into the District to live there, except temporarily the slaves, "necessary servants," of Government officers from slave-holding states. After January 1, 1850, all children born of slave mothers should be free, should be "reasonably supported and educated" by the owners of their mothers though owing "reasonable service" to such owners until arriving at an age to be determined. By these two provisions —no new slaves to be brought in and all children born of slaves to be free—and all living slaves in the District certain to die sometime, there would be a definite, calculable day when slavery would have vanished from the District. The President, Secretary of State and Secretary of the Treasury should be a board to determine the value of such slaves as owners "may desire to emancipate." Yet Congress must not impose its will on the District; therefore let it provide an election where all "free white male" voters could say whether they wanted such emancipation.

One proviso was to make trouble for Lincoln then and for years after. Washington authorities would be "empowered and required" to arrest and deliver to owners "all fugitive slaves escaping into said District." Lincoln said that he had shown his proposals to 15 leading citizens of the District and "he had authority to say that every one of them desired that some proposition like this should pass." The cry came from several members, "Who are they? Give us their names," to which Lincoln made no answer. In the many debates of various angles of the slavery question, he kept silence. Angry Free-Soilers, anxious antislavery and proslavery Whigs and Democrats clashed in wild disputes, and Lincoln sat still. He had begun waiting for unforeseen events sure to come.

He saw "Old Zach" inaugurated March 4, did his best at reaching the new Whig President and having him appoint Ned Baker to the Cabinet, but it didn't come off. He began writing letters and for months was to go on with letters asking the President or department heads to appoint this or that good Whig to this or that office. For several old friends he landed places, but he made some enemies; there were always the disgruntled and suspicious. He was to write to the Secretary of State that Taylor's habit of throwing appointments over to department heads was fixing in the public mind "the unjust and ruinous character of [the President] being a mere man of straw," and it could "damn us all inevitably."

Admitted March 7 to practice before the U.S. Supreme Court he argued a case appealed from an Illinois court, and lost it.

Back in Springfield, for months he carried on a furious

and snarled campaign of letter writing, conferences, wire-pulling, aimed at getting for himself or for some other Illinois Whig, the appointment of Commissioner of the General Land Office at Washington, salary $3,000 a year. The politics of the affair seemed to narrow down to where Lincoln would have to go after the office for himself or it would be lost to southern Illinois Whigs. Early in June he wrote to many: "Would you as soon I should have the General Land Office as any other Illinoian? If you would, write me to that effect at Washington, where I shall be soon. No time to lose." In June in Washington wearing a linen duster, he offered reasons why he, an original Taylor man, should be named over the Clay man who landed it. Justin Butterfield won through northern Illinois and Chicago influence, besides that of Daniel Webster and Henry Clay. When Secretary of State John M. Clayton notified Lincoln August 10, 1849, of his appointment as Secretary of the Territory of Oregon, he replied, "I respectfully decline the office" but he would be "greatly obliged" if the place be offered to Simeon Francis, editor of the oldest and leading Whig paper of the state.

Chapter 8

Back Home in Springfield

Back in Springfield picking up law practice again he still had his sense of humor and the advice he had long ago given Speed that when feeling sad work is a cure. He liked the law. He was a born lawyer. He went to it, later writing, "From 1849 to 1854, both inclusive, I practiced law more assiduously than ever before." He traveled the Eighth Circuit, staying two days to two weeks in each county seat, in some years from September till Thanksgiving and from March till June away from his Springfield home. He kept in close touch with the people, their homes, kitchens, barns, fields, their churches, schools, hotels, saloons, their ways of working, worshiping, loafing.

In February 1850 the four-year-old boy Edward Baker Lincoln died. He could call to Eddie and the boy had no living ears to hear. The mother took it hard and it was his place to comfort and restore, if he could, a broken woman.

From the funeral sermon by the Reverend James Smith of the First Presbyterian Church, a friendship grew between the Lincoln family and Mr. Smith. He had been a wild boy in Scotland, a scoffer at religion, then a preacher in Kentucky; he could tell a story—he and Lincoln were good company. The Lincolns rented a pew; Mrs. Lincoln took the sacrament, and joined in membership. Mr. Smith presented Lincoln with his book, *The Christian's Defense*, a reply to infidels and atheists. Lincoln read the book, attended revival meetings, was interested, but when asked to join the church he said he "couldn't quite see it."

Close friends, such as Herndon and Matheny, saw Lincoln as a sort of infidel, saying he told them he couldn't see the Bible as the revelation of God, or Jesus as the Son of God. Lincoln, however, read the Bible closely, knew it from cover to cover, its famous texts, stories and psalms; he quoted it in talks to juries, in speeches, in letters. There were evangelical Christian church members who saw him as solemn, reverent, truly religious. Jesse W. Fell of Bloomington felt that Lincoln's views had likeness to those of the noted preachers, Theodore Parker and William Ellery Channing. Fell gave Lincoln a complete collection of Channing's sermons.

Over the year 1850 Lincoln could read in newspapers and the *Congressional Globe* of the tumults and hazards of political drama in Washington. Only by slender circumstance and hair-trigger chances was the Union saved. In Senate and House men of both sides of the Great Compromise shook their fists and cried threats. A Mississippi Senator, Foote, called a Missouri Senator, Benton, a "calumniator," a liar. Benton walked straight toward Foote, who pulled a revolver and cocked it. Benton tore open his coat and shirt, shouting, "I disdain to carry arms. Let him fire!

Stand out of the way and let the assassin fire!" Other Senators rushed in, took the revolver from Foote, and the debate went on.

In January Henry Clay, whom Lincoln was to term "my beau ideal of a statesman," had introduced the omnibus bills and argued that only by compromise, by give and take, by each side north and south making concessions, could the Union be saved. As his bills came out of a special committee they would let California into the Union as a Free State; New Mexico and Utah would become territories, without reference to slavery; Texas would be paid for giving up boundary claims in New Mexico and having her other boundaries fixed; the slave trade in the District of Columbia would be abolished but slavery would continue so long as it was insisted on by Maryland, which had ceded the District land to the Federal Government. Last and most fiercely disputed was the proposed new Fugitive Slave Law, "with teeth in it"; the Negro claimed as a slave could not have a jury trial and could not testify; a Federal official would be empowered to decide ownership and if he decided for the Negro his fee was $5.00 but if his decision was for the owner his fee was $10; also anyone helping a runaway Negro was made liable to fine and imprisonment.

Daniel Webster on March 7 made a three-hour speech to crowded galleries. The eyes of the audience left him a few moments when the foremost interpreter of the doctrine of states' rights and secession, the aged John C. Calhoun, who was to die 24 days later, had his gaunt and bent form in a black cloak helped to the seat he had held so many years. Webster spoke for the Great Compromise, bill by bill, as the only agreement by which the Union could be held together. Mr. Lincoln out in Illinois must have dwelt with keen eyes on Mr. Webster's passionate exclamations toward his close: "Secession! Peaceable secession! Sir, your eyes and mine are never destined to see that miracle. The dismemberment of this vast country without convulsion! The breaking up of the great deep without ruffling the surface! Who is so foolish . . . as to expect to see any such things? . . . There can be no such thing as a peaceable secession." Webster had tried, in private conferences, to provide jury trial for the fugitive slave, but that was one of many matters to which in that hour he could not refer. Webster, wrote one of his intimate friends, was "a compound of strength and weakness, dust and divinity."

Henry Clay spoke, again and again, at times to storms of applause from crowded galleries. He rebuked personal ambitions. An individual man is "an atom, almost invisible without a magnifying glass . . . a drop of water in the great deep, which evaporates and is borne off by the winds; a grain of sand, which is soon gathered to the dust from which it sprung. Shall a being so small, so petty, so fleeting, so evanescent, oppose itself to onward march of a great nation, to subsist for ages and ages to come? . . . Forbid it God!"

President Taylor, it was known, had made up his mind that if Texans, as they were threatening, moved their troops to interfere with the New Mexico boundary, "I will take command of the army myself to enforce the laws." To the Southern Whigs, Toombs and Stephens, who called on him and said his action would bring civil war and dissolve the Union, he said, "If you men are taken in rebellion against the Union, I will hang you with less reluctance than I hanged spies and deserters in Mexico." Taylor was 65 and scandals, quarrels and insoluble problems had worn him. He sat three hours in the hot sun near the Washington Monument ceremonial on the Fourth of July, listening to orations calling for conciliation and national harmony. He drank ice water, went home to the White House and ate from a basket of cherries, disobeyed his doctor and drank goblets of iced milk and ate more cherries. He died July 9, saying, "I have endeavored to do my duty." With his death hope ran higher of passing the Great Compromise.

Serving as floor captain for the worn men, Clay and Webster, was Senator Douglas; he traded and rounded up votes; he framed provisions of the three most important bills; he maneuvered against the outspoken threats of immediate secession, made speeches for an ocean-to-ocean republic. He replied in anger and scorn to the Massachusetts Free-Soiler, Senator Charles Sumner, who called Douglas "a Northern man with Southern principles." Doug-

las heard and would never forget and would come back
to it again and again that the Whig Senator from New
York, William H. Seward, declared, ". . . there is a higher
law than the Constitution, which regulates our authority . . ." He kept a wary eye on new Free-Soil Senators
who held the Fugitive Slave Law to be infamous and said
so. Douglas kept close to the new Whig President, Millard
Fillmore, chubby-faced, moderate, suave, doing his best
for the Great Compromise. By majorities of about one-
third or more, the omnibus bills, some of them slightly mod-
ified, passed and became law. From January on through
part of August the great debate had raged in Washington
and spread over the country. Now cannon boomed over
Washington, bonfires blazed, processions roared through
the streets, stopping for speeches at the homes of Webster,
Douglas and others. Drinking men said the occasion called
for nothing less than every patriot to get stone blind drunk,
which many of them did. And over the country there settled a curious, quiet, bland, enigmatic peace. In many a
house men breathed easier and slept better because secession and possibly war had been stood off. The quiet was
broken only by the abolitionists, Free-Soilers, antislavery
men in both of the old parties, delivering their shrill or gut-
tural curses on the new Fugitive Slave Law. Lincoln, two
years later, in eulogizing Clay, would say of this new peace,
"The nation has passed its perils, and is free, prosperous,
and powerful."

In late May 1849 Dennis Hanks wrote Lincoln of the
illness of his father Thomas Lincoln and, "He Craves to
See you all the time & he wonts you to Come if you ar able
to git hure, for you are his only Child that is of his own
flush & blood . . . he wonts you to prepare to meet him in
the unknown world, or in heven, for he think that ower
Savour has a Crown of glory, prepared for *him* I wright
this with a bursting hart . . ." A few days later came a letter from Augustus H. Chapman, who married a grand-
daughter of Sarah Bush Lincoln; the father was out of
danger and would be well in a short time.
When later word came of his father on the Coles County

farm dying in January 1851 Lincoln wrote to his step-brother John D. Johnston:

> I feel sure you have not failed to use my name, if necessary, to procure a doctor, or any thing else for Father in his present sickness. My business is such that I could hardly leave home now, if it were not, as it is, that my own wife is sick-abed. (It is a case of baby-sickness, and I suppose is not dangerous.) I sincerely hope Father may yet recover his health; but at all events, tell him to remember to call upon, and confide in, our great, and good, and merciful Maker; who will not turn away from him in any extremity. He notes the fall of a sparrow, and numbers the hairs of our heads; and He will not forget the dying man, who puts his trust in Him. Say to him that if we could meet now, it is doubtful whether it would not be more painful than pleasant; but that if it be his lot to go now, he will soon have a joyous meeting with many loved ones gone before; and where the rest of us, through the help of God, hope ere-long to join them.

When death came close, with a murmur from deep rivers and a cavern of dark stars, Lincoln could use Bible speech. The father died January 17, 1851, and the only son, with a crowded court calendar, including three Supreme Court cases, did not go to the funeral. Lincoln's final somber words to his father could be construed several ways. To be at the deathbed of one for whom you have even a small crumb of affection is definitely "more painful than pleasant." Thomas Lincoln to the last was a churchgoing, religious man, his invariable grace at meals, as reported by a local paper: "Fit and prepare us for humble service, we beg for Christ's sake. Amen."

When in Congress, Lincoln had written to his father, "I very cheerfully send you the twenty dollars, which sum you say is necessary to save your land from sale . . . Give my love to Mother, and all the connections. Affectionately your Son." Could there have been no slight pride or tone of warmth in his often quoting wise proverbs or quaint humor as coming from his father? "If you make a bad bargain, *hug* it the tighter." "Every man must skin his own skunk."

A local paper reported, "One day when alone with her husband, Mrs. Lincoln said, 'Thomas, we have lived together a long time and you have never yet told me whom you like best, your first wife or me.' Thomas replied, 'Oh, now, Sarah, that reminds me of old John Hardin down in Kentucky who had a fine-looking pair of horses, and a neighbor coming in one day and looking at them said, "John, which horse do you like best?" John said, "I can't tell; one of them kicks and the other bites and I don't know which is wust." ' It is plain to see where Abraham Lincoln got his talent for wit and apt illustration." When a third boy baby come to the Lincoln family in 1850 he was named William Wallace: the fourth one in 1853 was named Thomas after his grandfather, so Mrs. Lincoln wrote in a letter to Sarah Bush.

The next summer Lincoln as sole heir deeded the west 80 acres of his father's 120-acre farm to John D. Johnston, subject to Sarah Bush Lincoln's dower right. This stepbrother bothered him; Lincoln gave Johnston more free, sharp, peremptory advice than he did anyone else. While in Congress he refused to loan Johnston $80, well aware that Johnston was somewhat of a dude, handy with the girls, at times selling liquor by the jug. "You are not *lazy*, and still you *are* an *idler*. I doubt whether since I saw you, you have done a good whole day's work, in any one day . . . This habit of uselessly wasting time, is the whole difficulty." Lincoln promised that for every dollar Johnston would earn he would pay him another dollar. "You say you would almost give your place in Heaven for $70 or $80. Then you value your place in Heaven very cheaply . . . You have always been [kind] to me, and I do not now mean to be unkind to you . . . Affectionately Your brother."

On hearing that Johnston was going to sell his land and move to Missouri, he wrote, "What can you do in Missouri, better than here? Is the land any richer? Can you there, any more than here, raise corn, & wheat & oats, without work? Will any body there, any more than here, do your work for you? . . . Squirming & crawling about

from place to place can do no good . . . part with the land
you have, and my life upon it, you will never after, own a
spot big enough to bury you in. Half you will get for the
land, you spend in moving to Missouri, and the other half
you will eat and drink, and wear out, & no foot of land
will be bought . . . The Eastern forty acres I intend to keep
for Mother while she lives—if you *will not cultivate it;* it
will rent for enough to support her . . . Her Dower in the
other two forties, she can let you have, and no thanks to
[me] . . . Your thousand pretences . . . deceive no body
but yourself. *Go to work* is the only cure for your case."

To this was added a postscript which might be termed
the only known letter Lincoln wrote to his beloved stepmother, who was to say, "Abe was the best boy I ever saw.
His mind and mine, what little I had, seemed to run together, more in the same channel." The postscript read:

> A word for Mother:
> Chapman tells me he wants you to go and live with
> him. If I were you I would try it awhile. If you get
> tired of it (as I think you will not) you can return to
> your own home. Chapman feels very kindly to you;
> and I have no doubt he will make your situation very
> pleasant. Sincerely your Son A. Lincoln

Later Lincoln had to warn Johnston not to sell land be-
longing to his mother. Johnston married a nice 16-year-old
girl, got her parents to sell their land, and with the money
moved to Arkansas, bought land, failed as a farmer and
small-scale whisky distiller. Years later Lincoln saw a young
son of Johnston in jail at Urbana for stealing a watch; Lincoln spent hours with the boy and then in kindly talk persuaded the owners of the watch to drop action against the
boy.

After 11 years of marriage Lincoln and Mary Todd had
stood together at the cradles of four babies, at the grave of
one. For these little ones Lincoln was thankful. To handle
them, play with them and watch them grow, pleased his
sense of the solemn and the ridiculous.

The father and mother had come to understand that each was strong and each was weak. Habits held him that it was useless for her to try to break. If he chose to lie on the front room carpet, on the small of his back, reading, that was his way. If he came to the table in his shirt sleeves and ate his victuals absently, his eyes and thoughts far off, that too was his way. She tried to stop him from answering the front doorbell and leave it to the servant. But he would go to the front door in carpet slippers and shirt sleeves to ask what was wanted. Once two fine ladies came to see Mrs. Lincoln; he looked for her and asked the callers in, drawling, "She'll be down soon as she gets her trotting harness on."

When his wife wrangled with the iceman claiming an overcharge or when she screamed at John Mendonsa that she would pay only ten cents a quart for berries, that they were not worth 15 cents, he spoke quietly to her as "Mary," and did his best to straighten things. Mary had sewed her own clothes, had sewed clothes for the children; he let her manage the house. In Springfield she was quoted as once saying, "Money! He never gives me any money; he leaves his pocketbook where I can take what I want."

In many matters Lincoln trusted her judgment. Herndon wrote much against her yet he noted: "She was an excellent judge of human nature, a better reader of men's motives than her husband and quick to detect those who had designs upon and sought to use him. She was, in a good sense, a stimulant. She kept him from lagging, was constantly prodding him to keep up the struggle. She wanted to be a leader in society. Realizing that Lincoln's rise in the world would elevate and strengthen her, she strove in every way to promote his fortunes, to keep him moving, and thereby win the world's applause." When Lincoln ordered bricks for a front fence to be "about two feet above ground" and when later they rebuilt the upper half-story, making a two-story house, Lincoln naturally consulted her every wish.

Talk about her over Springfield ran that she economized in the kitchen to have fine clothes; she had a terrible temper and tongue. That her husband had married her a thousand dollars in debt, that he charged low fees and had careless habits, that he trusted her and let her have her own way in the household economy, didn't fit well into the gossip. That she was at times a victim of mental disorder, that she was often sorry and full of regrets after a wild burst of temper, didn't make for exciting gossip.

She knew he liked cats and kittens as he did no other animals. She had written to him gaily from Kentucky of fun and trouble with kittens. Staying with one of the Grigsbys in Indiana a cat's yowling in the night broke all sleep and Lincoln got out of bed, held and quieted the cat and enjoyed it.

In July 1850 and in Chicago on a law case, Whigs pressed Lincoln to memorialize Zachary Taylor. He spoke as a Whig to Whigs, by inference defending the Whig policy toward the Mexican War. How Lincoln himself might wish to behave in crises when other men were losing their heads, he intimated in saying of Taylor: "He could not be *flurried,* and he could not be *scared* . . . He was alike averse to *sudden,* and to *startling* quarrels; and he pursued no man with *revenge.*"

When Henry Clay died in June 1852, Springfield stores closed, and after services in the Episcopal Church, a procession moved to the Hall of Representatives where Lincoln sketched Clay's long life, how Clay on occasions by his moderation and wisdom had held the Union together when it seemed ready to break. He quoted Clay on the American Colonization Society: "There is a moral fitness in the idea of returning to Africa her children, whose ancestors have been torn from her by the ruthless hand of fraud and violence. Transplanted in a foreign land, they will carry back to their native soil the rich fruits of religion, civilization, law and liberty." How desperate this hope, Lincoln was to learn at cost. Over the South were 3,204,000 slaves valued on tax books at more than one and one-half billion dollars. How to pay for them as property, if that were conceivable, and then "transplant" them to Africa, was the problem. With Henry Clay, Lincoln leaned on the hope of buying slave property and colonizing it in Africa, both laying blame on radical abolitionists who were saying they would welcome a breakup of the Union, and laying equal blame on proud Southern hotheads who saw slavery as a sanctioned institution for which they were ready to secede from the Union.

Lincoln in 1852 had for 20 years been a loyal Whig party leader who had shaken hands with nearly all active local Whig leaders over Illinois. He seemed to be merely a party wheel horse in his seven speeches in the 1852 campaign, discussing candidates and personalities rather than any great issues. Of Franklin Pierce, the Democratic candidate for President, he noted, "The first thing ever urged in his favor as a candidate was his having given a strange boy a cent to buy candy with." The inflation of Pierce as a heroic brigadier general in the Mexican War reminded him of oldtime militia rules. "No man is to wear more than five pounds of cod-fish for epaulets, or more than thirty yards of bologna sausages for a sash; and no two men are to dress alike, and if any two should dress alike the one that dresses most alike is to be fined."

He belittled statements of Douglas with a relentless logic that became comic and had an audience splitting its sides. He had never read Seward's "supposed proclamation of a 'higher law' " but if it was intended to "foment a disobedience to the constitution, or to the constitutional laws of the country, it has my unqualified condemnation." He praised General Winfield Scott, a hero of two wars, the third military candidate of the Whigs for President. He had seen Southern Whigs favoring the Whig President Fillmore for the nomination but Seward and the extreme antislavery Whigs had swung the nomination to Scott. When Scott in the November election carried only four states, the question was asked by good Whigs, "Is the party falling to pieces?"

Herndon wrote that Lincoln was "the most secretive man" he ever knew. A Danville man said, "Lincoln doesn't show at first all that is in him." A lawyer who had tried cases with him, said, "You can never tell what Lincoln is going to do till he does it." Once during a criminal trial, Lincoln had been giving away one point after another, and as Lincoln was speaking to the jury, a colleague, Amzi Mc-Williams, whispered to other attorneys, "Lincoln will pitch in heavy now, for he has hid." Of two friendly lawyers, one said Lincoln "was harmless as a dove and wise as a serpent," and the other, "He respectfully listened to all advice, and rarely, if ever, followed it." Still another saw him as elusive: "While guilty of no duplicity, he could hide his thoughts and intentions more efficiently than any man with a historical record."

About the year 1850, wrote Herndon, he and Lincoln were driving in Lincoln's one-horse buggy to the Menard County Court. The case they were to try would touch on hereditary traits. "During the ride he spoke, for the first time in my hearing, of his mother, dwelling on . . . qualities he inherited from her. He said, among other things, that she was the illegitimate daughter of Lucy Hanks and a well-bred Virginia farmer or planter; and he argued that from this last source came his power of analysis, his logic, his mental activity, his ambition . . . His theory . . . had been, that, for certain reasons, illegitimate children are oftentimes sturdier and brighter than those born in lawful wedlock . . . The revelation—painful as it was—called up the recollection of his mother, and, as the buggy jolted over the road, he added ruefully, 'God bless my mother; all that I am or ever hope to be I owe to her,' and immediately lapsed into silence . . . We rode on for some time without exchanging a word."

Of this statement, a keen and thorough analyst of Herndon was to write that when Herndon related a fact as of his own observation, it might generally be accepted without question, while his derivations and guesses regarding the recollections of others might be full of errors. "As a matter of fact, the weight of independent evidence supports the truth of the statement, although proof beyond the possibility of a doubt has never been assembled. Even if it should be established that Nancy Hanks was born in lawful wedlock—a development which does not seem likely—Herndon's reliability would not necessarily be impaired. *The question is so difficult of solution that it would not be strange if Lincoln himself had been mistaken.*"

Herndon in 1840 had married Mary Maxcy, the daughter of Virginia-born James Maxcy, the first town constable of Springfield. Her quiet beauty was likened to a summer daisy in a meadow corner. She bore him six children, read books for him, gave him ease after his restless hours. Their home held rare happiness, and in a sense, they had a lifelong romance. This home Herndon would leave for the office which he opened at eight o'clock in the morning. Lincoln, when in town, would arrive at nine, and, wrote Herndon, "The first thing he did was to pick up a newspaper, spread himself out on an old sofa, one leg on a chair, and read aloud, much to my discomfort." Lincoln once explained to him, "When I read aloud two senses catch the idea: first, I see what I read; second, I hear it, and therefore I can remember it better."

Each of them had climbed narrow stairs, crossed a dark hallway, entered by a glass-paned door, to see worn familiar things of use—the sofa, the stove, two tables (one of them somewhat jack-knifed), a secretary with pigeonholes and drawers stuffed with papers, an earthenware inkpot with quill pens in reach, dingy windows looking out on a lonesome alley. Here they prepared cases, Lincoln writing most of the papers introduced in court, Herndon often doing the heavy research work on authorities and precedents.

Lincoln's silk stovepipe hat was part of his office, Herndon writing that it was his desk and memorandum book, holding bank book, letters and scribbled ideas placed in the hatband. To a fellow lawyer Lincoln once wrote of a lost letter, "I put it in my old hat, and buying a new one the next day, the old one was set aside, and so, the letter lost sight of for a time." Yet amid this seeming disorder the firm of Lincoln & Herndon in 1850 had 18 per cent of all cases in Sangamon County Circuit Court, in 1853 34 per cent, in 1854 30 per cent, and they rated as a leading law firm in a city of 6,000 having an exceptionally able set of attorneys. Herndon had moods of disgust with the law, once writing, "If you love the stories of murder—rape—fraud &c. a law office is a good place." The partners bothered little with bookkeeping, dividing fees equally, Lincoln sometimes putting money in an envelope he marked with the name of the case and "Herndon's half." Herndon only occasionally went on the circuit. Each appeared in many cases alone or with other lawyers, the rule being that they were never to be opposing counsel.

Herndon was bothered at times by Lincoln telling the same funny story on the same day to one client or politician after another. He saw, too, in other hours, Lincoln with a "woestruck face," gazing at the office floor or out the window, in a dark silence Herndon didn't dare interrupt. He tried to solve Lincoln's melancholy, whether it went back to heredity, environment, glands, slow blood circulation, or constipation, or thwarted love. Yet Herndon knew that his partner was, in degree, a steadying force in his own life, a sort of elder brother or affectionate uncle. When Herndon spoke as a red-hot abolitionist, Lincoln would tell him, "Billy, you're too rampant and spontaneous." He noted Lincoln's walk. "He put the whole foot flat down on the ground at once, not landing on the heel; he likewise lifted his foot all at once, not rising from the toe . . . The whole man, body and mind, worked slowly, as if it needed oiling." Then came Herndon as a brain specialist: "The convolutions of his brain are long; they do not snap quickly like a short, thick man's brain," which was pretentious guesswork, not commanding the respect that might be accorded his writing: "The enduring power of Mr. Lincoln's brain is wonderful. He can sit and think without food or rest longer than any man I ever met."

It came hard for Herndon when the boys, Willie and Tad, came to the office with their father on a Sunday morning while the mother was at church; the boys pulled books off shelves, upset ink bottles, threw pencils into the spittoon, their father at his desk working as though the office were empty. It lingered with Herndon that Lincoln said to him more than once, "I shall meet with some terrible end." Out of what shadowed meditations could such a premonition come to be spoken? He took Shakespeare in his carpetbag

on the circuit, it was known, but that wouldn't explain why
one of his original bent would speak lines like Hamlet.
When Joshua Speed said he had a quick mind, he denied it.
"I am slow to learn, and slow to forget . . . My mind is
like a piece of steel—very hard to scratch anything on it,
and almost impossible after you get it there to rub it out."

An angry family trying to break a will, a man who with
a knife had cut another man in the eye, a client of Lincoln's
found guilty of manslaughter and sentenced to eight years
at hard labor, the first three months in solitary confinement,
another Lincoln client, a one-legged Mexican War veteran
found guilty of robbing the mails of $15,000 in bank notes
and sentenced to ten years—the likes of these came before
Lincoln's eyes, their faces and voices beyond forgetting.

"She charges," he wrote in behalf of Eliza Jane Hel-
mick, "that said complainant, while he yet lived with her,
for the purpose of contriving evidence to procure a divorce
from her, at various times, and in different ways, attempted
to induce different men to make attempts upon the chastity
of your Respondent." He wrote another lawyer of how he
hadn't "pressed to the utmost" his case against a man: "I
am really sorry for him—*poor* and a *cripple* as he is." In
several cases he defended whisky sellers—and again at a
trial in DeWitt County attended by more than a hundred
women he defended nine women charged with riot; they
had warned a saloonkeeper to close his place and when he
didn't they smashed barrels and bottles and left him no
whisky to sell; the jury found them guilty but the judge let
them off with a fine of $2.00 each. More often came the
humdrum cases involving properties and payments, estates,
promissory notes, defaults, claims, mortgages, foreclosures,
ejectments.

Little Harriet Beecher Stowe in 1852 had published a
novel, *Uncle Tom's Cabin*, and by the device of dramatiz-
ing a black Christ lashed by a Yankee-born Satan, had led
millions of people to believe that in the Slave States south
of the Ohio River was a monstrous wrong. She ended her
book with a prophecy: "This is an age of the world when
nations are trembling and convulsed. A mighty influence is

abroad, surging and heaving the world, as with an earthquake. And is America safe? Every nation that carries in its bosom great and unredressed injustice has in it the elements of this last convulsion."

Lincoln at a Springfield, Illinois, meeting wrote the resolutions of sympathy for Louis Kossuth and Hungarians in revolution against an arrogant and cruel monarchy. In notes for possible use, he wrote of "a society of equals" where every man had a chance. He had heard Southern men declare slaves better off in the South than hired laborers in the North. He would observe, "There is no permanent class of hired laborers amongst us. Twenty-five years ago, I was a hired laborer. The hired laborer of yesterday, labors on his own account to-day; and will hire others to labor for him to-morrow . . . Although volume upon volume is written to prove slavery a very good thing, we never hear of the man who wishes to take the good of it, *by being a slave himself* . . . As Labor is the common *burthen* of our race, so the effort, of *some* to shift their share of the burthen on to the shoulders of *others,* is the great, durable, curse of the race."

Emerson, the Concord preacher, saw war, revolution, violence, breeding in the antagonisms of bold, powerful men. "Vast property, gigantic interests, family connection, webs of party, cover the land with a network that immensely multiplies the dangers of war."

Lincoln caught the feel of change in the national air. He had seen the frontier move far west. He had seen St. Louis, with its 5,000 people, grow to 74,000 in 20 years, and Springfield from 700 to 6,000. Senator Douglas was telling of "a power in this nation greater than either the North or the South—a growing, increasing, swelling power, that will be able to speak the law to this nation, and to execute the law as spoken. That power is the country known as the great West—the Valley of the Mississippi." The human inflow from Europe kept coming into Illinois—Germans, Irish and English by tens of thousands. Fourteen steamboats, ice-locked in the Mississippi River near Cairo in the winter of 1854, were loaded with 2,000 German and Irish immigrants. Of new and old societies, unions, lodges, churches, it seemed that Lincoln belonged only to the Whig party and the American Colonization Society.

Between 1850 and 1860, the country's 23,000,000 people become 31,000,000, this being 2,000,000 more than Great Britain. In ten years 2,600,000 people arrive from overseas, in a single year 400,000. The East grows 21 per cent, the South 28 per cent, the Northwest 77 per cent, in population. Little towns peep up on the prairies where before were only gophers and jack rabbits.

Washington wrangles about the public lands, millions of acres northwest and southwest. Land speculators, interests powerful in Washington, for reasons of their own do not want free land for actual settlers. A few Senators try to get a free homestead law and fail. Free land bills keep coming up in Congress.

The transcontinental railroad, the iron-built, ocean-going steamship, the power-driven factory—the owners and man agers of these are to be a new breed of rulers of the earth. Between seaboard and the Mississippi comes the "iron horse" hauling pork and grain of the West to factory towns of the East, to vessels sailing to Europe; the cars return with sewing machines, churns, scissors, saws, steel tools. New reaping and threshing machinery comes. Singlehanded, a farmer gathers the crop on a quarter section. Grain drills, corn planters, wagons and buggies with springs under the boxes and seats are bought by the farmers. New churns and sewing machines help the farmer's wife. Steam fire engines, gas lighting systems, the use of anesthesia, the Hoe revolving cylinder press, vulcanized rubber, photography, arrive.

A territory of Kansas is organized, and from slave-soil Missouri, men with rifles ride over into Kansas and battle with abolitionists from New England for political control of Kansas. Emerson peers into years ahead and cries, "The hour is coming when the strongest will not be strong enough." On a late afternoon of any autumn day in those years, Abraham Lincoln in his rattletrap buggy over the prairie might have been lost deep in the swirl of his thoughts and his hope to read events to come.

Lincoln bought a book on logic, studied how to untangle fallacies and derive inexorable conclusions from established facts. On the circuit when with other lawyers, two in a bed, eight or ten in one hotel room, he read Euclid by the light of a candle after others had dropped off to sleep. Herndon and Lincoln had the same bed one night, and Herndon noticed his partner's legs pushing their feet out beyond the footboard of the bed, as he held Euclid close to the candlelight.

John T. Stuart saw Lincoln as a hopeless victim of melancholy. "Look at him now," said Stuart, in the McLean County Courthouse. "I turned a little," wrote Henry C. Whitney, Lincoln's fellow lawyer at Urbana, "and there beheld Lincoln sitting alone in the corner . . . wrapped in gloom." He seemed to be "pursuing in his mind some specific, sad subject, . . . through various sinuosities, and his sad face would assume, at times, deeper phases of grief . . . He was roused by the breaking up of court, when he emerged . . . like one awakened from sleep."

Herndon once found Lincoln covering sheets of paper with figures, signs, symbols. He told Herndon he was trying to square the circle. After a two days' struggle, worn down, he gave up trying to square the circle.

He penned notes trying to be as absolute as mathematics: "If A. can prove, however conclusively, that he may, of right, enslave B., why may not B. snatch the same argument, and prove equally, that he may enslave A?—You say A. is white, and B. is black. It is *color*, then; the lighter, having the right to enslave the darker? Take care. By this rule, you are to be slave to the first man you meet, with a fairer skin than your own. You do not mean *color* exactly? —You mean the whites are *intellectually* the superiors of the blacks, and, therefore have the right to enslave them? Take care again. By this rule, you are to be slave to the first man you meet, with an intellect superior to your own. But, say you, it is a question of *interest;* and, if you can make it it your *interest*, you have the right to enslave another. Very well. And if he can make it his interest, he has the right to enslave you." Thus his private memorandum.

He wrote of the legitimate object of government being

"to do for the people what needs to be done, but which they can not, by individual effort, do at all, or do so well, for themselves," such as "Making and maintaining roads, bridges, and the like; providing for the helpless young and afflicted; common schools; and disposing of deceased men's property." Military and civil departments were necessary. "If some men will kill, or beat, or constrain others, or despoil them of property, by force, fraud, or noncompliance with contracts, it is a common object with peaceful and just men to prevent it."

Out of the silent working of his inner life came forces no one outside of himself could know; they were his secret, his personality and purpose. He was in the toils of more than personal ambition. Politely, gently but firmly, he had told those who wanted him to run for the legislature or for Congress, that he wasn't in the running.

Chapter 9

Restless Growing America

The California "gold rush" of 1849 and what followed had the eyes of the world. San Francisco had become a world port. Sacramento, four lone houses in April 1849, became in six months a roaring crazy city of 10,000. Ten men in one week had shaken from the gravel in their hand-screens a million dollars in gold nuggets. More than once a single spade had sold for $1,000. Courts and law broke down in San Francisco and a Committee of Vigilantes took over the government.

Over the Great Plains moved wagon trains, a traveler counting 459 wagons in ten miles along the Platte River. A Peoria newspaper in 1854 counted 1,473 wagons in one month, movers going to Iowa. In a single week 12,000 immigrants arrived on railroad trains in Chicago. Cyrus Mc-

Cormick's Chicago factory in 1854 sold 1,558 farming machines, mostly for both reaping and sowing, and was planning for 3,000 machines in 1855. The Department of State reported that Irish immigrants alone had in three years sent back to the old country nearly $15,000,000 for their kinfolk. A restless young growing America was moving toward a future beyond reading.

The peace of the Great Compromise had held up fairly well, broken by the endless crying of antislavery men against the new Fugitive Slave Law. The case of the slave, Anthony Burns, shook the country. He escaped from a Virginia plantation, stowed away on a ship for Boston, was arrested, and by a Federal commissioner ordered back to Virginia. A mob led by a minister broke into the courthouse to save Burns and in the fighting with Federal officers a deputy U.S. marshal was killed. Stores closed, doors and windows were draped in black, crowds lined the streets when the one lone Negro slave was marched to his Virginia-bound ship, escorted by dragoons, marines, loaded artillery, 12 companies of infantry, 120 personal friends of the U.S. marshal carrying drawn swords and loaded pistols. The affair cost the Government over $40,000. Like incidents, less dramatic, happened here and there over the country. In Chicago a fugitive slave was slipped out a courtroom window and when the Federal commissioner asked, "Where is the prisoner at the bar?" the answer came, "He is at rest in the bosom of the community."

Amid these changing scenes and issues, Douglas had become the foremost dramatic leader of the Democratic party, speaking, as he said, for "Young America" as against "Old Fogies," meaning Cass, Buchanan and other figures of hesitation. A younger element of the party boomed him for President in 1852 and he was only 39 when in the Democratic national convention on the 30th and 31st ballots he had more votes than any other candidate. He made his home in Chicago, where he bought land for a few dollars and sold one tract for $80,000. To the young University of Chicago he donated ten acres. He was close to all interests that wanted a railway to the Pacific. His tenacity had

brought a rail route from the Great Lakes to the Gulf; the
Illinois Central was thankful to him and let him have private cars for travel.

After the death of his wife in early 1853, when he went
back to Congress he was noticed as bitter, bad-tempered, a
sloven in dress, chewing tobacco and careless where he spat.
He went abroad several months, seeing Russia and the Near
East, and came back the oldtime Douglas who could put his
hands on the shoulders of an old colleague or a young precinct worker and say, as though they were chums, "You—
I count on your help." He was three years later to marry
Adèle Cutts, a great-niece of Dolly Madison, a beautiful,
warmhearted woman who proved to be a perfect helpmeet
for a combative and furiously active husband. He made
many long speeches, wrote few letters and those having
little of self-revelation, kept no diary, seemed seldom if
ever to have time for meditations on himself in particular
or the whence and whither of all mankind.

In early 1854 came a bold, challenging action of Douglas
that set the slavery issue boiling in a wild turmoil, Douglas
having predicted, "It will raise a hell of a storm." Now 41,
a battler, magnetic, with flashing blue eyes, chin drawn in,
pivoting, elusive, he made a daring, spectacular play for
reasons better known to himself than any he gave to the
public. His lionlike head, his black pompadour swept back
in waves, his deep bass voice, were seen and heard. Toiling,
sweating, crying, he had coaxed, guided and jammed
through Congress the Nebraska Bill, as it came to be
known. It created two territories, Kansas on the south, Nebraska on the north; in each the voters would decide
whether it should be free or slave soil. Nebraska then
stretched far and wide, its area including all or part of the
later states of Nebraska, North and South Dakota, Wyo-
ming and Montana. There, in the future, under "popular
sovereignty," said Douglas, "they could vote slavery up or
down." Southern members had insisted on, and got, a provision expressly repealing the hitherto sacred Missouri
Compromise; the line it drew between slave and free soil
was wiped out.

As the news went across the country, not in the memory

of living men had there been such recoils and explosions of opinion and passion over a political act and idea. Lincoln was roused as "by the sound of a fire-bell at night." In New England, 3,050 clergymen signed a widely published memorial to the U.S. Senate: "IN THE NAME OF ALMIGHTY GOD, AND IN HIS PRESENCE," we "solemnly protest against the passage of . . . the Nebraska bill." In Chicago 25 clergymen signed a like protest, followed by 500 ministers in the Northwest. Several longtime Democratic party leaders in Illinois gave it out that they were anti-Nebraska men. Traveling to Illinois, Douglas could see from his car window the burning of dummies bearing his name; in Ohio some women managed to present him with 30 pieces of silver. In Chicago in front of North Market Hall, on the hot night of September 1, he defied and insulted those against him; a crowd of 8,000 interrupted with questions, hisses, groans, boos, catcalls. They howled and hooted him till he looked at his watch, jammed his silk hat on his head, and left.

Among those who led in hooting Douglas were the Know-Nothings, members of the secret "Order of the Star Spangled Banner." When asked what the order stood for, members answered, "I know nothing." Each member on joining swore he would never vote for a foreigner or a Catholic for any office. Their slogans were, "Americans must rule America" and "No papacy in the Republic." Of millions of Irish and German immigrants, a large part were Catholic and they had become a power in large cities, throwing their strength most often to the Democrats, such as Douglas, who were more friendly to them than the Whigs in general. Two Catholic churches in Massachusetts had been wrecked and gutted—and a convent burned. A Protestant procession of 2,000 people in Newark, New Jersey, met an Irish mob and the fighting left one man dead and many wounded. Hibernian parades had been broken up by rioting Know-Nothings. Being secret in their operations, it was hard to guess what the Know-Nothings would show in the year's elections. Being openly anti-Nebraska and antislavery, they had drawn toward them many Democrats and an element of Whigs.

Before the year closed the Know-Nothings would surprise the country by electing mayors of Philadelphia and Washington. In alliance with Free-Soilers and former Whigs, they were to sweep Massachusetts with 63 per cent of all ballots, electing a Know-Nothing governor and legislature. They would have swept New York State but for the longtime proven friendships of Seward and Weed with groups of foreigners and Catholics. Lincoln gave out no word publicly but when Know-Nothings called on him he was reported as saying the red man in breechclout and with tomahawk was the true native American. "We pushed them from their homes, and now turn on others not fortunate enough to come over so early as we or our forefathers." He told of an Irishman who was asked why he wasn't born in America, and the answer, "Faith, I wanted to, but me mither wouldn't let me."

On a State Fair day in Springfield thousands who hated or loved Douglas stood in the cool night air of October 2 to see him on the Chenery House porch, torches lighting his face. His eyes flashed and lips trembled. "I tell you the time has not yet come when a handful of traitors in our camp can turn the great State of Illinois, with all her glorious history and traditions, into a negro-worshiping, negro-equality community." The next afternoon Douglas spoke three hours in the Statehouse. Had not the Missouri Compromise been practically wiped out by the Omnibus Bill of 1850? Was not the real question whether the people should rule, whether the voters in a territory should control their own affairs? If the people of Kansas and Nebraska were able to govern themselves, they were able to govern a few miserable Negroes. The crowd enjoyed it; cries came, "That's so!" "Hit 'em again." Lincoln comforted a pretty young woman abolitionist: "Don't bother, young lady. We'll hang the judge's hide on the fence tomorrow."

The next afternoon Lincoln spoke to the same crowd. "Wherever slavery is, it has been first introduced without law." He gave reasons for hating it as a "monstrous injustice," and added: "When southern people tell us they are no more responsible for the origin of slavery, than we; I acknowledge the fact. When it is said that the institution

exists; and that it is very difficult to get rid of it, in any satisfactory way, I can understand and appreciate the saying. I
surely will not blame them for not doing what I should not
know how to do myself . . . What next? Free them, and
make them politically and socially, our equals? My own
feelings will not admit of this, and if mine would, we well
know that those of the great mass of white people will not.
Whether this feeling accords with justice and sound judgment, is not the sole question, if indeed, it is any part of it.
A universal feeling, whether well or ill-founded, can not be
safely disregarded."

And yet, while he could not say what should be done
about slavery where it was already established and operating, he was sure it would be wrong to let it spread north.
"Inasmuch as you do not object to my taking my hog to
Nebraska, therefore I must not object to you taking your
slave. Now, I admit this is perfectly logical, if there is no
difference between hogs and negroes." And what should be
done first of all? "The Missouri Compromise ought to be
restored. For the sake of the Union, it ought to be restored." In Peoria 12 days later, he gave much the same
speech to a crowd of thousands, wrote it out for publication, and it became widely known as the "Peoria Speech."

In the October elections of 1854, anti-Nebraska voters of
all shades—former Whigs and Democrats, Know-Nothings,
Fusionists—won by startling majorities. A combination in
Pennsylvania elected 21 anti-Nebraska Congressmen as
against four Nebraska. A Know-Nothing legislature in
Massachusetts elected a Know-Nothing U.S. Senator.
Maine, for years Democratic, saw the Anti-Nebraska Fu-
sion Party electing a governor and carrying every congressional district, the same break from the past occurring in
Iowa, Vermont and other states. Anti-Nebraska men rolled
up a majority of 70,000, elected a Congressman in every
Ohio district; they carried all but two districts in Indiana.
Lincoln mentioned in his Peoria speech these sweeping
political smashups, with a changed public opinion. He rebuked the "desperate assumption" of Douglas: "If a man
will stand up and assert, and repeat, and re-assert, that two
and two do not make four, I know nothing in the power of

argument that can stop him . . . In such a case I can only commend him to the seventy thousand answers just in from Pennsylvania, Ohio, and Indiana."

At meetings in Ripon, Wisconsin, and Jackson, Michigan, citizens opposed to slavery extension, and coming from all parties, resolved in favor of a new party with a new name gathering anti-Nebraska Whigs and Democrats, also Free-Soilers, under one banner, and, "we will cooperate and be known as 'Republicans.' " In Wisconsin and Vermont conventions the name Republican was adopted. The New York *Tribune*'s Whig Almanac designated the 21 Congressmen from Ohio as Republicans, and in October 1854 Greeley was writing, "We consider the Whig party a thing of the past." In several county and congressional districts over Illinois the name Republican had been adopted, an Ottawa Democratic paper saying the Republican convention there was made up of "Whigs, abolitionists, know nothings, sore heads, and fag ends."

A group of radical abolitionists met in Springfield October 5 to organize an Illinois Republican party. Herndon, then calling himself an abolitionist, sat in with the group, and suddenly went in a hurry to Lincoln, saying, "Go home at once . . . Drive somewhere into the country and stay till this thing is over." And Lincoln, sending word to the radicals that he had law business in Tazewell County, drove away in his one-horse buggy. Herndon wrote, "On grounds of policy it would not do for him to occupy at that time such advanced ground as we were taking. On the other hand, it was equally as dangerous to refuse a speech for the Abolitionists." Later when Lincoln was named a member of the new state central committee of the new Republican party, he declined the honor, as without his authority, and refused to attend their meetings.

In the November 7 election the Democrats elected only four of the nine Illinois Congressmen, and to the legislature only 41 regular Democrats against 59 anti-Nebraska members of differing shades. Lincoln wrote the names of all members in alphabetical order and studied his chances for election to the seat of U.S. Senator James Shields. Late in 1854 he sent out many letters in the tone of one: "I have really got it into my head to try to be United States Senator; and if I could have your support my chances would be reasonably good." In February 1855 he watched in the Statehouse the election for U.S. Senator. He got 45 votes. Six more would have elected him. The balloting went on, his vote slumped to 15. The minute came when Lincoln saw that if he held his 15 loyal votes Governor Joel A. Matteson, a Douglas and tricky Nebraska Democrat playing what Lincoln termed "a double game," would be elected. Lincoln begged his steadfast 15 votes to go to Lyman Trumbull, anti-Nebraska bolter from the Democratic party. On the tenth ballot Trumbull was elected. The affair was snarled and shadowed, filled with strategies keen and subtle, and with treacheries plain and slimy.

Lincoln wrote to a friend: "I regret my defeat moderately, but I am not nervous about it." By not being stubborn he had won friends. He gave a dinner for all anti-Nebraska members of the legislature. Mrs. Lincoln had watched the balloting from the gallery and was bitter about it. Julia Jayne, the wife of Trumbull, had been bridesmaid at her wedding; they had joined in writing verse and letters to the *Sangamo Journal,* but forever after the night of Trumbull's election Mrs. Lincoln refused to speak to Julia or to receive a call from her.

Lincoln wrote to Speed: "I think I am a whig; but others say there are no whigs, and that I am an abolitionist . . . I now do no more than oppose the *extension* of slavery. I am not a Know-Nothing. That is certain. How could I be? How can any one who abhors the oppression of negroes, be in favor of degrading classes of white people? Our progress in degeneracy appears to me to be pretty rapid. As a nation, we began by declaring '*all men are created equal.*' We now practically read it 'all men are created equal, *except negroes.*' When the Know-Nothings get control, it will read 'all men are created equal, except negroes, *and foreigners, and catholics.*' When it comes to this I should prefer emigrating to some country where they make no pretence of loving liberty—to Russia, for instance, where despotism can be taken pure, and without the base alloy of hypocracy."

Polly, a free Negro woman in Springfield, had a son who worked on a steamboat to New Orleans where, not having papers to show he was a free Negro, he was jailed. The steamboat left without him and after a time he was advertised for sale to pay jail expenses. Polly came to Lincoln and Herndon about it. They went to Governor Matteson who said he could do nothing. Lincoln with Herndon and others raised by subscription the money to pay jail charges, and brought the boy back to Polly.

In August 1855 Lincoln wrote to Owen Lovejoy, "Not even *you* are more anxious to prevent the extension of slavery than I; and yet the political atmosphere is such, just now, that I fear to do any thing, lest I do wrong." Know-Nothing elements would be needed to combat the pro-Nebraska Democrats. "About us here, they [the Know-Nothings] are mostly my old political and personal friends; and I have hoped their organization would die out without the painful necessity of my taking an open stand against them. Of their principles I think little better than I do of those of the slavery extensionists. Indeed I do not perceive how any one professing to be sensitive to the wrongs of the negroes, can join in a league to degrade a class of white men." Few they were to whom Lincoln could write a letter of such candor which if published in that hour could do him harm. A peculiar bond of trust and understanding ran between him and the rugged Congregational minister over at Princeton, Illinois, who was a radical antislavery man.

One night in Danville at the McCormick House, the ladies' parlor was turned into a bedroom for Judge David Davis, who had a bed to himself, and for Lincoln and Henry C. Whitney, who slept two in a bed. Whitney wrote of it: "I was awakened early—before daylight—by my companion sitting up in bed, his figure dimly visible by the ghostly firelight, and talking the wildest and most incoherent nonsense all to himself. A stranger to Lincoln would have supposed he had suddenly gone insane. Of course I knew Lincoln and his idiosyncrasies, and felt no alarm, so I listened and laughed. After he had gone on in this way for, say, five minutes, while I was awake, and I knew not how long *before* I was awake, he sprang out of bed, hur-

riedly washed, and jumped into his clothes, put some wood
on the fire, and then sat in front of it, moodily, dejectedly,
in a most sombre and gloomy spell, till the breakfast bell
rang, when he started, as if from sleep, and went with us
to breakfast."

In 1856, on the Missouri and Kansas border, 200 men,
women and children were shot, stabbed or burned to death
in the fighting between free- and slave-state settlers and
guerrillas. The money loss, in crops burned, cattle and
horses stolen or killed, ran about $2,000,000. Each side
aimed to settle Kansas with voters for its cause. In May, as
the first state convention to organize the Republican party
of Illinois was meeting in Bloomington, the town of Lawrence, Kansas, had been entered by riding and shooting men
who burned the Free State Hotel, wrecked two printing
offices and looted homes.

Senator Charles Sumner of Massachusetts, speaking on
"The Crime Against Kansas," had lashed verbally South
Carolina Senator Andrew P. Butler, saying Butler "has
chosen a mistress . . . who, though ugly to others, is always
lovely to him—I mean the harlot, Slavery." Butler had
"with incoherent phrases, discharged the loose expectora-
tion of his speech" on the people of Kansas. "He cannot
open his mouth, but out there flies a blunder." And Congressman Preston Brooks, a nephew of Butler, had walked
into the Senate chamber, and over the head and backbone
of the seated Sumner had rained blows that broke to pieces
a gutta-percha cane, beating his victim near to death. Over
the North raged a fury almost tongue-tied. In the South was
open or secret exultation; the man they hated and loathed
more than any other in Congress had met punishment and
would leave the Senate and suffer years before his wounds
healed.

These events were in the air when political elements of
Illinois and other states were holding conventions to organize state parties and to get up a national Republican party.
Of delegates at Bloomington about one-fourth were regularly elected; others had appointed themselves. All stripes
of political belief outside of the pro-Nebraska Democratic

party were there: Whigs, bolting anti-Nebraska Democrats, Free-Soilers, Know-Nothings, abolitionists. Some who came were afraid that wild-eyed radicals would control.

The convention met in Major's Hall, upstairs over Humphrey's Cheap Store, near the courthouse square. The platform denounced Democratic policies and declared Congress had power to stop the extension of slavery and should use that power. After several delegates spoke, there were calls for Lincoln. He stood up. There were cries, "Take the platform," which he did. He observed, according to a Whitney version written many years later, "We are in a trying time"; then suddenly came the thrust, "Unless popular opinion makes itself very strongly felt, and a change is made in our present course, *blood will flow on account of Nebraska, and brother's hand will be raised against brother!* . . . We must not promise what we ought not, lest we be called on to perform what we cannot . . . We must not be led by excitement and passion to do that which our sober judgments would not approve in our cooler moments." He noted that the delegates had been collected from many different elements. Yet they were agreed, *"Slavery must be kept out of Kansas."* The Nebraska Act was usurpation; it would result in making slavery national. "We are in a fair way to see this land of boasted freedom converted into a land of slavery in fact."

A terribly alive man stood before them. Joseph Medill, of the Chicago *Tribune,* and other newspaper writers felt their pencils slip away. Herndon and Whitney had started to take notes, then forgot they had pencils. Listeners moved up closer to the speaker. "I read once in a law book, 'A slave is a human being who is legally not a *person* but a *thing.*' And if the safeguards of liberty are broken down, as is now attempted, when they have made *things* of all the free negroes, how long, think you, before they will begin to make *things* of poor white men?"

He summarized history to show that freedom and equality, sacred to the men of the American Revolution, had become words it was fashionable to sneer at. He rehearsed current violent events. Should force be met with force? He could not say. "The time has not yet come, and if we are true to ourselves, may never come. Do not mistake that the ballot is stronger than the bullet." Applause came regularly. He was saying what the convention wanted said. He was telling why the Republican party was being organized. As applause roared and lingered, the orator walked slowly toward the back of the platform, looked at notes in his hand, took a fresh start and worked toward the front. To Bill Herndon and others he seemed taller than ever before. "He's been baptized," said Herndon, hearing Lincoln declare that no matter what was to happen, "We will say to the Southern disunionists, *We* won't go out of the Union, and you *shan't!*" The delegates rose from their seats, applauded, stamped, cheered, waved handkerchiefs, threw hats in the air, ran riot. He was their tongue and voice. He had deepened the passions and unified the faith of adherents of a partisan cause.

After it was all over, Whitney did the best he could at making notes of the speech. If Lincoln had written out the speech the record of it would be accurate and responsible. But it was known that what he said, if written and printed, would be taken as wild-eyed and radical, that a published text of his passionate declarations would bring fierce denunciations and would alienate moderates from his party. Delegates wrung Lincoln's hand, and William Hopkins of Grundy burst out, "Lincoln, I never swear, but that was the damnedest best speech I ever heard."

Anti-Nebraska "Long John" Wentworth, two inches taller than Lincoln, wrote in the Chicago *Democrat*, "Abraham Lincoln for an hour and a half held the assemblage spellbound by the power of his argument, the intense irony of his invective, the brilliancy of his eloquence. I shall not mar any of its fine proportions by attempting even a synopsis of it." He suggested, "Mr. Lincoln must write it out and let it go before all the people." This advice Lincoln also heard from others and refused to follow it. The speech carried drama, irony, anger, storm, and could be twisted too many ways to please the opposition. He would let it be a memory.

An Alton editor's brief summary of the speech, at the time the only one published, caught no single syllable of passionate oratory, and closed: "The Black Democracy were endeavoring to cite Henry Clay to reconcile old Whigs to their doctrine, and repaid them with the very cheap compliment of National Whigs." Whitney's version, written many years later, from notes made after the speech, had Lincoln closing: "While, in all probability, no resort to force will be needed, our moderation and forbearance will stand us in good stead when, if ever, we must make an appeal to battle and to the God of Hosts!!" Such a daring and flaming utterance, in those exact words, may not have come from Lincoln, but words of equally high and challenging import came from him that day in Bloomington. He delivered cold logic that he would have been willing to see in print. And he broke loose with blazing outbursts in regard to human freedom and the Union of States, which for that particular political hour were better kept out of print.

In the McLean County Circuit Court, Lincoln represented the Illinois Central Railroad, his retainer $200. He lost his case; the decision was that the railroad must pay a tax in every county through which it passed. The cost in taxes would mount into millions and bankrupt the corporation. Lincoln appealed to the Supreme Court, argued the case twice, and in January 1856 won a decision reversing the lower court. He presented to an official at their Chicago office his bill for $2,000. The official looked at it: "Why, this is as much as a first-class lawyer would have charged!" adding it was "as much as Daniel Webster himself would have charged."

Back on the circuit when he told other lawyers of it, they didn't know whether to laugh or cry; the corporation had been saved millions of dollars through Lincoln's victory in court. Lincoln started a suit against the Illinois Central for a fee of $5,000. The case was called; the lawyer for the railroad didn't show up; Lincoln was awarded his $5,000 one morning. When the railroad lawyer arrived and begged for a retrial, Lincoln was willing. The case was called later, and Lincoln read a statement signed by six of the highest-priced lawyers in Illinois that the sum of $5,000 for the services rendered in the case "is not unreasonable." Before the jury went out he told them he had been paid $200 by the railroad and they should make the verdict for $4,800. Which they did.

Thirty-eight days went by and the railroad company failed to pay the $4,800 fee. An execution was issued directing the sheriff to seize property of the railroad. Then the fee was paid. And high officers of the railroad explained, "The payment of so large a fee to a western lawyer would embarrass the general counsel with the board of directors in New York."

Lincoln deposited the $4,800 in the Springfield Marine and Fire Insurance Company, and later, in handing Herndon half the fee, he pushed it toward his partner, then held it back an instant, and said with a smile, "Billy, it seems to me it will be bad taste on your part to keep saying severe things I have heard from you about railroads and other corporations. Instead of criticizing them, you and I ought to thank God for letting this one fall into our hands." And Herndon wrote, "We both thanked the Lord for letting the Illinois Central Railroad fall into our hands."

He was more and more trusted with important affairs of property. The McLean County Bank retained him to bring suit against the City of Bloomington. In Springfield, the gasworks asked him to make certain their title to the two city lots on which they were located, which Lincoln did, later sending the gasworks a bill for $500.

A caller in his office one day asked Lincoln to use his influence in a certain legal quarter, offering him $500. Herndon wrote, "I heard him refuse the $500 over and over again. I went out and left them together. I suppose Lincoln got tired of refusing, for he finally took the money; but he never offered any of it to me; and it was noticeable that whenever he took money in this way, he never seemed to consider it his own or mine. In this case, he gave the money to the Germans in the town, who wanted to buy themselves a press. A few days after, he said to me in the coolest way, 'Herndon, I gave the Germans $250 of yours the other day.' 'I am glad you did, Mr. Lincoln,' I answered. Of course I could not say I was glad he took it."

On May 6, 1856, the steamboat *Effie Afton* rammed into a pier of the Rock Island Railroad bridge, took fire, and burned to a total loss, while part of the bridge burned and tumbled into the river. The owners of the *Effie Afton* sued the bridge company for damages. Lincoln represented the company at the hearing in Chicago, with Judge McLean presiding. In his argument Lincoln pointed to the growing travel from east to west being as important as the Mississippi traffic. It was ever growing larger, this east-to-west traffic, building up new country with a rapidity never before seen in the history of the world. In his own memory he had seen Illinois grow from almost empty spaces to a population of 1,500,000. One man had as good a right to cross a river as another had to sail up or down it. He asked if the products of the boundless, fertile country lying west must for all time be forced to stop on a western bank, be unloaded from the cars and loaded on a boat, and after passage across the river be reloaded into cars on the other side. Civilization in the region to the west was at issue. The jury listened two weeks and were locked up; when they came out they had agreed to disagree; their action was generally taken as a victory for railroads, bridges and Chicago, as against steamboats, rivers and St. Louis.

During noon recess of a case tried in Rock Island, it was told, Lincoln walked out to the railroad bridge and came to a boy sitting on the end of a tie with a fishing pole out over the water. And Lincoln, fresh from the squabbles and challenges of the courtroom, said to the boy, "Well, I suppose you know all about this river." And the boy, "Sure, mister, it was here before I was born and it's been here ever since." Lincoln smiled, "Well, it's good to be out here where there is so much fact and so little opinion."

A check for $500 came into Lincoln's hands, thus far his largest retaining fee. Cyrus H. McCormick of Chicago was bringing suit against John H. Manny of Rockford, claiming that Manny's patents, not lawful and valid, infringed on the McCormick rights. If McCormick could win his case he would stop the Manny factory at Rockford and get $400,000 as damages. His lawyers were Edward M.

Dickerson and Reverdy Johnson, while Manny had George Harding, Edwin M. Stanton, Peter H. Watson and Abraham Lincoln.

Lincoln went to Rockford, saw the Manny reaper in the making, and went on to Cincinnati to argue before Judge McLean. Lincoln's colleague, Edwin M. Stanton, was a serious owl-eyed man, strict in language, dress, duty. When his eyes lighted on Lincoln at the Burnet House in Cincinnati, wearing heavy boots, loose clothes, farmer-looking, he used language reported as: "Where did that long-armed baboon come from?"

Up and down the courtroom walked Lincoln, in his coat pocket a manuscript of his argument. The moment came when Stanton told the court that only two arguments would be made for the defense. Lincoln was out, his carefully planned speech not delivered. The defense won, though not by his services. Back in Springfield he divided a $2,000 fee, half and half, with Herndon, saying he had been "roughly handled by that man Stanton," and mentioned Judge McLean as "an old granny," and, "If you were to point your finger at him and a darning needle at the same time he never would know which was the sharpest."

A woman client had Lincoln survey and lay off into lots a piece of land she owned near the Springfield city limits. He found that by some mistake the woman had become owner of three more acres of land than she was entitled to, and Charles Matheny, the former owner, was the loser of the three acres. Lincoln notified her she ought to pay the heirs of Matheny the price per acre first agreed on. The woman couldn't see it. Lincoln wrote her again; the Matheny heirs were poor and needed the money. And again he wrote explaining what seemed to him plain justice. One day the woman sent him payment in full and he hunted up the heirs and paid them out their money.

Whitney told of a murder case in which Lincoln "hedged" after getting into it. Leonard Swett and Whitney had spoken for the defense, and believed they would get a verdict of acquittal. Then Lincoln spoke to the jury, took up the facts and the evidence, and was all of a sudden making arguments and admissions that spoiled the case for the

prisoner at the bar. The jury came in with a verdict that
sent the client to the penitentiary for three years. And the
case got to working in Lincoln's mind. Somehow he hadn't
done just right. Having helped get the man in the penitentiary, he worked to get him out, and in a year handed him
a pardon from the governor.

All other law cases were out when Lincoln threw himself
into the defense of William ("Duff") Armstrong, the son
of Hannah Armstrong. Before a coroner's jury a house
painter named Charles Allen from Petersburg swore that
he saw the fight between ten and eleven o'clock at night,
and, by the light of a moon shining nearly straight over
them, he saw Armstrong hit Metzker with a slung shot and
throw away the slung shot which he, Allen, picked up.

In the trial at Beardstown Lincoln aimed to have young
men on the jury; young, hot blood would understand his
case better; the average age of the jurymen as finally picked,
was 23. With each witness Lincoln tried to find some
ground of old acquaintance. "Your name?" he asked one.
"William Killian." "Bill Killian? Tell me, are you the son of
old Jake Killian?" "Yes, sir." "Well, you are a smart boy if
you take after your dad."

Again Allen swore he saw Armstrong by the light of a
moon nearly overhead, on a clear night, hit Metzker with
a slung shot. Nelson Watkins testified that he had been to
camp meeting the day after the fight, that he had with him
a slung shot, and that he had thrown it away because it was
too heavy and bothersome to carry. He had made the slung
shot himself, he testified; he had put an eggshell into the
ground, filled it with lead, poured melted zinc over the lead,
but the two metals wouldn't stick; then he had cut a cover
from a calfskin boot leg, sewed it together with a squirrel-
skin string, using a crooked awl to make the holes; and he
had then cut a strip from groundhog skin that he had
tanned, and fixed it so it would fasten to his wrist.

Lincoln took out his knife, cut the string with which the
cover was sewed, showed it to be squirrel-skin, and then
took out the inside metals and showed they were of two
different sorts that did not stick together—the slung shot
Allen testified he had picked up was identical with the one

Watkins testified he had made and thrown away. Meantime he had sent out for an almanac, and when the moment came he set the courtroom into a buzz of excitement, laughter, whispering, by showing that, instead of the moon being in the sky at "about where the sun is at ten o'clock in the morning," as the leading witness testified, a popular, well-known family almanac showed that on the night of August 29, 1857, the moon had set and gone down out of sight three minutes before midnight, or exactly 11:57 P.M. The almanac raised the question whether there was enough light by which a murder could be competently and materially witnessed.

Lincoln told the jury he knew the Armstrongs; the wild boy, Duff Armstrong, he had held in his arms when Duff was a baby at Clary's Grove; he could tell good citizens from bad and if there was anything he was certain of, it was that the Armstrong people were good people; they were plain people; they worked for a living; they made their mistakes; but they were kindly, loving people, the salt of the earth. He had told the mother of Duff, "Aunt Hannah, your son will be free before sundown." And it so happened. As the jury had filed out to vote, one of the jurymen winked an eye at Duff, so he afterwards told it.

Lincoln was easygoing sometimes about collecting money owed to him by clients. John W. Bunn, the Springfield banker, was asked by a Chicago firm to have a local attorney help them in an attachment suit involving several thousand dollars; Lincoln won the suit and charged $25. The Chicago firm wrote Bunn, "We asked you to get the best lawyer in Springfield, and it certainly looks as if you had secured one of the cheapest."

A lease on a valuable hotel property in Quincy was handled by Lincoln for George P. Floyd, who mailed a check for $25, Lincoln replying: "You must think I am a high-priced man. You are too liberal with your money. Fifteen dollars is enough for the job. I send you a receipt for fifteen dollars, and return to you a ten-dollar bill." In co-operation with a Chicago lawyer he saved a farm in Brown County for Isaac Hawley, a Springfield man, and Hawley had $50 ready to pay a fee; Lincoln smiled into Hawley's face and

216 THE PRAIRIE YEARS

drawled, "Well, Isaac, I think I will charge you about ten dollars." To another client he said, "I will charge you $25, and if you think that is too much I will make it less." A woman gave him a check to push a real-estate claim in court; he found the claim no good and told the woman on her next visit to his office that there was no action; she thanked him, took her papers and was going, when Lincoln said, "Wait—here is the check you gave me."

In the case of Samuel Short, living near Taylorville, Lincoln cleared him of charges of maliciously and feloniously firing a shotgun at boys stealing watermelons on Short's farm; Short didn't pay his fee and Lincoln collected it through a suit in the court of a justice of the peace. Ending a letter that notified a client his case was won, he wrote, "As the dutch Justice said when he married folk 'Now, vere ish my hundred tollars?'" There was a personal tang or smack in slight things he did. A man asked him for advice on a point of law and he told the man he'd have to look it up; meeting the man again, he gave the advice wanted, but when the man wished to know the fee, Lincoln answered there would be no fee because it was a point he ought to have known without looking it up.

On Herndon asking him why he was so prompt in always paying Herndon half the fees, the answer was, "Well, Billy, there are three reasons: first, unless I did so I might forget I had collected the money; secondly, I explain to you how and from whom I received the money, so that you will not be required to dun the man who paid it; thirdly, if I were to die you would have no evidence that I had your money."

A client complained to Whitney about the way he and Lincoln had managed a case; Whitney tried to get Lincoln to smooth it over with the client, Lincoln's answer being, "Let him howl." Usually he was calm, bland, easygoing with other lawyers; but sometimes he wasn't; Amzi McWilliams, handling a witness on Lincoln's side of a case, called out, "Oh! No! No!! No!!!" which brought Lincoln undoubling out of a chair with a slow yelling of, "Oh! Yes! Yes!! Yes!!!" putting a stop to the bulldozing of the witness.

A horse thief in the Champaign County jail told his local lawyer, William D. Somers, that he wanted Lincoln to help in the defense. When Lincoln and Somers arrived at the jail they found their client talking with his wife, who was in a delicate condition of health, Lincoln noticed. When the client handed Lincoln $10 and said that was all the money he had, Lincoln looked at the woman and asked: "How about your wife? Won't she need this?" The answer was, "She'll get along somehow," which didn't satisfy Lincoln. He handed the woman $5.00, and divided the other five with Somers.

He had to take losses; once all around the circuit his cases were for defendants, and he was beaten every time; so he told Bunn, the banker, in Springfield. And he told of himself that people had said, without disturbing his self-respect, "Well, he isn't lawyer enough to hurt him."

Lincoln defended a man who had 35 indictments against him for obstruction of the public highway. He took to the Supreme Court of the state a case involving a dispute over the payment of $3.00 in a hog sale. He became versed in the questions whether a saloon license can be transferred, whether damages can be collected from a farmer who starts a prairie fire that spreads to other farms, whether the divorced wife of a man can compel him to give her custody of her children and to supply her the means for their support. A merchant set fire to his stock of goods, collected the insurance, bought a new stock, and was sued by the insurance company for possession of the new stock. A man and his wife were threatened with being put off a railroad train because they refused to pay excess cash fare, claiming that the station agent had no tickets to their point of destination; they sued the railroad company. Lincoln's memory was cross-indexed with tangled human causes.

They had their fun and stories on the circuit. Once in Champaign County Court Judge Davis absent-mindedly sentenced a young fellow to seven years in the *legislature* of the State of Illinois. Prosecutor Lamon whispered to the judge, who then changed legislature to *penitentiary*. Lincoln, one morning in Bloomington, meeting a young lawyer whose case had gone to the jury late the night before, asked what had become of his case; the young lawyer bemoaned, "It's gone to hell," and Lincoln, "Oh, well, then you'll see it again." Lincoln enjoyed quoting to other lawyers from a book he had read about a man who far from being a liar "had such great regard for the truth that he spent most of his time embellishing it."

To illustrate a point, he would tell a fable: "A man on foot, with his clothes in a bundle, coming to a stream which he must ford, made elaborate preparations by stripping off his garments, adding them to his bundle, and, tying all to the top of a stick, which enabled him to raise the bundle high over his head to keep them dry during the crossing. He then fearlessly waded in and carefully made his way across the rippling stream, and found it in no place up to his ankles." In a law case having to do with hogs breaking through a fence and damaging crops, he told about a fence so crooked that whenever a hog went through a hole in it, the hog always came out on the same side from which it started.

A rich newcomer to Springfield wanted Lincoln to bring suit against an unlucky, crackbrained lawyer who owed him $2.50; Lincoln advised him to hold off; he said he would go to some other lawyer who was more willing. So Lincoln took the case, collected a $10 fee in advance, entered suit, hunted up the defendant and handed him half of the $10 and told him to show up in court and pay the debt. Which was done. And all litigants and the lawyer were satisfied.

On a 36-mile drive one October night, Lincoln, Swett and his wife, and Whitney were in a two-seated carriage; dark had come on as they rode into a river-bottom road in heavy timber with deep ditches alongside; and the horses and hubs plugged through mud. The driver stopped the horses; someone would have to go ahead and pilot; he didn't want to tip over as one of Frink & Walker's stages had done. Whitney jumped out, Lincoln after him; they rolled up their trousers, and arm in arm went ahead, calling back every minute or so. Lincoln sang, "Mortal man with face of clay, Here tomorrow, gone today," and other verses he made up. They drove into Danville later, laughing at October night weather and autumn mud.

He made safe, moderate investments. Speculations beckoned to others, but not to him. At hotels he took what was offered him with no complaint. He told his fellow lawyer Joe Gillespie he never felt easy when a waiter or a flunky was around. At a meeting of Republican editors in Decatur, he said he was a sort of interloper, and told of a woman on horseback meeting a man on a horse on a narrow trail. The woman stopped her horse, looked the man over: "Well for the land's sake, you are the homeliest man I ever saw!" The man excused himself, "Yes, Ma'am, but I can't help that," and the woman: "No, I suppose not, but you might stay at home."

Before posing for an ambrotype he ran his fingers through his hair to rumple it; on the stump or in jury speeches his hands wandered over his head and put the hair in disorder. Always, it was noticed, the linen he wore was clean; his barbers didn't let the sign of a beard start; he blacked his own boots. As to haircuts, grammar and technicalities, he wasn't so particular. In jury arguments and before a big crowd in Springfield, he wiped sweat from his face with a red silk handkerchief.

He read Joe Miller and repeated some of the jokes though he had a thousand fresher ones of his own; they sprouted by the waysides of his travel. For lawyers he would mimic a country justice: "If the court understand *herself* and she think she do." And there was John Moore, driving a yoke of red steers to Bloomington one Saturday, starting home with a jug, and emptying the jug into himself. Driving through timber a wheel hit a stump and threw the pole out of the ring of the yoke. The steers ran away; Moore slept till morning in the cart, and when he awoke and looked around, he said, "If my name is John Moore, I've lost a pair of steers; if my name ain't John Moore, I've found a cart."

And Lincoln had heard a farmer brag about his hay crop one year: "We stacked all we could outdoors, and then we put the rest of it in the barn." On a paper written by a lawyer, with too many words and pages, he remarked, "It's like the lazy preacher that used to write long sermons, and the explanation was, he got to writin' and was too lazy to stop."

Lincoln and Henry Grove of Peoria were attorneys at

Metamora for the defense of 70-year-old Melissa Goings, indicted for the murder of her husband, a well-to-do farmer of 77. Testimony indicated he was choking her and she broke loose, got a stick of stove wood, and fractured his skull. The dead man had a name for quarreling and hard drinking and his last words were, "I expect she has killed me. If I get over it I will have revenge." Melissa Goings was held in $1,000 bail. Public feeling ran overwhelmingly in her favor. Indications were that Lincoln held a conference with the prosecuting attorney, and that on the day set for trial Mrs. Goings was granted time for a short conference with her lawyer, Mr. Lincoln. Then she left the courthouse, was never again seen in Metamora, and the next day the case against her bondsmen was stricken from the docket. A court bailiff, Robert T. Cassell, later said that when he couldn't produce the defendant for trial he accused Lincoln of "running her off." Lincoln replied, "Oh no, Bob. I did not run her off. She wanted to know where she could get a good drink of water, and I told her there was mighty good water in Tennessee."

Friendships with Swett, Whitney and others on the circuit grew and deepened for Lincoln, and particularly that with fair-haired and pink-faced Judge David Davis, six years younger, five inches shorter, a hundred pounds heavier. A graduate of Kenyon College, Davis had come west and grown up with Bloomington. He had a keen eye for land deals and owned thousand-acre tracts. On his large farm near Bloomington he had a frame mansion where Lincoln stayed occasionally. In many ways the destinies of Davis and Lincoln were to interweave.

Chapter 10

The Deepening Slavery Issue

The Democratic national convention opened June 2, 1856, in Cincinnati, gave unanimous endorsement to the Nebraska Act, voted 138 to 120 against a Pacific railway, and after the 15th ballot went into a deadlock with 168½ votes for James Buchanan for President, 118½ for Douglas, a two-thirds vote being required to nominate. Douglas sent a letter saying the "embittered state of feeling" was a danger to the party and as Buchanan had a majority he was entitled to the nomination. On the 17th ballot Buchanan was nominated by unanimous vote. Buchanan had been away as minister to England, had taken no hand in the Kansas-Nebraska mess, and was rated a "safe" candidate. He and the platform faced to the past. The most human touch in the platform struck at the Know-Nothings; "a political crusade . . . against Catholics and foreign-born" had no place in the American system.

A fresher air and new causes moved the first national Republican convention in Philadelphia in mid-June. The newly born party's platform faced to the future; no extension of slavery, admission of Kansas as a Free State, "a railroad to the Pacific Ocean, by the most central and practicable route." No delegates came from the Deep South, only a few from the Border States; the party was sectional.

The nomination for President went to John C. Frémont; he had served as U.S. Senator from the Free State of California; as an explorer and "pathfinder in western wilds he had made a name for daring and enduring hardship. He was overly dignified, an egotist, a greenhorn in politics, yet somehow he had never said or done anything radical that could harm him or the party. He was nominated by 359 votes, 196 going to U.S. Supreme Court Justice John Mc-

Lean. Lincoln had favored the veteran Whig McLean as the man to draw the votes of the conservative Old Line Whigs. For Vice-President William L. Dayton of New Jersey, an able lawyer and former U.S. Senator, was nominated, the first ballot giving him 259 votes and Abraham Lincoln 110. The news reaching Lincoln, he laughed that it must be "some other Lincoln."

A February convention of Know-Nothings in Philadelphia had declared that only "*native*-born citizens" should hold office, and the foreign-born should vote only after "continued residence of twenty-one years." This political convention of the American party took a proslavery stand endorsing the Kansas-Nebraska Bill, an antislavery faction walking out. Millard Fillmore, while in Europe, was nominated for President, and coming home, accepted. Fillmore had been a Whig Vice-President, had become a Whig President on the death of President Taylor, had a strong Whig following that would vote for him. And Lincoln in letters and in more than 50 speeches hammered it home that a Whig vote for Fillmore was a vote against the Republicans and a vote for Buchanan, the Democrat. He mentioned Frémont often but never with any slight flowering of praise. Also he handled Fillmore respectfully and tenderly, with no belittlement, saying nothing of the Know-Nothings who created and sponsored Fillmore as a candidate. He kept quiet about a convention of Old Line Whigs, presided over by Judge Edward Bates of Missouri, which in September endorsed Fillmore, "without adopting the peculiar doctrines" of the American party.

Lincoln stressed the slavery question most often. "The slaves of the South, at a moderate estimate, are worth a thousand million of dollars. Let it be permanently settled that this property may extend to new territory, without restraint, and it greatly *enhances,* perhaps quite *doubles,* its value at once." In Belleville, where Germans were in high proportion, the *Weekly Advocate* said that Lincoln referred to "the noble position" taken by the Germans, and, "When he called down the blessings of the Almighty on their heads, a thrill of sympathy and pleasure ran through his whole audience." The *Advocate* mentioned Lincoln as "this associate" of Frederick K. F. Hecker and carried banners reading, "Lincoln and Hecker." A revolutionary favoring a constitutional government to replace the monarchy, Hecker had been exiled from Germany. Hecker's home in St. Clair County had been burned down while he was making a Frémont speech. Lincoln had raised a fund to rebuild and wrote Hecker, "I hope you will not decline to accept."

At Galena July 23, 1856, Lincoln went radical. He spoke there in what was probably the tone of his "Lost Speech." In no other published speech did he refer to the naked might and force that could in the future be called into play. Fillmore in an Albany speech had charged that if the Republicans elected a President the event would dissolve the Union. "Who are the disunionists, you or we?" Lincoln asked. "We, the majority, would not strive to dissolve the Union; and if any attempt is made it must be by you, who so loudly stigmatize us as disunionists. But the Union, in any event, won't be dissolved. We don't want to dissolve it, and if you attempt it, *we won't let you*. With the purse and sword, the army and navy and treasury in our hands, and at our command, you *couldn't do it*. This Government would be very weak, indeed, if a majority, with a disciplined army and navy, and a well-filled treasury, could not preserve itself, when attacked by an unarmed, undisciplined, unorganized minority. All this talk about the dissolution of the Union is humbug—nothing but folly. *We won't* dissolve the Union, and *you shan't*." Thus it was published in Galena and Springfield newspapers.

Of his day at Dixon, the Amboy *Times* said Lincoln "is about six feet high, crooked-legged, stoop-shouldered, spare-built, and anything but handsome in the face," but "as a close observer and cogent reasoner, he has few equals and perhaps no superior in the world . . . He attacks no man's character or motives, but fights with arguments." He spoke at Princeton with Lovejoy who was running for Congress, and at several meetings was joined with Senator Trumbull and William "Deacon" Bross of the Chicago *Daily Democratic Press*. He spoke at Atlanta (Illinois) in early September and again in late October. At a Shelbyville rally of Democrats, he debated with a local leader, the

Register at Springfield saying his three-hour speech "was prosy and dull . . . all about 'freedom,' 'liberty' and niggers. He . . . dodged every issue."

His law practice got little of his time as he rode on trains, in buggies and wagons, to speak at many points including Bloomington, Urbana, Sterling, Paris, Grand View, Charleston, Oregon, Vandalia, Decatur, Lacon, the State Fair at Alton, Ottawa, Joliet, Peoria, Clinton, Pittsfield, Jacksonville, four speeches in Springfield, occasionally two speeches in one day. A crowd of 10,000 heard him in Kalamazoo, Michigan, where an abolitionist wrote he was "far too conservative and Union-loving."

In his own home Lincoln's arguments failed. Mrs. Lincoln wrote to a sister: "My weak woman's heart was too Southern in feeling to sympathize with any but Fillmore . . . he made so good a President & is so just a man & feels the *necessity* of keeping foreigners within bounds."

When the October and November election returns were all in, Buchanan had 174 electoral votes, Frémont 114, Fillmore 8. The popular vote was 1,838,169 for Buchanan, 1,341,264 for Frémont, 874,534 for Fillmore. Buchanan carried all the Slave States except Maryland, which Fillmore carried. Lincoln's fears of the Fillmore vote were seen in Illinois where the vote was 105,000 for Buchanan, 96,000 for Frémont, and 37,000 for Fillmore. Yet there was comfort. The Republicans had elected a Mexican War veteran, Colonel William H. Bissell, governor, and the state ticket had swept in.

The New York *Times* and the *Evening Post* reported that $150,000 was sent into Pennsylvania from the slaveholding states; that August Belmont of New York had contributed $50,000 for the Democrats; and that other Wall Street bankers and brokers, fearing disorder and damage to business from disunion, raised still another $100,000. "Very nearly $500,000" was spent by the Democrats, the New York *Times* estimated, while the Republican expenses were somewhat less. Enough was known to show that behind the Pennsylvania contest were special interests paying big money toward winning that state.

At a Chicago banquet Lincoln spoke the toast: *"The*

Union—the North will maintain it—the South will not depart therefrom." All who didn't vote for Buchanan made a majority of 400,000. "We were divided between Frémont and Fillmore. Can we not come together, for the future . . . Let bygones be bygones. Let past differences, as nothing be." The central idea should be not "all citizens as citizens are equal" but the broader and better "all *men* are created equal." He was sure, "The human heart *is* with us—God is with us."

On March 6, 1857, in the U.S. Supreme Court room on the ground floor of the north wing of the Capitol, a hushed crowd listened to get every word read for three hours from a document by a man out of the past, an 81-year-old man, thin of body and furrowed of face, frail and fading, his voice at times a whisper. He had been Attorney General and Secretary of the Treasury under President Jackson who appointed him Chief Justice. He was Roger Brooke Taney, Maryland-born, a devout Catholic, free from scandal, highly respected in his profession, one lawyer terming him "apostolic" in conduct. He came from the tobacco-planting, slaveholding tidewater strip of Maryland but he had freed the slaves he inherited, except two or three too old to work whom he supported. At this time he was not yet over the shock of his wife's death from yellow fever and the death the next day of their last child, a beloved and beautiful daughter. He read for three hours the Supreme Court decision in the case of Dred Scott, a slave suing for freedom because he had been taken into territory where slavery was illegal under the Missouri Compromise; the Supreme Court of Missouri had sent him back into slavery because he had voluntarily returned to a Slave State. Four of the nine judges of the U.S. Supreme Court dissented, five being from Slave States. The decision declared that Congress did not have power to prohibit slavery in the Territories; the Missouri Compromise was unconstitutional; a slave was property and if a slaveowner took his property into a territory where the U.S. Constitution was the high law, his property could not be taken from him; a Negro slave or a free Negro whose ancestors were slaves, could not become a U.S. citizen. Negroes "were not intended to be included under the word 'citizens' " in the Constitution. "They had for more than a century before been regarded as beings of an inferior order, and altogether unfit to associate with the white race, either in social or political relations; and so far inferior that they had no rights which the white man was bound to respect, and that the negro might justly and lawfully be reduced to slavery for his benefit. He was bought and sold, and treated as an ordinary article of merchandise and traffic, whenever a profit could be made by it." Quoting from the Declaration of Independence "that all men are created equal," Taney read: "The general words above quoted would seem to embrace the whole human family . . . But it is too clear for dispute that the enslaved African race were not intended to be included."

Taney had hoped good would come from this decision but it set the slavery question seething. The New York *Tribune* said 6,000,000 people in the South had more weight in the Supreme Court than 16,000,000 people in the Free States. Lincoln, from now on for years, was to stress more than ever what he believed the Declaration of Independence meant by the clause "that all men are created equal." The question would recur, "If those who wrote and adopted the Constitution believed slavery to be a good thing, why did they insert a provision prohibiting the slave trade after the year 1808?" Into Lincoln's speech was to come more often that phrase "the Family of Man" as though mankind has unity and dignity.

Douglas in Springfield in June spoke for the court's decision. "Whoever resists the final decision of the highest judicial tribunal aims a deadly blow at our whole republican system of government." Lincoln two weeks later replied, "We know the court that made it, has often over-ruled its own decisions, and we shall do what we can to have it to over-rule this. We offer no *resistance* to it." Lincoln then quoted from a message of President Jackson in open resistance to a Supreme Court decision against a national bank, remarking, "Again and again have I heard Judge Douglas denounce that bank decision, and applaud Gen. Jackson for disregarding it."

He mentioned Taney's lengthy insistence "that negroes were no part of the people" who made the Declaration of Independence or the Constitution. Lincoln then quoted from a dissenting court opinion showing that in five of the 13 original states, free Negroes were voters. He read from Douglas' speech that the signers of the Declaration of Independence "referred to the white race alone, and not to the African, when they declared all men to have been created equal—they were speaking of British subjects on this continent being equal to British subjects born and residing in Great Britain." Thus, said Lincoln, not only Negroes but, the "French, Germans and other white people of the world are all gone to pot along with the Judge's inferior races."

Of course the Declaration signers did not intend to declare "all men equal in all respects" but they did consider all men equal in "certain inalienable rights, among which are life, liberty and the pursuit of happiness." He mentioned Douglas being "horrified at the thought of mixing blood by the white and black races," and commented, "In 1850 there were in the United States, 405,523 mulattoes. Very few of these are the offspring of whites and *free* blacks; nearly all have sprung from black *slaves* and white masters . . . In 1850 there were in the free states, 56,649 mulattoes; but for the most part they were not born there— they came from the slave States, ready made up. In the same year the slave States had 348,874 mulattoes all of home production . . . Could we have had our way, the chances of these black girls, ever mixing their blood with that of white people, would have been diminished at least to the extent that it could not have been done without their consent. But Judge Douglas is delighted to have them decided to be slaves."

Taney assumed "that the public estimate of the black man is more favorable *now* than it was in the days of the Revolution" yet in states where formerly the free Negro could vote, that right had been taken away. More and more state constitutions forbade the legislature to abolish slavery or slaveowners to free slaves. Of the chattel slave Lincoln spoke a fateful and strangely cadenced meditation:

All the powers of earth seem rapidly combining against him. Mammon is after him; ambition follows, and philosophy follows, and the Theology of the day is fast joining the cry. They have him in his prison house; they have searched his person, and left no prying instrument with him. One after another they have closed the heavy iron doors upon him, and now they have him, as it were, bolted in with a lock of a hundred keys, which can never be unlocked without the concurrence of every key; the keys in the hands of a hundred different men, and they scattered to a hundred different and distant places; and they stand musing as to what invention, in all the dominions of mind and matter, can be produced to make the impossibility of his escape more complete than it is.

Never ending for months had been the unrest and the high crying over "Bleeding Kansas." Between November 5, 1855, and December 1, 1856, about 200 persons had been killed and far more wounded from guns and knives. The Emigrant Aid Society, with large eastern funds, had sent out thousands of antislavery settlers and the legislature was strongly antislavery. But by registration trickery in test oaths, by thousands of ballots from counties having only a few score of settlers, by threats of violence, and by refusal of thousands of antislavery voters to vote in a special election where they said their votes wouldn't be counted, the proslavery party "elected" a constitutional convention which met in Lecompton under Federal troop guard. The Lecompton constitution which they wrote, proslavery in its mumbo-jumbo clauses, was sent to Washington for approval by Congress.

While the debate dragged on for months in Congress, President Pierce sent two governors to Kansas, Buchanan sent another and another, and each failed at bringing order and peace. John W. Geary and Robert J. Walker were, in the aftermath, estimated to have been shrewd, keen and fair umpires in meeting demands from the desperate proslavery men who saw themselves more and more with every month outnumbered by antislavery settlers and immigrants—and whenever a fair election was held the proslavery party lost. A congressional committee went to Kansas, heard hundreds of witnesses and its report ran 1,206 pages. Only a long story, reciting election frauds, disputes, bickerings, burnings of houses and barns, shooting and stabbing affairs could begin to picture the tragic and moaning chaos of Kansas. Poll books stolen, election judges driven from their seats, illegal ballots by hundreds, voters coming to the polls hearing men with guns and knives, "Cut his throat!" "Tear his heart out!"—the witnesses gave names, dates, places.

Guerrillas, bushwackers, roving outlaw gangs were common after the "Pottawatomie Creek Massacre." Tall, bearded John Brown, 56 years old, haunted by five free-state men killed, made a decision. He would kill five slave-state men, saying to one of his men, Townley, who didn't like the idea, "I have no choice. It has been decreed by Almighty God, ordained from eternity, that I should make an example of these men." On the night of May 24, 1857, he took two men and his four obedient sons, Owen, Frederick, Salmon and Oliver, each with a rifle, pistol and cutlass, and they went to three different cabins. In the Doyle cabin, the wife and mother begged to be let alone, but out into the night they dragged her husband and two sons, found next morning on the grass 200 yards from the cabin, the father shot in the head and stabbed in the breast, one son with arms and fingers cut off and a hole in his throat, the other son with holes in side, head and jaw. At Wilkinson's cabin past midnight they forced him to open the door, heard his sick wife plead, but he was found next day dead, with gashes in head and side. At the third cabin they took William Sherman who was found next morning with his skull split open and left hand cut off. The butchery was done mainly with two-edged cutlasses Brown had brought from Ohio.

Over the country in press and pulpit, on the platform, on sidewalks and in cigar stores and saloons, each side made its claims on the basis of distorted and incomplete reports. The sad fact that didn't come out till complete evidence was in made it clear that the victims slaughtered so coldly were merely plain illiterate farmers making a scant living and definitely not proslavery agitators. One son of Brown who didn't go along asked his father, "Did you have anything to do with that bloody affair on the Pottawatomie?" And John Brown: "I approved of it." The son: "Whoever did it, the act was uncalled for and wicked." And John Brown: "God is my judge. The people of Kansas will yet justify my course."

What with governors appointed by Pierce and Buchanan and more than a thousand U.S. Regular troops in Kansas, disorder and violence there slowed down, but in Washington in December 1857 the Lecompton constitution split the Democratic party wide open. At a coming election in Kansas the voters were to ballot, not on the constitution a rump convention had adopted, but on the single question of whether they adopted the constitution "with slavery" or "without slavery." Buchanan favored this election.

Douglas, before crowded galleries, made one of his great dramatic speeches. He denied the President's assertion that the Nebraska Act had carried an obligation merely to submit the slavery question and not the whole constitution. The election now arranged for this December in Kansas, said Douglas, offered Louis Napoleon's choice: Vote *yes* and be protected, vote *no* and be shot. Those in favor of it could vote for it, those against it couldn't vote at all. He had asked men who framed the Lecompton constitution about it. "They said that if they allowed a negative vote, the constitution would have been voted down by an overwhelming majority, and hence the fellows shall not be allowed to vote at all. [laughter] . . . If this constitution is to be forced down our throats, under a mode of submission that is a mockery and insult, I will resist it to the last." This speech was in a political year when the Boston scholar, George Ticknor, wrote to an English friend that American politics is "completely inexplicable."

In the eyes of some Republican leaders in the east Douglas became a hero; they suggested that Illinois Republicans in 1858 should support Douglas for Senator. Lincoln wrote to Trumbull in late December 1857: "What does the *New-*

York Tribune mean by it's constant eulogising, and admiring, and magnifying Douglas? . . . Have they concluded that the republican cause, generally, can be best promoted by sacrificing us here in Illinois? . . . I am not complaining. I only wish a fair understanding."

Three months later when Buchanan was throwing out of office men put in by Douglas, postmasters, marshals, land and mail agents, Herndon wrote to Trumbull, "Lincoln and I are glad to death that Douglas has been crushed." But Douglas was far from crushed. With his Democratic following in Congress, joined with Republicans, he defeated Buchanan's proslavery measures for Kansas. Over the nation and in a large segment of his party Douglas had never before had such a peculiarly high and honorable standing. Many, however, in Republican and other circles, held that he was no particular hero in having done what he had to do; when Buchanan wanted to make a mockery of "popular sovereignty," his only course was to oppose Buchanan, even if it should smash party unity. He kept on saying he didn't care "whether slavery was voted up or down," and in that posture he was the same old Douglas.

Meantime the country was still staggering under the financial panic of 1857 with its bank wrecks, tumbling stocks, property value shrinkages. Processions of thousands of men marched in the Northern large cities with banners reading: "Hunger Is a Sharp Thorn" and "We Want Work."

Chapter 11

The Great Debates

The political letters of Lincoln early in 1858 showed more and more a rare skill in the management of men. He wrote Lovejoy that he had been in Lovejoy's district and the danger had been that the Democrats "would wheedle some republican to run against you." The letter was strictly confidential, "not that there is anything wrong in it; but that I have some highly valued friends who would not like me any the better for writing it." He wrote in other letters that he was not "setting stake" against Seward, that Greeley was honest though "a drag upon us," that the enemy trick was "to try to excite all sorts of suspicions and jealosies amongst us," and that "we need nothing so much as to get rid of unjust suspicions of one another." He wrote to Norman B. Judd, the Chicago railroad and corporation lawyer who was chairman of the state central committee, that if Herndon had been talking of Judd being "treacherous," he could promise it wouldn't be repeated. He wrote to Congressman Elihu B. Washburne that he never did believe rumors afloat about Washburne going for Douglas and, "I am satisfied you have done no wrong, and nobody has intended any wrong to you."

To another he wrote June 1 that he supposed it wasn't "necessary" that county conventions should make known their choice for U.S. Senator, though Lincoln must have known that an amazing number of county conventions would name him. The Chicago *Tribune* said on June 14 that the unprecedented action of 95 county Republican conventions endorsing Lincoln was a "remonstrance against outside intermeddling" by Greeley and easterners favoring Douglas.

Many Republicans were saying when their state convention met in Springfield June 16, 1858, "We know Douglas, we have fought him for years, and now we're going to give him the run of his life." On a unanimous vote the resolution passed, saying, "Abraham Lincoln is the first and only choice of the Republicans of Illinois for the U.S. Senate as the successor of Stephen A. Douglas." In the evening in the hall of the House of Representatives, Lincoln came, bowed to applause and cheers, murmured, "Mr. President and Gentlemen of the convention." Then he read a speech from manuscript. He had worked harder on it, revised it with more care, than any other speech in his life; he had read it the evening before to a group of party leaders who advised him not to deliver it. Now he read:

"If we could first know *where* we are, and *whither* we

are tending, we could better judge *what* to do, and *how* to do it. We are now far into the *fifth* year, since a policy was initiated, with the *avowed* object, and *confident* promise, of putting an end to slavery agitation. Under the operation of that policy, that agitation has not only, *not ceased*, but has *constantly augmented*. In *my* opinion, it *will* not cease, until a *crisis* shall have been reached, and passed. 'A house divided against itself cannot stand.' I believe this government cannot endure, permanently half *slave* and half *free*. I do not expect the Union to be *dissolved*—I do not expect the house to *fall*—but I *do* expect it will cease to be divided. It will become *all* one thing, or *all* the other."

This was so plain that two farmers fixing fences on a rainy morning could talk it over. The speaker read on: "Either the *opponents* of slavery, will arrest the further spread of it, and place it where the public mind shall rest in the belief that it is in the course of ultimate extinction; or its *advocates* will push it forward, till it shall become alike lawful in *all* the States, *old* as well as *new*, *North* as well as *South*." He put together this and that circumstance and argued that while on the face of them the people could not be sure there was a conspiracy on foot to nationalize slavery, yet explanations were required. "Put *that* and *that* together, and we have another nice little niche, which we may, ere long, see filled with another Supreme Court decision, declaring that the Constitution of the United States does not permit a *state* to exclude slavery from its limits . . . Such a decision is all that slavery now lacks of being alike lawful in all the States." What interested the country most, as many newspapers published the speech in full, was its opening paragraph. It became known as the "House Divided" speech. It went far.

A court official in Springfield once asked Lincoln what special ability was most valuable for a winning politican, and quoted Lincoln's answer: "To be able to raise a cause which will produce an effect, and then fight the effect."

Douglas in Washington told a group of Republicans, "You have nominated a very able and a very honest man." To John W. Forney he said: "I shall have my hands full.

Lincoln is the strong man of his party, the best stump speaker in the West." And again, "Of all the damned Whig rascals about Springfield, Abe Lincoln is the ablest and the most honest."

Douglas started west in June, his daily movements watched by the country. The Chicago *Times* reprinted from the Philadelphia *Press:* "Senator Douglas, accompanied by his beautiful and accomplished wife, arrived at the Girard House, en route for Chicago." Sixty miles out from Chicago, a special Illinois Central train with a brass band, flags and pennants met the Douglas party July 9 and escorted the statesman to Chicago. As he stepped out on the Lake Street balcony of the Tremont House that night, rockets and red fire lit the street. The crowd in the street was getting over a fight with hack drivers who had tried to plow through the mass of people and deliver guests at the Tremont House. One man was knocked down with the butt end of a whip, one driver pulled off his seat three times. As horses, people, and hack drivers were untangled, Judge Douglas began an hour and a half speech.

Lincoln heard Douglas refer to him as "a kind, amiable, and intelligent gentleman, a good citizen and an honorable opponent." He heard Douglas say to the swarming thousands on the street: "Mr. Lincoln advocates boldly and clearly a war of sections, a war of the North against the South, of the free States against the slave States—a war of extermination—to be continued relentlessly until the one or the other shall be subdued, and all the States shall either become free or become slave."

The next night Lincoln spoke from the same Tremont House balcony to a crowd somewhat smaller; rockets blazed; the brass band of the German Republican Club from the Seventh Ward rendered music. And amid much on issues of the day Lincoln said: "I do not pretend that I would not like to go to the United States Senate, I make no such hypocritical pretense, but I do say to you that in this mighty issue, it is nothing to you—nothing to the mass of the people of the nation—whether or not Judge Douglas or myself shall ever be heard of after this night."

It was in this same month that A. P. Chapman wrote Lincoln of "Grand Mother Lincoln" (Sarah Bush) doing well, and, "I often take my Republican papers and read Extracts from them that Eulogise you you can hardly form an idea how proud it makes her. She often says Abram was always her best child & that he always treated her like a son. I told her I was a going to write you to day & and she says tell you she sent a heap of love to you & wants to see you once more very much . . ."

Lincoln wrote a challenge to debate and Douglas accepted. The two men would meet on platforms and clash on issues in cities in seven different parts of the state, all Illinois watching, the whole country listening. By the short-hand writing newly invented, reporters would give the country "full phonographic verbatim reports," newspapers told their readers.

In the Ottawa public square 12,000 listeners sat or stood in a broiling summer sun August 21 for the first debate. For three hours they listened. A train of 17 cars had come from Chicago. By train, boat, wagon, buggy and afoot people had arrived, waved flags, paraded and escorted their heroes.

Acres of people listened and, the speaking ended, they surged around their heroes and formed escorts. A dozen grinning Republicans lifted Lincoln to their shoulders, and a Republican crowd headed by a brass band saw him carried to Mayor Glover's home. "With his long arms about his carriers' shoulders, his long legs dangling nearly to the ground, his long face was an incessant contortion to wear a winning smile that succeeded in being only ghastly," said a Democratic newspaper. The Philadelphia *Press* reporter noted of Lincoln: "Poor fellow! he was writhing in the powerful grasp of an intellectual giant. His speech amounted to nothing." The New York *Evening Post* reporter wrote: "In repose, I must confess that 'Long Abe's' appearance is *not* comely. But stir him up and the fire of genius plays on every feature. Listening to him, calmly and unprejudiced, I was convinced that he has no superior as a stump speaker."

Next came Freeport, far in the northwestern corner of Illinois. A torchlight procession met Douglas; the Chicago *Times* counted 1,000 torches, the Chicago *Press* and *Tribune* 74. Lincoln rode to the speaking stand in a covered wagon drawn by six big white horses. Fifteen thousand people sat and stood listening through three hours of cloudy, chilly weather; mist and a fine drizzle drifted across the air. Some had come on the new sleeping cars from Chicago the night before. One train on the Galena road had 16 cars and 1,000 passengers.

Then debaters and shorthand reporters dropped south 300 miles, to a point south of Richmond, Virginia. The Jonesboro crowd numbered about 1,400—most of them rather cool about the great debate. The place was on land wedged between the Slave States of Kentucky and Missouri; several carloads of passengers had come from those states to listen. The Chicago *Times* noted: "The enthusiasm in behalf of Douglas is intense; there is but one purpose, to reelect him to the Senate where he has won for himself and the State such imperishable renown." As to Lincoln's remarks, the Louisville *Journal* noted: "Let no one omit to read them. They are searching, scathing, stunning. They belong to what some one has graphically styled the *tomahawking* species."

Three days later debaters and reporters were up at Charleston, and there, said the Missouri *Republican*, "The joint discussion between the Tall Sucker and the Little Giant came off according to programme." Twelve thousand people came to the county fairgrounds—and listened.

On October 7, in the itinerary, came Galesburg, in Knox County. Twenty thousand people and more sat and stood hearing Lincoln and Douglas speak while a raw northwest wind tore flags and banners to rags. The damp air chilled the bones of those who forgot their overcoats. For three hours the two debaters spoke to people who buttoned their coats tighter and listened. They had come from the banks of the Cedar Fork Creek, the Spoon River, the Illinois, Rock and Mississippi Rivers, many with hands toughened on the plow handles, legs with hard, bunched muscles from tramping the clods behind a plow team. With ruddy and wind-bitten faces they were of the earth; they could stand the raw winds when there was something worth hearing and remembering.

Six days later, in Quincy, on the Mississippi River, 12,000 people came from Illinois, Iowa, Missouri, and sat and stood three hours hearing the debaters. And two days later, farther down river, looking from free-soil Illinois across to slave-soil Missouri, the debaters had their final match, in Alton, before 6,000 listeners.

One young man, Francis Grierson, kept a sharp impression of Lincoln at Alton. He "rose from his seat, stretched his long, bony limbs upward as if to get them into working order, and stood like some solitary pine on a lonely summit."

Two men had spoken in Illinois to audiences surpassing any in past American history in size and in eagerness to hear. Yet they also spoke to the nation. The main points of the debates reached millions of readers. Newspapers in the larger cities printed the reports in full. A book of passion, an almanac of American visions, victories, defeats, a catechism of national thought and hope, were in the paragraphs of the debates. A powerful fragment of America breathed in Douglas' saying at Quincy: "Let each State mind its own business and let its neighbors alone! . . . If we will stand by that principle, then Mr. Lincoln will find that this republic can exist forever divided into free and slave States . . . Stand by that great principle and we can go on as we have done, increasing in wealth, in population, in power, and in all the elements of greatness, until we shall be the admiration and terror of the world, . . . until we make this continent one ocean-bound republic."

Those who wished quiet about the slavery question, and those who didn't, understood Lincoln's inquiry: "You say it [slavery] is wrong; but don't you constantly . . . argue that this is not the right place to oppose it? You say it must not be opposed in the free States, because slavery is not here; it must not be opposed in the slave States, because it is there; it must not be opposed in politics, because that will make a fuss; it must not be opposed in the pulpit, because it is not religion. Then where is the place to oppose it? There is no suitable place to oppose it."

So many could respond to the Lincoln view: "Judge Douglas will have it that I want a negro wife. He never can be brought to understand that there is any middle ground on this subject. I have lived until my fiftieth year, and have never had a negro woman either for a slave or a wife, and I think I can live fifty centuries, for that matter, without having had one for either." Pointing to the Supreme Court decision that slaves as property could not be voted out of new territories, Lincoln said, "His [Douglas'] Supreme Court cooperating with him, has *squatted* his Squatter Sovereignty out." The argument had got down as thin as "soup made by boiling the shadow of a pigeon that had starved to death."

Douglas said he would not be brutal. "Humanity requires, and Christianity commands that you shall extend to every inferior being, and every dependent being, all the privileges, immunities and advantages which can be granted to them consistent with the safety of society." America was a young and growing nation. "It swarms as often as a hive of bees . . . In less than fifteen years, if the same progress that has distinguished this country for the last fifteen years continues, every foot of vacant land between this and the Pacific ocean, owned by the United States, will be occupied . . . And just as fast as our interests and our destiny require additional territory in the north, in the south, or on the islands of the ocean, I am for it, and when we acquire it will leave the people, . . . free to do as they please on the subject of slavery and every other question."

Lincoln cited a Supreme Court decision as "one of the thousand things constantly done to prepare the public mind to make property, and nothing but property, of the negro in all the states of this Union." Why was slavery referred to in "covert language" and not mentioned plainly and openly in the U.S. Constitution? Why were the words "negro" and "slavery" left out? Was it not always the single issue of quarrels? "Does it not enter into the churches and rend them asunder? What divided the great Methodist Church into two parts, North and South? What has raised this constant disturbance in every Presbyterian General Assembly that meets?" It was not politicians; this fact and issue of slavery operated on the minds of men and divided them in every avenue of society, in politics, religion, literature, morals. "That is the issue that will continue in this country when these poor tongues of Judge Douglas and myself shall be silent. It is the eternal struggle between these two principles . . . The one is the common right of humanity and the other the divine right of kings. It is the same . . . spirit that says, 'You work and toil and earn bread, and I'll eat it.' No matter in what shape it comes, whether from the mouth of a king who seeks to bestride the people of his own nation and live by the fruit of their labor, or from one race of men as an apology for enslaving another race, it is the same tyrannical principle."

At Freeport Lincoln put a series of questions to Douglas, one of them, "Can the people of a United States Territory, in any lawful way, against the wish of any citizen of the United States, exclude slavery from its limits prior to the formation of a State Constitution?" The answer of Douglas amounted to saying, "Yes." It raised a storm of opposition to him in the South, and lost him blocks of northern Democratic friends who wanted to maintain connections in the South.

When Douglas twisted his antislavery position into one of race equality, Lincoln replied it was an arrangement of words by which a man can prove a horse chestnut to be a chestnut horse. At Charleston he shook a finger at a man's face: "I assert that you are here to-day, and you undertake to prove me a liar by showing that you were in Mattoon yesterday. I say that you took your hat off your head, and you prove me a liar by putting it on your head. That is the whole force of Douglas' argument."

Of Lincoln's face in a hotel room in Quincy, David R. Locke wrote: "I never saw a more thoughtful face. I never saw a more dignified face. I never saw so sad a face." Nor could Locke forget that Lincoln had his boots off and explained, "I like to give my feet a chance to breathe."

On October 30, several thousand farmers out around Springfield hitched up their teams and drove into town to a

Republican rally; Lincoln was to make his last speech of the campaign. Nine cars had come from Jacksonville and way stations. The Chicago & Alton brought 32 cars from McLean and Logan Counties, seats and aisles full, tops of the cars and two engine pilots crowded with passengers. Ten thousand swarmed around the Statehouse square, waves of people facing toward the speakers' stand.

Lincoln began his speech about two o'clock: "I stand here surrounded by friends—some *political, all personal friends,* I trust. May I be indulged, in this closing scene, to say a few words of myself? I have borne a laborious, and, in some respects to myself, a painful part in the contest."

He knew Galesburg to the north would vote about two to one for him and Jonesboro to the south three to one against him. He faced toward Jonesboro and all the South rather than Galesburg and the North. "The legal right of the Southern people to reclaim their fugitives I have constantly admitted. The legal right of Congress to interfere with their institution in the states, I have constantly denied . . . To the best of my judgment I have labored *for,* and not *against* the Union."

The issues were so immense, the required decisions so delicate, it was an hour for considerations beyond the personal. "As I have not felt, so I have not expressed any harsh sentiment towards our Southern bretheren. I have constantly declared, as I really believed, the only difference between them and us, is the difference of circumstances. I have meant to assail the motives of no party, or individual; and if I have, in any instance (of which I am not conscious) departed from my purpose, I regret it."

Then came words strange with a curious bittersweet. "I have said that in some respects the contest has been painful to me. Myself, and those with whom I act have been constantly accused of a purpose to destroy the union; and bespattered with every imaginable odious epithet; and some who were friends, as it were but yesterday have made themselves most active in this. I have cultivated patience, and made no attempt at a retort."

And in the same tone, he ended. "Ambition has been ascribed to me. God knows how sincerely I prayed from the first that this field of ambition might not be opened. I claim no insensibility to political honors; but today could the Missouri restriction be restored, and the whole slavery question replaced on the old ground of 'toleration' by *necessity* where it exists, with unyielding hostility to the spread of it, on principle, I would, in consideration, gladly agree, that Judge Douglas should never be *out,* and I never *in,* an office, so long as we both or either, live."

The speech may have been longer. What he wrote that survived took less than 15 minutes. Packed with momentous meanings for people south and north, it was a sober appeal in an hour of hair-trigger tension. The local reporters raved over "the outpouring," "the gaily decorated stores and public buildings," "banners and flags flying," the Springfield *Journal* printing six columns of labored description, stilted narrative in commonplace style. The speech that would have taken a half column had this unconsciously silly and blandly ignorant report in the *Journal:* "At two o'clock, the vast multitude being congregated around the stand, Mr. Lincoln began his speech. We have neither time nor room to give even a sketch of his remarks to-day. Suffice it to say, the speech was one of his very best efforts, disdistinguished for its clearness and force, and for the satisfactory manner in which he exposed the . . . misrepresentations of the enemy. The conclusion of this speech was one of the most eloquent appeals ever addressed to the American people. It was received with spontaneous bursts of enthusiasm unequalled by any thing ever before enacted in this city." And not a paragraph, not a line or phrase, of the brief and great speech itself!

Henry Villard of the New York *Staats-Zeitung* wrote that a thunderstorm had come up the night before Election Day. Lincoln with Villard, at a flag station 20 miles west of Springfield, crawled into a railroad boxcar. They sat on the floor, chins on knees, talking in the dark. Villard felt the laughs "peculiar" as Lincoln rambled on about himself for U.S. Senator. "I am convinced that I am good enough for it; but, in spite of it all, I am saying to myself every day: 'It is too big a thing for you; you will never get

it.' Mary [Mrs. Lincoln] insists, however, that I am going
to be Senator and President of the United States, too."

And there was light enough in the boxcar for Villard to
see Lincoln, with arms hugging knees, roaring another long
laugh, and shaking in legs and arms at his wife's ambition
for him to be President. The fun of it swept him as he shook
out the words, "Just think of such a sucker as me as President!"

November 2, Election Day, arrived, wet and raw in
northern Illinois. And though Lincoln had a majority of
4,085 votes over Douglas, Douglas because of a gerry-
mander held a majority of the legislature. Lincoln wrote
to loyal friends, "Another explosion will soon come." Douglas managed to be supported as the best instrument both
to *break down* and to *uphold* the slave power. "No in-
genuity can keep this deception . . . up a great while."
He was glad he made the race. "Though I now sink out of
view, and shall be forgotten, I believe I have made some
marks which will tell for the cause of civil liberty long
after I am gone." And he joked; he was like the boy who
stubbed his toe, "It hurt too bad to laugh, and he was too
big to cry."

On January 5 the legislature elected Douglas. After the
news Lincoln sat alone in his law office with his thoughts
a while, blew out the light, locked the door, stepped down
to the street, and started home. The path, worn pig-backed,
was slippery. One foot slipped and knocked the other foot
from under him. He was falling. He made a quick twist,
caught himself, and said with a ripple, "It's a slip and not a
fall!" The streak of superstition in him was touched. He
said it again, "A slip and not a fall!"

And far off in Washington, Stephen A. Douglas was
reading a telegram, from the *State Register,* "Glory to God
and the Sucker Democracy, Douglas 54, Lincoln 46."

In November 1858 the *Illinois Gazette* at Lacon, the
Chicago *Democrat,* the Olney, Illinois, *Times,* nominated
Lincoln for President. The Cincinnati *Gazette* printed a
letter nominating him, and a mass meeting at Sandusky,
Ohio, called for him to head the Republican ticket in 1860.

In Bloomington, in December, Jesse Fell saw Lincoln coming out of the courthouse door. Fell was a land trader in thousand-acre tracts, a railroad promoter, a contractor for large lots of railroad ties off his timberland holdings. He was of Quaker blood, antislavery, Republican, a little below medium height, smooth-faced, honest-spoken, trusted and liked in Bloomington. He stepped across the street and asked Lincoln to go with him to the law office of his brother, Kersey H. Fell. A calm twilight was deepening, as Fell said: "Lincoln, I have been East, . . . travelling in all the New England States, save Maine; in New York, New Jersey, Pennsylvania, Ohio, Michigan, and Indiana; and everywhere I hear you talked about. Very frequently I have been asked, 'who is this man Lincoln, of your state?' . . . Being, as you know, an ardent Republican, and your friend, I usually told them, we had in Illinois, two giants instead of one; that Douglas was the little one, as they all knew, but that you were the big one which they didn't all know. But, seriously, Lincoln, Judge Douglas being so widely known, you are getting a national reputation through him . . . your speeches in whole or in part . . . have been pretty extensively published in the East . . . I have a decided impression, that if your popular history and efforts on the slavery question can be sufficiently brought before the people, you can be made a formidable, if not a successful, candidate for the Presidency."

Lincoln heard and, as Fell told it, replied: "Oh, Fell, what's the use of talking of me for the Presidency, whilst we have such men as Seward, Chase, and others, who are . . . so intimately associated with the principles of the Republican party. Everybody knows them. Nobody, scarcely, outside of Illinois, knows me."

Then Fell analyzed. Yes, Seward and Chase stood out as having rendered larger service to the Republican cause than Lincoln. "The truth is," said Fell, "they have rendered too much service, . . . have both made long records . . . and have said some very radical things, which, however just and true . . . would seriously damage them . . . if nominated . . . What the Republican party wants, to insure success in 1860, is a man of popular origin, of acknowledged ability, committed against slavery aggressions, who has no record to defend, and no radicalism of an offensive character . . . You have sprung from the humble walks of life . . . and if we can only get these facts sufficiently before the people, depend upon it, there is some chance for you."

And Fell went on, "Now, Mr. Lincoln, I come to the business part of this interview. My native State, Pennsylvania, will have a large number of votes to cast for somebody . . . Pennsylvania don't like, overmuch, New York and her politicians; she has a candidate, Cameron, of her own, but he will not be acceptable to a larger number of her own people, much less abroad, and will be dropped. Through an eminent jurist and essayist of my native county in Pennsylvania, favorably known throughout the state, I want to get up a well-considered, well-written newspaper article, telling the people who you are, and what you have done, that it may be circulated not only in that state, but elsewhere, and thus help in manufacturing sentiment in your favor. I know your public life and can furnish items that your modesty would forbid, but I don't know much about your private history: when you were born, and where, the names and origin of your parents, what you did in early life, what were your opportunities for education, etc., and I want you to give me these. Won't you do it?"

Lincoln had been listening and said: "Fell, I admit the force of much that you say, and admit that I am ambitious, and would like to be President; I am not insensible to the compliment you pay me, and the interest you manifest in the matter, but there is no such good luck in store for me, as the Presidency of these United States; besides, there is nothing in my early history that would interest you or anybody else; and as Judge Davis says, 'It won't pay.' "

Rising, Lincoln wrapped a thick gray and brown wool shawl around his bony shoulders, spoke good night, and started down the stairway, with Fell calling out that Lincoln must listen and do as he asked. Newspapers in small towns in Midwest states had begun asking, "Why not Abraham Lincoln for President of the United States?" Calls for Lincoln to speak, as the foremost Republican figure of the

West, were coming from Kansas, Buffalo, Des Moines, Pittsburgh. Thurlow Weed, the New York boss, wired to Illinois, "Send Abram Lincoln to Albany immediately." Long John Wentworth, editor of the Chicago *Democrat*, a Republican paper, saw Lincoln looming, and told him he "needed somebody to run him"; in New York Seward had Weed to run him. Lincoln laughed, "Only events can make a President."

Chapter 12

Strange Friend and Friendly Stranger

Lincoln was 51 years old. With each year since he had become a grown man, his name and ways, and stories about him, had been spreading among plain people and their children. So tall and so bony, with so peculiar a slouch and so easy a saunter, so sad and so haunted-looking, so quizzical and comic, as if hiding a lantern that lighted and went out and that he lighted again—he was the Strange Friend and the Friendly Stranger. Like something out of a picture book for children—he was. His form of slumping arches and his face of gaunt sockets were a shape a Great Artist had scrawled from careless clay.

He looked like an original plan for an extra-long horse or a lean tawny buffalo, that a Changer had suddenly whisked into a man-shape. Or he met the eye as a clumsy, mystical giant that had walked out of a Chinese or Russian fairy story, or a bogy who had stumbled out of an ancient Saxon myth with a handkerchief full of presents he wanted to divide among all the children in the world.

He didn't wear clothes. Rather, clothes hung upon him as if on a rack to dry, or on a loose ladder up a windswept chimney. His clothes, to keep the chill or the sun off, seemed to whisper, "He put us on when he was thinking about something else."

He dressed any which way at times, in broadcloth, a

silk hat, a silk choker, and a flaming red silk handkerchief, so that one court clerk said Lincoln was "fashionably dressed, as neatly attired as any lawyer at court, except Ward Lamon." Or again, people said Lincoln looked like a huge skeleton with skin over the bones, and clothes covering the skin.

The stovepipe hat he wore sort of whistled softly: "I am not a hat at all; I am the little garret roof where he tucks in little thoughts he writes on pieces of paper." The hat, size seven and one-eighth, had a brim one and three-quarters inches wide. The inside band in which the more important letters and notes were tucked, measured two and three-quarters inches. The cylinder of the stovepipe was 22 inches in circumference. The hat was lined with heavy silk and, measured inside, exactly six inches deep. And people tried to guess what was going on under that hat. Written in pencil on the imitation satin paper that formed part of the lining was the signature "A. Lincoln, Springfield, Ill.," so that any forgetful person who might take the hat by mistake would know where to bring it back. Also the hatmaker, "George Hall, Springfield, Ill.," had printed his name in the hat so that Lincoln would know where to get another one just like it.

The umbrella with the name "Abraham Lincoln" stitched in, faded and drab from many rains and regular travels, looked sleepy and murmuring. "Sometime we shall have all the sleep we want; we shall turn the law office over to the spiders and the cobwebs; and we shall quit politics for keeps."

There could have been times when children and dreamers looked at Abraham Lincoln and lazily drew their eyelids half shut and let their hearts roam about him—and they half-believed him to be a tall horse chestnut tree or a rangy horse or a big wagon or a log barn full of new-mown hay—something else or more than a man, a lawyer, a Republican candidate with principles, a prominent citizen—something spreading, elusive, and mysterious—the Strange Friend and the Friendly Stranger.

In Springfield and other places, something out of the ordinary seemed to connect with Abraham Lincoln's past, his birth, a mystery of where he came from. The wedding certificate of his father and mother was not known to be on record. Whispers floated of his origin as "low-flung," of circumstances so misty and strange that political friends wished they could be cleared up and made respectable. The wedding license of Thomas Lincoln and Nancy Hanks had been moved to a new county courthouse—where no one had thought to search.

The year of the big debates a boy had called out, "There goes old Mr. Lincoln," and Lincoln hearing it, remarked to a friend, "They commenced it when I was scarcely thirty years old." Often when people called him "Old Abe" they meant he had the texture and quaint friendliness of old handmade Bibles, old calfskin law books, weather-beaten oak and walnut planks, or wagon axles always willing in storm or stars.

A neighbor boy, Fred Dubois, joined with a gang who tied a string to knock off Lincoln's hat. "Letters and papers fell out of the hat and scattered over the sidewalk," said Dubois. "He stooped to pick them up and us boys climbed all over him." As a young man he played marbles with boys; as an older man he spun tops with his own boys, Tad and Willie.

When William Plato of Kane County came to his office with the little girl, Ella, he stood Ella on a chair and told her, "And you're not as tall as I am, even now." A girl skipping along a sidewalk stumbled on a brick and fell backward, just as Lincoln came along. He caught her, lifted her up in his arms, put her gently down and asked, "What is your name?" "Mary Tuft." "Well, Mary, when you reach home tell your mother you have rested in Abraham's bosom."

Old Aesop could not have invented a better fable than the one about the snakes in the bed, to show the harm of letting slavery into the new territories. "If there was a bed newly made up, to which the children were to be taken, and it was proposed to take a batch of young snakes and put them there with them, I take it no man would say there was any question how I ought to decide."

When Tad was late bringing home the milk he hunted

the boy and came home with Tad on his shoulders and carrying the milk pail himself. Once he chased Tad and brought the little one home, holding him at arm's length; the father chuckled at his son's struggle to kick him in the face. Once as he lugged the howling Willie and Tad, a neighbor asked, "Why, Mr. Lincoln, what's the matter?" The answer: "Just what's the matter with the whole world. I've got three walnuts and each wants two."

In Rushville and towns circling around, they remembered the day he was there. The whole town turned out, among them young women of Rushville society, as such. One of the belles dangled a little Negro doll baby in Lincoln's face. He looked into her face and asked quietly, "Madam, are you the mother of that?" At many a corn shucking and Saturday night shindig, this incident had been told.

Germans and Irishmen had greetings from him. "I know enough German to know that Kaufman means merchant, and Schneider means tailor—am I not a good German scholar?" Or, "That reminds me of what the Irishman said, 'In this country one man is as good as another; and for the matter of that, very often a great deal better.'"

He told of the long-legged boy "sparking" a farmer's daughter when the hostile father came in with a shotgun; the boy jumped through a window, and running across the cabbage patch scared up a rabbit; in about two leaps the boy caught up with the rabbit, kicked it high in the air, and grunted, "Git out of the road and let somebody run that knows how." He told of a Kentucky horse sale where a small boy was riding a fine horse to show off points. A man whispered, "Look here, boy, hain't that horse got the splints?" and the boy, "Mister, I don't know what the splints is, but if it's good for him, he has got it; if it ain't good for him, he ain't got it."

Riding to Lewistown, an old acquaintance, a weather-beaten farmer, spoke of going to law with his next neighbor. "Been a neighbor of yours for long?" "Nigh onto fifteen year." "Part of the time you get along all right, don't you?" "I reckon we do." "Well, see this horse of mine? I sometimes get out of patience with him. But I know his faults; he does fairly well as horses go; it might take me a long time to get used to some other horse's faults; for all horses have faults."

Lincoln told of a balloonist going up in New Orleans, sailing for hours, and dropping his parachute over a cotton field. The gang of Negroes picking cotton saw a man coming down from the sky in blue silk, in silver spangles, wearing golden slippers. They ran—all but one old-timer who had rheumatism and couldn't get away. He waited till the balloonist hit the ground and walked toward him. Then he mumbled: "Howdy, Massa Jesus. How's yo' Pa?"

He liked to tell of the strict judge of whom it was said: "He would hang a man for blowing his nose in the street, but he would quash the indictment if it failed to specify which hand he blew it with."

He could write an angry letter, with hard names and hot epithets—and then throw it in the stove. He advised it was a help sometimes to write a hot letter and then burn it. On being told of a certain man saying, "I can't understand those speeches of Lincoln," he laughed, "There are always some fleas a dog can't reach."

Though the years had passed, he still believed, "Improvement in condition—is the order of things in a society of equals." And he still struggled under the load of that conundrum of history he had written ten years back: "As Labor is the common *burthen* of our race, so the effort of *some* to shift their share of the burthen on to the shoulders of *others,* is the great, durable, curse of the race."

He defended Peachy Harrison who killed Greek Grafton, a law student in the office of Lincoln & Herndon. On the witness stand came old Peter Cartwright, the famous circuit rider, grandfather of the accused murderer. "How long have you known the prisoner?" "I have known him since a babe; he laughed and cried on my knee." And Lincoln led on with more questions, till old Peter Cartwright was telling the last words that slowly choked out from the murdered man, three days after the stabbing: "I am dying; I will soon part with all I love on earth and I want you to say to my slayer that I forgive him. I want to leave this earth with a forgiveness of all who have in any way injured me." Lincoln had then begged the jury to be as forgiving as the murdered man. The handling of the grandfather as a witness cleared Peachy Harrison and set him free.

Over a period of some 20 years Lincoln had signed 20 petitions for pardons for convicted men, the governors of Illinois granting pardons in 14 cases. He had served as attorney for 14 of the convicted men and in some cases wrote his opinions and beliefs why the men should be set free. He wrote as to one of his clients that he was of a young family, had lost one arm, and had served five-sixths of his sentence, of another that it was "a miscarriage of justice," of two brothers sentenced to one year for stealing five shoats valued at $10 that the public was "greatly stirred" in their favor.

The name of the man had come to stand for what he was, plus beliefs, conjectures and guesses. He was spoken of as a "politician" in the sense that politics is a trade of cunning, ambitious, devious men. He chose a few issues on which to explain his mind fully. Some of his reticences were not evasions but retirements to cloisters of silence. Questions of life and destiny shook him close to prayers and tears in his own hidden corners and byways; the depths of the issues were too dark, too pitiless, inexorable, for a man to open his mouth and try to tell what he knew.

In the cave of winds in which he saw history in the making he was far more a listener than a talker. The high adventure of great poets, inventors, explorers, facing the unknown and the unknowable, was in his face and breath, and had come to be known, to a few, for the danger and bronze of it.

There was a word: democracy. Tongues of politics played with it. Lincoln had his slant at it. "As I would not be a *slave*, so I would not be a *master*. This expresses my idea of democracy. Whatever differs from this, to the extent of the difference, is no democracy."

He had faced men who had yelled, "I'll fight any man that's goin' to vote for that miserable skunk, Abe Lincoln." And he knew homes where solemn men declared, "I've seen Abe Lincoln when he played mournin' tunes on their heartstrings till they mourned with the mourners." He was taken, in some log cabins, as a helper of men. "When I went over to hear him at Alton," said one, "things looked onsartin. 'Peared like I had more'n I could stand up under. But he hadn't spoken more'n ten minutes afore I felt like I never had no load. I begin to feel ashamed o' bein' weary en complainin'."

He loved trees, was kin somehow to trees, his favorite the hard maple. Pine, cedar, spruce, cypress, had each their pine family ways for him. He could pick crossbreeds of trees that plainly belonged to no special family. He had found trees and men alike; on the face of them, the outside, they didn't tell their character. Life, wind, rain, lightning, events, told the fiber, what was clean or rotten.

What he said to a crowd at Lewistown one August afternoon of 1858 had been widely printed and many a reader found it deeply worth reading again and again. His theme was the Declaration of Independence and its phrase, "that all men are created equal," and have unalienable rights to "life, liberty and the pursuit of happiness." That document was a "majestic" interpretation:

> This was their lofty, and wise, and noble understanding of the justice of the Creator to His creatures. [Applause.] Yes, gentlemen, to *all* His creatures, to the whole great family of man . . . They grasped not only the whole race of man then living, but they reached forward and seized upon the farthest posterity . . . Wise statesmen as they were, they knew the tendency of prosperity to breed tyrants, and so they established these great self-evident truths, that when in the distant future some man, some faction, some interest, should set up the doctrine that none but rich men, or none but white men, were entitled to life, liberty and the pursuit of happiness, their posterity might look up again to the Declaration of Independence and take courage to renew the battle which their fathers began . . . I charge you to drop every paltry and insignificant thought for any man's success. It is nothing; I am nothing; Judge Douglas is nothing. *But do not destroy that immortal emblem of Humanity—the Declaration of American Independence.*

Once in 1858 Lincoln wrote a meditation he didn't use in any of the debates. It was a private affair between him and his conscience:

> . . . Yet I have never failed—do not now fail—to remember that in the republican cause there is a higher aim than that of mere office. I have not allowed myself to forget that the abolition of the Slave-trade by Great Brittain was agitated a hundred years before it was a final success; that the measure had it's open fire-eating opponents; it's stealthy "dont-care" opponents; it's dollar and cent opponents; it's inferior race opponents; its negro equality opponents; and its religion and good order opponents; that all these opponents got offices, and their adversaries got none. But I have also remembered that though they blazed, like tallow-candles for a century, at last they flickered in the socket, died out, stank in the dark for a brief season, and were remembered no more, even by the smell . . . I am proud, in my passing speck of time, to contribute an humble mite to that glorious consummation, which my own poor eyes may not last to see.

And that year he read at Bloomington a lecture on "Discoveries and Inventions," repeating it later in Springfield. Scheduled a second time at Bloomington he met so small an audience that he didn't bother to read his paper; he soon dropped the idea of being a "popular lecturer." What he read revealed him as a droll and whimsical humorist, a scholar and thinker, a keen observer and a man of contemplation who, if fate ordained, could have a rich and quiet life entirely free from political ambitions. He touched on man's first discovery or invention of clothes, of speech, of wind power for sailing, of the alphabet, of printing. Rulers and laws in time past had made it a crime to read or to own books. "It is difficult for us, *now* and *here,* to conceive how strong this slavery of the mind was; and how long it did, of necessity, take, to break it's shackles, and to get a habit of freedom of thought, established." A new country, such as America, "is most favorable—almost necessary—to the immancipation of thought, and the consequent advancement of civilization and the arts." Briefly and ironically, in passing, he went political, mentioning "the invention of negroes, or, of the present mode of using them, in 1434." Dominant in the paper he read was love of books, of pure science, of knowledge for its own sake, of a humanity creeping out of dark mist toward clear light.

Somewhere in this period Milton Hay of Springfield heard Lincoln speak offhand a rule or maxim in politics. Hay later passed it on to Joseph Fifer of Bloomington who found it so simple and so nicely singsong that he couldn't forget it: "You can fool some of the people all of the time, and all of the people some of the time, but you can't fool all of the people all of the time."

At a remark in Mayor Sanderson's house in Galesburg that he was "afraid of women," Lincoln laughed, "A woman is the only thing I am afraid of that I know can't hurt me." He told Whitney he hated going through the act of telling a hayrack full of girls in white gowns, each girl one state of the Union, "I also thank you for this beautiful basket of flowers." After a tea party at the home of Mayor Boyden of Urbana, the mayor and Whitney excused themselves for an hour, and left Lincoln alone with Mrs. Boyden, Mrs. Whitney, and her mother. Whitney, on returning, found Lincoln "ill at ease as a bashful country boy," eyes shifting from floor to ceiling and back, arms behind and then in front, then tangled as though he tried to hide them, and his long legs tying and untying themselves. Whitey couldn't understand it unless it was because he was alone in a room with three women.

A woman wrote her admiration of his course in politics, and he thanked her in a letter. "I have never corresponded much with ladies; and hence I postpone writing letters to them, as a business which I do not understand." Men knew of his saying, after giving money or time or a favor in answer to a pathetic but probably bogus appeal, "I thank God I wasn't born a woman."

Herndon believed Lincoln cloaked his ways with women by a rare and fine code, writing, "Mr. Lincoln had a strong, if not terrible passion for women. He could hardly keep his hands off a woman, and yet, much to his credit, he lived a pure and virtuous life. His idea was that a woman had as much right to violate the marriage vow as the man—no more and no less. His sense of right—his sense of justice —his honor forbade his violating his marriage vow. Judge Davis said to me, 'Mr. Lincoln's honor saved many a woman.' This I know. I have seen Lincoln tempted and I have seen him reject the approach of woman!"

A woman charged with keeping a house of ill fame was a client of Lincoln & Herndon; they asked for a change of venue; and Lincoln drove across the prairies from one town to another with the madam of the house and her girls. After the trial the madam was asked about Lincoln's talk with her. Yes, he told stories, and they were nearly all funny. Yes, but were the stories proper or improper, so to speak? Well—the madam hesitated—they were funny; she and all the girls laughed—but coming to think it over she believed the stories could have been told "with safety in the presence of ladies anywhere." Then she added, as though it ought to be told, "But that is more than I can say for Bill Herndon."

A curious friend and chum of Lincoln was Ward Hill Lamon, his Danville law partner, a young Virginian, daunt-less, bull-necked, melodious, tall, commanding, often racy and smutty in talk, aristocratic and, drinking men said, magnificent in the amount of whisky he could carry. The first time he and Lincoln met, Lamon wore a swallow-tailed coat, white neckcloth, and ruffled silk shirt, and Lincoln: "Going to try your hand at law, are you? I don't think you would succeed at splitting rails." As the years passed a strange bond of loyalty between the two men grew. "Sing me a little song," was Lincoln's word to Lamon, who brought out a banjo and struck up "Cousin Sally Downard," or "O Susanna," or the sad "Twenty Years Ago."

Women, music, poetry, art, pure science, all required more time than Lincoln had to give them. He liked to tell of the Indiana boy blurting out, "Abe, I don't s'pose there's anybody on earth likes gingerbread better'n I do—and gets less'n I do."

Herndon told of his partner coming to the office sometimes at seven in the morning when his usual hour to arrive was nine. Or of Lincoln at noon, having brought to the office a package of crackers and cheese, sitting alone eating. Mrs. Lincoln and Herndon hated each other. While Herndon was careless as to where he spat, she was not merely scrupulously neat and immaculate as to linen and baths, she was among the most ambitious women in Springfield in the matter of style and fashion. She knew of such affairs as Herndon getting drunk with two other men and breaking a windowpane that her husband had to hustle the money for so that the sheriff wouldn't lock up his law partner. She didn't like it that her husband had a drinking partner reckless with money, occasionally touching Lincoln for loans. She carried suspicions and nursed misgivings as to this swaggering upstart, radical in politics, transcendentalist in philosophy, antichurch.

At parties, balls, social gatherings, she moved, vital, sparkling, often needlessly insinuating or directly and swiftly insolent. If the music was bad, what was the need of her making unkind remarks about the orchestra? Chills, headaches, creepers of fear came; misunderstandings rose in waves so often around her; she was alone, so all alone, so like a child thrust into the Wrong Room.

At parties, balls, social gatherings, she trod the mazy waltzes in crinoline gowns, the curves of the hoop skirts shading down the plump curves of her figure. Once when talk turned to Lincoln and Douglas, she had said, "Mr. Lincoln may not be as handsome a figure, but people are perhaps not aware that his heart is as large as his arms are long."

She wrote to a sister in September 1857 of a trip east with her husband when he had law business in New York. A moment of happy dreaminess ran through part of her letter. "The summer has so strangely and rapidly passed away. Some portion of it was spent most pleasantly in traveling East. We visited Niagara, Canada, New York and other points of interest."

How often good times shone for them, only they two could tell. They were intense individuals, he having come through hypochondria, and she moving by swirls toward a day when she would cry out that hammers were knocking nails into her head, that hot wires were being drawn through her eyes. Between flare-ups and regrets, his was most often the spirit of accommodation. He was ten years older than she, with a talent for conciliation and adjustment.

There were times when she made herself pretty for him. One picture of her after 15 years of marriage shows dark ringlets of hair down her temples and about her ears, a little necklace circling her bare neck, three roses at her bosom, and a lily in her shapely hands.

Lincoln in 1857 sent an editor, John E. Rosette, a letter marked "Private":

> Your note about the little paragraph in the Republican was received yesterday, since which time I have been too unwell to notice it. I had not supposed you wrote or approved it. The whole originated in mistake. You know by the conversation with me that I thought the establishment of the paper unfortunate, but I always expected to throw no obstacle in its way, and to patronize it to the extent of taking it and paying for one copy. When the paper was brought to my house, my wife said to me, "Now are you going to take another worthless little paper?" I said to her *evasively*, "I have not directed the paper to be left." From this, in my absence, she sent the message to the carrier. This is the whole story.

A lawyer was talking business to Lincoln once at home and suddenly the door opened. Mrs. Lincoln put her head in and snapped the question whether he had done an errand she told him to do. He looked up quietly, said he had been busy, but would attend to it as soon as he could. The woman wailed; she was neglected, abused, insulted. The door slammed; she was gone. The visiting lawyer, openeyed, muttered his surprise. Lincoln laughed, "Why, if you knew how much good that little eruption did, what a relief it was to her, and if you knew her as well as I do, you would be glad she had had an opportunity to explode."

She was often anxious about her boys, had mistaken fears about their safety or health, exaggerated evils that might befall them. She gave parties for them and wrote with her own pen, in a smooth and even script, gracious invitations.

Mary Todd had married a genius who made demands; when he wanted to work, it was no time for interruptions or errands. For this brooding and often somber man she

Drawn by Otto J. Schneider from Lincoln's hat and umbrella in Chicago Historical Society

was wife, housekeeper, and counselor in personal and political affairs in so far as he permitted. She watched his "browsing" in the pantry and tried to bring him to regular meals. She had kept house years ago, too poor for a hired girl; they burned wood then; now they had a coal cookstove with four lids and a reservoir to warm rain water. She had chosen the beautiful, strong black-walnut cradle, into which she had put, one after the other, four boy babies.

She knew of the money cost in 1858 when he dropped nearly all law cases for months and paid his way at hotels and in 4,200 miles of travel, writing in one letter after the campaign closed, "I am absolutely without money now for even household purposes." At times he did the shopping, Herndon saying that of a winter's morning he might be seen around the market house, a basket on his arm, "his old gray shawl wrapped around his neck."

With their rising income and his taking place as the outstanding leader of his party, Mary Lincoln in the late 1850's enjoyed giving parties occasionally for two or three hundred people. Isaac N. Arnold noted of these evenings "everything orderly and refined," and "every guest perfectly at ease," with a table "famed for the excellence of many rare Kentucky dishes, and in season, loaded with venison, wild turkeys, prairie chickens, quail and other game." She had moved with him from lean years to the comforts of the well-to-do middle class. With ownership of his house and lot, with farm lands, and collectible bills he had out, Lincoln in 1859 had property worth perhaps $15,000 or more.

Chapter 13

"Only Events Can Make a President"

Joseph W. Fifer, later a governor of Illinois, a man of unusually accurate and tenacious memory, heard Lincoln speak in 1858 to an immense crowd in Bloomington. He stood ten feet from where Lincoln was speaking, turned around for a look, "And the faces of those listening thousands were as if carved out of rock on a mountainside— so still, so set!" The voice they heard was "metallic, clear, ringing, very penetrating." Fifer heard the voice at one point regarding the Negro, "In the right to eat the bread his own hands have earned he is the equal of Judge Douglas, or of myself, or of any living man." Then Lincoln "raised high his long right arm with the clenched hand on the end of it—high above his head—and he shook it in the air and then brought it down. And when he did that it —it made the hair on a man's head stand up, and the breath stop in his throat."

Lincoln's name had spread far as a speaker and thinker.

In 1859 he made speaking trips in Illinois, Indiana, Ohio, Wisconsin, Iowa, Kansas, and had to refuse many invitations to speak. On these trips he met leading men of the Republican party. They could judge whether he was presidential timber. He had said, "Only events can make a president," and there were friends saying events might dictate that each other candidate was either too old, too radical or too conservative and that Lincoln was on points the one most available. Also on these speaking trips Lincoln kept in touch with undercurrents of politics and public feeling; he met men who were to be delegates to the national Republican party convention the next year.

At no time in his many addresses of this year did he hint that he might be a candidate for President the next year and when good Republican party men said something about Lincoln for President he brushed it off with remarks that he wasn't fit or, as he had told Fell, there were greater men than he the party could choose. Yet his speeches in Ohio had a simple finality, a merciless logic, often a solemnity woven with Bible verses. He tore to ribbons the pretenses of Douglas, Buchanan, Chief Justice Taney; his lamentations over the possible outspreading of slavery had a dark music. There were listeners who couldn't help thinking and feeling he stood before them a consecrated man with a warm heart, a cool head, and he might make an able President.

He tried to guide party policy, writing in June 1859 to Governor Chase about the Ohio Republican party platform demand for the "repeal of the atrocious Fugitive Slave Law." The proposition was "already damaging us here" in Illinois. If brought up in the next Republican national convention it would "explode" the convention and the party.

In May 1859 banker Jacob Bunn handling the deal, Lincoln bought for $400 the weekly German-language newspaper of Springfield, the *Illinois Staats-Anzeiger*. By the contract, Lincoln owned the type, press and other equipment, and Theodore Canisius, the editor, was to continue publishing a Republican paper in German with occasional articles in English. Those handling the deal kept it a secret; Lincoln said nothing of it to Herndon; no news of it was published. Editor Canisius had written Lincoln asking where he stood on the Massachusetts Act of 1859 providing that no foreign-born naturalized citizen could hold office or vote until two years after his naturalization. Lincoln wrote, "I am against it's adoption in Illinois, or in any other place, where I have a right to oppose it." Having "notoriety" for his efforts in behalf of the Negro, he would be "strangely inconsistent" if he favored "any project for curtailing the existing rights of *white men*, even though born in different lands, and speaking different languages from myself." Canisius published this letter and it was widely copied in other papers.

The census of the next year would show 1,300,000 foreigners in the country, 700,000 of them Germans, chiefly in the Northern States. They held a balance of political power in many states. Their editors and political leaders were many of them German university graduates who had taken a hand in the revolutions of 1830 or 1848 in Germany; some had served prison terms or escaped; they had been hunted men, coming to America as refugees and fugitives; they had their bitterness over the Fugitive Slave Law. One of the hunted was Lincoln's friend at Belleville, Gustave Koerner, who to escape arrest, fled Germany to France, then to St. Louis, later to become a Supreme Court justice in Illinois and lieutenant governor. Lincoln was now openly allying himself with these men. He had helped Germans write a resolution passed by the Republican state convention in 1856 declaring that "our naturalization laws . . . being just in principle, we are opposed to any change being made in them intended to enlarge the time now required to secure the rights of citizenship." This resolution a German editor had taken to the Philadelphia national convention of the Republican party where it was, in substance, adopted.

In September at Columbus, Ohio, Lincoln held the spread of slavery to be the only thing that ever had threatened the Union. Amid his sober reasonings and solemn appeals there was laughter at his saying of Douglas, "His explanations explanatory of explanations explained are interminable" and again of Douglas' logic, "It is as impudent and absurd as if a prosecuting attorney should stand up before a jury, and ask them to convict A as the murderer of B, while B was walking alive before them."

Next day in Cincinnati, he declared: "We must prevent the outspreading of the institution . . . We must prevent the revival of the African slave trade and the enacting by Congress of a territorial slave code." To Kentuckians particularly, he wished to say: "We mean to remember that you are as good as we; that there is no difference between us other than the difference of circumstances. We mean to recognise and bear in mind always that you have as good hearts in your bosoms as other people, or as we claim to have, and treat you accordingly. We mean to marry your girls when we have a chance—the white ones I mean—and I have the honor to inform you that I once did have a chance in that way."

On the morning of September 30, 1859, at the Wisconsin State Fair in Milwaukee, Lincoln spoke as philosopher and scientist, even as a sort of inventor. "I have thought a good deal, in an abstract way, about a Steam Plow." In the four years past the ground planted with corn in Illinois had produced about 20 bushels to the acre. "The soil has never been pushed up to one-half of its capacity." He recommended "deeper plowing, analysis of soils, experiments with manures, and varieties of seeds, observance of seasons."

He saw the country as new and young; the hired laborer could get a farm for himself. "There is no such thing as a freeman being fatally fixed for life, in the condition of a hired laborer." Some reasons held: "Labor is prior to, and independent of, capital; that, in fact, capital is the fruit of labor, and could never have existed if labor had not *first* existed,—that labor can exist without capital, but that capital could never have existed without labor. Hence . . . labor is the superior—greatly the superior—of capital."

Was the working class to be the mudsills on which the structure of the upper class rested? "According to that theory," Lincoln told his farmers, "a blind horse upon a tread-mill, is a perfect illustration of what a laborer should be—all the better for being blind, that he could not tread out of place, or kick understandingly." By that theory education for the workers was regarded as dangerous. "A Yankee who could invent a strong *handed* man without a head would receive the everlasting gratitude of the 'mudsill' advocates." He spoke in simple words: "As each man has one mouth to be fed, and one pair of hands to furnish food, it was probably intended that that particular pair of hands should feed that particular mouth—that each head is the natural guardian, director, and protector of the hands and mouth inseparably connected with it; and that being so, every head should be cultivated, and improved, by whatever will add to its capacity for performing its charge. In one word Free Labor insists on universal education."

He walked around seeing the prize bulls and stallions, the blue-ribbon hens and roosters, and, chaffing with a bunch of farmers, patted a boy on the head: "My little man, I hope you live to vote the Republican ticket." The boy's father broke in, "If he ever does, I'll break his neck." And where a short strong man was lifting heavy weights, Lincoln tried his muscles at lifting, looking down at the short strong man and said, "Why, I could lick salt off the top of your head." In the evening at the Newhall House he made an offhand political speech and the next afternoon spoke in Beloit and in the evening at Janesville.

The editor of the *Wisconsin Pinery* at Stevens Point wrote: "He looks as if he was made for wading in deep water. He looks like an open-hearted, honest man who has grown sharp in fighting knaves. His face is swarthy and filled with very deep long thought-wrinkles. His voice is not heavy, but has a clear trumpet tone that can be heard an immense distance."

Herndon brought from Boston a book that Lincoln read, *The Impending Crisis of the South*, by Hinton Rowan Helper, who came from a slaveholding family that had lived a hundred years in the Carolinas. Helper gave formidable statistics showing that under the free labor system the North was growing richer and the people of the South sinking deeper in debt and poverty. Of the 6,184,477 people in the Slave States in 1850 only 347,525 were slaveholders. "As a general rule, poor white persons are regarded with less esteem and attention than Negroes and though the condition of the latter is wretched beyond description, vast numbers of the former are infinitely worse off." The South was shocked and aghast at the book, forbade its sale, and its men in Congress lashed out at any and all who read it or quoted from it.

Edwin A. Pollard of Virginia in his book *Black Diamonds* called for the African slave trade to be made lawful; then Negroes fresh from the jungles could be sold in Southern seaports at $100 to $150 a head. "The poor man might then hope to own a negro." Senator James H. Hammond, son of a Connecticut Yankee who had emigrated to South Carolina, told the North: "Our slaves are hired for life and well compensated. Yours are hired by the day, not cared for, and scantily compensated . . . Why, you meet more beggars in one day in the city of New York than you would meet in a lifetime in the whole South . . . Your slaves are white, of your own race. Our slaves do not vote. Yours do vote . . . If they knew that the ballot box is stronger than an army of bayonets, and could combine, where would you be? Your society would be reconstructed, your government overthrown, your property divided."

Abolitionists had stood up and interrupted church services to cry out it was a crime that the U.S. Constitution sanctioned slavery. Garrison had publicly burned a copy of the Constitution of the United States, calling it "a covenant with hell"; Henry Ward Beecher had held mock auctions of Negro women in his Brooklyn church; *Uncle Tom's Cabin* had sold in many editions and as a stage play held audiences breathless. The next census was to show that the 3,204,000 slaves of 1850 had increased to 3,953,500.

Out of Kansas came a man who ran slaves to freedom, burned barns, stole horses, and murdered men and boys without trial or hearing. He had come to Kansas from Ohio and New York, a descendant of *Mayflower* Pilgrim Fathers; two of his grandfathers fought in the Revolutionary War; at his house his 19 children partook in prayer and Scripture reading morning and night. He told eastern abolitionists action was the need, bold deeds. He had a saying: "One man and God can overturn the universe." Funds for rifles, pikes, wagons and stores were raised by wealthy and respectable citizens who in secret code termed the affair a "speculation in wool."

On Monday, October 17, 1859, the telegraph carried strange news. At the junction of the Shenandoah and Potomac Rivers, where Virginia and Maryland touch borders, in the rocky little town of Harpers Ferry, a U.S. Government arsenal and arms factory had been captured, the gates broken and watchmen made prisoners, slaveholders taken prisoner and their slaves told to spread the word of freedom to slaves everywhere—all of this between Sunday night and Monday daybreak.

Would the next news tell of slaves in revolt repeating the Nat Turner insurrection, with men, women and children butchered, homes looted and burned? The country breathed easier on Tuesday's news that Colonel Robert E. Lee, commanding 80 marines, had rushed a little engine-house fort where 18 men inside had fought till all were dead or wounded except two.

In a corner of the engine house, an old man with a flowing long beard said his name was John Brown. "Who sent you here?" they asked. "No man sent me here. It was my own prompting and that of my Maker." "What was your object?" "I came to free the slaves. I think it right to interfere with you to free those you hold in bondage." "And you say you believe in the Bible?" "Certainly I do." "Don't you know you are a seditionist, a traitor?" "I was trying to free the slaves." "You are mad and fanatical." "And I think you people of the South are mad and fanatical. Is it sane to think such a system can last? Is it sane to talk of war rather than give it up?"

The State of Virginia gave him a fair trial on charges of murder, treason and inciting slaves to rebellion; Northern friends sent him able lawyers; he was found guilty and sentenced to be hanged. He spoke calmly to the court. "Had I taken up arms in behalf of the rich, the powerful, the intelligent . . . or any of their class, every man in this court would have deemed it an act worthy of reward rather than of punishment . . . I see a book kissed here which is the Bible, and which teaches me that all things that I would have men do unto me, so must I do unto them. I endeavored to act up to that instruction. I fought for the poor; and I say it was right, for they are as good as any of you . . . God is no respecter of persons . . . Now, if it be deemed necessary that I should forfeit my life for the furtherance of the ends of justice . . . I say, let it be done."

Friends planned to steal him away from the death watch. He sent them word he would be more useful to freedom when dead. He wished to be a memory among young men. He was 59, but the average age of those who fought and died for his cause was a little over 25. He wrote in the Charles Town jail a last message before going to the gallows: "I, John Brown, am now quite certain that the crimes of this guilty land will never be purged away but with blood. I had, as I now think, vainly flattered myself that without much bloodshed it might be done." Beyond the 3,000 guardsmen with rifles and bayonets, he could see blue haze and a shining sun over the Blue Ridge Mountains. "This is a beautiful country; I never had the pleasure of really seeing it before."

He had written to the young abolitionist, Frank B. Sanborn, that he had always been "delighted with the doctrine that all men are created equal" and "the Savior's command, 'Thou shalt love thy neighbor as thyself,'" then adding, "Rather than have the doctrine fail in the world or in these States, it would be better that a whole generation, men, women and children, should die a violent death." His mother and grandmother had died insane and a maternal aunt and three maternal uncles suffered from the same dread taint of blood. His mind, somewhat off balance, dwelt on wholesale killings and with no haunting regrets over murders by his hand and direction in Kansas. He believed in his own right to doom others, and the power of God to doom wrongdoers everlastingly. "All our actions, even all the follies that led to this disaster, were decreed to happen ages before the world was made." He was only walking as

God had ages ago foreordained. The sheriff asked, "Shall I give you the signal when the trap is to be sprung?" "No, no," came the even voice from the white beard. "Just get it over quickly."

John Brown's ghost did walk. The governor of Virginia, the jailer, spoke of how he died, without a quaver, cool, serene. Emerson, Thoreau, Victor Hugo compared him to Christ, to Socrates, to the great martyrs. Wendell Phillips said, "The lesson of the hour is insurrection." Abolitionists acclaimed him and spoke for disunion. The antislavery men had regrets; they knew the South was lashed and would retaliate. Senator Douglas called for a law to punish conspiracies, quoting Lincoln's House Divided and Seward's Irrepressible Conflict speeches to indicate that Republican politicians and their "revolutionary doctrines" had incited John Brown.

John Brown became a mystical and haunting challenge. Five of his moral and financial supporters crossed the Canadian border to be safe from investigation. His chief backer, Gerrit Smith, a quaint and lovable character who had expected a different performance from Brown, broke down in fear of indictment and misunderstanding; under "a troop of hallucinations," he was taken to the Utica, New York, Asylum for the Insane, where in six weeks he was restored to calm.

The New York *Herald* published, in full, Seward's Senate speech foretelling "the irrepressible conflict." Seward now said he was opposed to conspiracy, ambush, invasion and force as shown by Brown; he favored reason, suffrage and the spirit of the Christian religion. Yet his explanations could not wash away the radical stripes. Political observers commented that Seward's prestige as a candidate for President had been hard hit. Jesse Fell and Judge David Davis worked steadily on their plans to nominate their dark horse the coming May.

Lincoln in Elwood, Kansas, referred to the hanging of Brown, and speaking in the dining room of the Great Western Hotel, the Elwood *Free Press* reported, "He believed the attack of Brown wrong for two reasons. It was a violation of law and it was, as all such attacks must be, futile as far

as any effect it might have on the extinction of a great evil
. . . John Brown has shown great courage, rare unselfish-
ness, as even Gov. Wise testifies. But no man, North or
South, can approve of violence or crime."

Of the fierce issue shaking the country he said, "The
Slaves constitute one seventh of our entire population.
Wherever there is an element of this magnitude in a government it will be talked about." Kansas now had a constitution, a legislature, and was soon to ballot on territorial
officers and a delegate to Congress. Lincoln spoke for the
Republican ticket in Troy, Doniphan, Atchison, and at
Leavenworth the *Times* reported: "In Brown's hatred of
slavery the speaker sympathized with him. But Brown's in-
surrectionary attempt he emphatically denounced. He believed the old man insane, and had yet to find the first Republican who endorsed the proposed insurrection." He
warned the Southern element, according to the Leavenworth *Register,* "If constitutionally we elect a President,
and therefore you undertake to destroy the Union, it will
be our duty to deal with you as old John Brown has been
dealt with."

He rode in an open one-horse buggy on 20- and 30-mile
drives over frozen roads across treeless prairie, the scattered
sod houses of pioneers looking lonesome. Once on open
prairie he met Henry Villard, traveling eastward from Col-
orado. They chatted a few minutes and Villard noticed Lincoln shivering, a raw northwest wind cutting through where
the short overcoat left the legs poorly covered. Lincoln
was glad to accept Villard's offer of a buffalo robe.

Keeping company with Lincoln over his Kansas trip, and
having Lincoln as house guest in Leavenworth, was Mark
W. Delahay, who had known Lincoln in Illinois and whose
wife was distantly related to Lincoln's stepmother, Sarah
Bush Lincoln. Delahay, eight years younger than Lincoln,
was born in Maryland, had gone to Illinois and become a
lawyer, had helped nominate and elect Lincoln to Congress, in 1853 practicing law for a year in Mobile, Alabama,
then moving to Kansas. In Leavenworth as a Democrat he
started the *Territorial Register* and upheld Douglas' "popular sovereignty." But after six months of the violence and

terror of proslavery mobs and wild shooting horsemen from Missouri, he changed policy and his paper became an outspoken and vehement antislavery organ. While he was attending a Free State convention in 1855 at Lawrence, the proslavery "Kickapoo Rangers" wrecked his newspaper office and threw the type and part of the press into the Missouri River. He had helped organize the Republican party of Kansas and against a strong Seward-for-President opposition was doing his best for Lincoln. He had asked Lincoln to endorse him for U.S. Senator and Lincoln had replied, "Any open attempt on my part would injure you."

Delahay had a well-modeled face, a head of thick curly hair, a full beard and mustache, and habits of overtalking and overdrinking. At a small dinner party in his home, he rose from his chair, waved a carving knife and called out, "Gentlemen, I tell you, Mr. Lincoln will be our next president." Lincoln put in, "Oh, Delahay, hush," but Delahay shouted, "I feel it. I mean it." As the dishes were passed they may have discussed John A. Martin, later a governor of Kansas. As a sour and bitter pro-Seward man and as editor of the Atchison *Champion*, Martin let no item of news be printed in his paper about Lincoln's arrival in Atchison, reporting no word of Lincoln's speech to an Atchison audience.

Back in Springfield after nine days away, Lincoln wrote political letters. He tried to smooth over the bitter feud in the Republican party between Long John Wentworth and Norman B. Judd. Wentworth had published that Judd was linked with corruption and Judd had sued for libel, the Chicago *Tribune* backing him to the hilt. Lincoln suggested that Wentworth print a retraction and Judd drop his suit, for the sake of party unity, but no such actions came and in county and state conventions the Wentworth-Judd feud went on.

On December 20 Lincoln sent Jesse Fell the requested autobiography. His father and mother came from "second families." Indiana, where he grew up, "was a wild region." And his schooling? "There was absolutely nothing to excite ambition for education. Of course when I came of age I did not know much. Still somehow, I could read, write,

and cipher to the Rule of Three; but that was all. I have
not been to school since. The little advance I now have
upon this store of education, I have picked up from time to
time under the pressure of necessity." His country drawl
was there. "I was raised to farm work." He closed, saying
he had a "dark complexion, with coarse black hair, and
grey eyes—no other marks or brands recollected." He
noted for Fell, "There is not much of it, for the reason, I
suppose, that there is not much of me. Of course, it must
not appear to have been written by myself." Fell's Pennsylvania friend elaborated on the facts sent him and published in the *Chester County Times* a sketch going "all out"
for Lincoln for President, many other papers reprinting it.

Letters kept coming about the House Divided speech.
Just what did it mean? He would quote its opening paragraph, and write: "It puzzles me to make my meaning
plainer. Look over it carefully, and conclude I meant all I
said and did not mean anything I did not say, and you will
have my meaning." And to close, "If you . . . will state to
me some meaning which you suppose I had, I can, and will
instantly tell you whether that was my meaning."

To a letter about the tariff question, he replied, "I have
not thought much upon the subject recently . . . just now,
the revival of that question, will not advance the cause
itself, or the man who revives it . . . I should prefer, to
not now, write a public letter upon the subject. I therefore
wish this to be considered confidential." His decisions and
choices in politics were dictated by swift-moving events.
To Trumbull and all Republicans he made it clear he would
not try for the U.S. senatorshp in 1860; he and Trumbull
were not rivals. "And yet I would rather have a full term
in the Senate than in the Presidency," he wrote to Judd.

In April he had written T. J. Pickett, a Rock Island editor, "I must, in candor, say I do not think myself fit for
the Presidency." In July 1859 he had written Samuel Gallo-
way, a Columbus, Ohio, lawyer, "I must say I do not think
myself fit for the Presidency." In November he wrote to a
Pennsylvania man, W. E. Frazer, an intimation that he
might be in the running. "I shall labor faithfully in the
ranks, unless, as I think not probable, the judgment of the

party shall assign me a different position." He knew Frazer was "feeling him out" and made clear he could enter no "combination . . . to the prejudice of all others." Still later he seemed to have an understanding with Norman Judd that he was to run for U.S. Senator in 1864 and toward that goal it would help if the Illinois delegates in the coming national convention were an instructed unit to vote for him for the presidential nomination. He wrote Judd, "I am not in a position where it would hurt much for me to not be nominated on the national ticket; but I am where it would hurt some for me to not get the Illinois delegates."

For nearly a year Lincoln had on hand what he called his "Scrap-book," writing, "It cost me a good deal of labor to get it up." From duplicate newspaper files he had clipped column by column, with careful scissoring, his and Douglas' main speeches of 1858 along with the full text of the Lincoln-Douglas debates. His own speeches were clipped from the friendly Chicago *Press & Tribune* while Douglas' speeches were clipped from the Chicago *Times*. These clippings he pasted neatly, two columns to a page, in a scrapbook bound in black boards, nine inches wide by 14 long, 95 pages numbered. He wrote on margins a few corrections and in scores of places his pencil struck out "Applause" or "Laughter" or "Cheers" or remarks shouted from the audience. In one place Douglas had nodded to a man, saying he knew this man would not vote for Lincoln, which the man seconded with a fast and blunt, "I'll be d——d if I do," and this Lincoln edited out.

In December came a letter from high Republican leaders in Ohio asking "for publication in permanent form" of the great debates of 1858. Lincoln wrote December 19 he was grateful for "the very flattering terms" of their request and, "I wish the reprint to be precisely as the copies I send, without any comment whatever." In January the Chicago *Press & Tribune* carried news that Ohio Republicans were publishing the Lincoln-Douglas debates as a campaign document, the Springfield *Journal* clipping it and adding it was "a most delicate and expressive compliment . . . The name of 'Old Abe,' the leader of the great Republican army of the Northwest, has become a word of power and might." Other newspapers chimed in. That the book would come off the press and go to an immense audience of readers gave Lincoln a quiet pride in the first book for which he had furnished a manuscript.

There would be readers enjoying such sentences as, "The Judge has set about seriously trying to make the impression that when we meet at different places I am literally in his clutches—that I am a poor, helpless, decrepit mouse," or, "I don't want to have a fight with Judge Douglas, and I have no way of making an argument up into the consistency of a corn-cob and stopping his mouth with it." Or the grinding cadenced statement: "I believe the entire records of the world, from the date of the Declaration of Independence up to within three years ago, may be searched in vain for one single affirmation, from one single man, that the negro was not included in the Declaration of Independence. I think I may defy Judge Douglas to show that he ever said so, that Washington ever said so, that any President ever said so, that any member of Congress ever said so, or that any living man upon the whole earth ever said so, until the necessities of the present policy of the Democratic party, in regard to slavery, had to invent that affirmation."

The title page read: "Political Debates between Hon. Abraham Lincoln and Hon. Stephen A. Douglas, in the Celebrated Campaign of 1858, in Illinois," the publishers Follett, Foster & Company, Columbus, Ohio. The book held the awesome heave and surge of the slavery issue and its companion, the dark threat of the Union dissolved. It gave the passionate devotion of Douglas to an ocean-bound republic of free white men, with what he termed "the inferior races," the Negro, the Indian, the Chinese coolie, barred from citizenship—and Lincoln's thousand-faceted defense of the clause, "that all men are created equal," and his high cries against the spread of slavery. In a sense, the book was a master mural of the American people in a given year.

Lincoln one October morning in 1859 "came rushing into the office," wrote Herndon, in his hands a letter inviting him to lecture in Brooklyn, in Plymouth Church, on the platform of Henry Ward Beecher. He thought it over, consulted with Herndon and others, and wrote the committee chairman, "I believe, after all, I shall make a political speech of it." Then over the winter weeks of late 1859 and early 1860 he toiled on the speech, at the State Library sinking himself in the *Congressional Globe*, the *Annals of Congress*, fingering through old mellowed newspaper files, in his office worming his way through his own six-volume Elliot's *Debates on the Federal Constitution*. This was to be no stump speech to prairie farmers. He would face a sophisticated metropolitan audience. The Chicago *Press & Tribune* on February 16, 1860, had sweepingly endorsed Lincoln for president, his character "the peer of any man yet named . . . more certain to carry Illinois and Indiana than any one else . . . great breadth and acuteness of intellect" and Lincoln would "never be President by virtue of intrigue and bargain." On February 23, as Lincoln left Springfield for New York, the *Illinois State Register* took its fling as to the coming speech: "Subject, not known, Consideration, $200 and expenses. Object, presidential capital. Effect, disappointment."

Arriving in New York he learned that the Young Men's Republican Union of New York City had arranged for his speech to be given in Cooper Union. At the Astor House he saw visitors, refused invitations to speak in New Jersey, went on working at his speech, noticed the *Tribune* called him "a man of the people, a champion of free labor." A Springfield Democrat, M. Brayman, wrote a letter February 27 telling of being at dinner with Lincoln, and admirers came to their table. "He turned half round and talked 'hoss' to them—introduced me as a Democrat, but one so good tempered that he and I could 'eat out of the *same rack, without a pole between us.*' "

A snowstorm interfered with traffic, and on the night of February 27 the Cooper Union audience didn't fill all the seats. About 1,500 people came, most of them paying the 25 cents admission; the door receipts were $367. The *Tribune* said that "since the days of Clay and Webster" there hadn't been a larger assemblage of the "intellect and moral culture" of the city of New York.

The eminent attorney, David Dudley Field, escorted the speaker to the platform, where among distinguished guests sat the innocent-faced Horace Greeley. William Cullen Bryant, editor of the *Evening Post*, author of "Thanatopsis" and "To a Waterfowl," told the audience of Lincoln's majority for the senatorship in Illinois and the legislative apportionment that elected Douglas. Bryant closed, "I have only, my friends, to pronounce the name of Abraham Lincoln of Illinois [loud cheering], to secure your profoundest attention."

A tall, gaunt frame came forward, on it a long, new suit of broadcloth, hanging creased and rumpled as it came out of his satchel. Applause began; the orator smiled, put his left hand to the lapel of his coat, and so stood as the greeting slowed down. "Mr. *Cheer*man," he said with Kentucky tang in his opening. He was slow getting started. There were Republicans not sure whether to laugh or feel sorry. As he got into his speech there came a change. They saw he had thought his way deeply among the issues and angers of the hour. He quoted Douglas: "Our fathers, when they framed the Government under which we live, understood this question [of slavery] just as well, and even better, than we do now." And who might these "fathers" be? Included must be the 39 framers of the original Constitution and the 76 members of the Congress who framed the amendments. And he went into a crisscross of roll calls, quotations, documents in established history, to prove "the fathers" held the Republican party view of restricting slavery. Did any one of "the fathers" ever say that the Federal Government should *not* have the power to control slavery in the Federal Territories? "I defy any man to show that any one of them ever, in his whole life, declared that." He said "neither the word 'slave' nor 'slavery' is to be found in the Constitution, nor the word 'property' even." They called the slave a "person." His master's legal right to him was phrased as "service or labor which may be due." Their purpose was "to exclude from the Constitution the idea that there could be property in man."

If the Republican party was "sectional" it was because of the Southern sectional efforts to extend slavery. The

Republicans were not radical nor revolutionary but conservative and in line with the "fathers" who framed the Constitution. Yet, "I do not mean to say we are bound to follow implicitly in whatever our fathers did. To do so, would be to discard all the lights of current experience—to reject all progress—all improvement." There were those saying they could "not abide the election of a Republican President," in which event they would destroy the Union. "And then, you say, the great crime of having destroyed it will be upon us! That is cool. A highwayman holds a pistol to my ear, and mutters through his teeth, 'Stand and deliver, or I shall kill you, and then you will be a murderer!' "

Slave insurrections couldn't be blamed on the young Republican party; 23 years before the slave Nat Turner led a revolt in Virginia where three times as many lives were lost as at Harpers Ferry. "In the present state of things in the United States, I do not think a general, or even a very extensive slave insurrection, is possible . . . The slaves have no means of rapid communication . . . The explosive materials are everywhere in parcels; but there neither are, nor can be supplied, the indispensable connecting trains. Much is said by Southern people about the affection of slaves for their masters and mistresses; and a part of it, at least, is true." In any uprising plot among 20 individual slaves, "some one of them, to save the life of a favorite master or mistress, would divulge it . . . John Brown's effort . . . was an attempt by white men to get up a revolt among slaves, in which the slaves refused to participate. In fact, it was so absurd that the slaves, with all their ignorance, saw plainly enough it could not succeed."

In the quiet of some moments the only sound competing with the speaker's voice was the steady sizzle of the burning gaslights. The audience spread before him in a wide quarter-circle. Thick pillars sprang from floor to ceiling, white trunks dumb, inhuman. But the wide wedges of faces between were listening. "And now, if they would listen—as I suppose they will not—I would address a few words to the Southern people." Then he dealt in simple words with the terrible ropes of circumstance that snarled and meshed the two sections of the country:

"The question recurs, what will satisfy them? Simply this: We must not only let them alone, but we must, somehow, convince them that we do let them alone . . . Wrong as we think slavery is, we can yet afford to let it alone where it is, because that much is due to the necessity arising from its actual presence in the nation; but can we, while our votes will prevent it, allow it to spread into the National Territories, and to overrun us here in these Free States? If our sense of duty forbids this, then let us stand by our duty, fearlessly and effectively."

He reasoned: "All they ask, we could readily grant, if we thought slavery right; all we ask, they could as readily grant, if they thought it wrong. Their thinking it right, and our thinking it wrong, is the precise fact upon which depends the whole controversy. Thinking it right, as they do, they are not to blame for desiring its full recognition, as being right; but, thinking it wrong, as we do, can we yield to them? Can we cast our votes with their view, and against our own?" To search for middle ground between the right and the wrong would be "vain as the search for a man who should be neither a living man nor a dead man." He finished: "Let us have faith that right makes might, and in that faith, let us, to the end, dare to do our duty as we understand it."

Applause came, outcries and cheers; hats went in the air and handkerchiefs waved; they crowded to shake the speaker's hand; a reporter blurted, "He's the greatest man since St. Paul" and scurried away to write: "No man ever before made such an impression on his first appeal to a New York audience."

The committee member, Charles C. Nott, walked with Lincoln, saw him limping and asked, "Are you lame, Mr. Lincoln?" No, he wasn't lame; his new boots hurt his feet. They boarded a horse-drawn streetcar, and rode to where Nott had to hop off for the nearest way home. He told Lincoln just to keep on riding and the car would take him to the Astor House. And Nott watching the car go bumping up the street wasn't sure he had done right to get off; Lincoln looked sad and lonesome like a figure blown in with the drifts of the snowstorm.

In the morning Lincoln saw that four papers printed his speech in full, and learned there would be a pamphlet reprint of it. Brady photographed him; as the picture came out he looked a little satisfied with himself; it wasn't the usual sad face. But people liked it.

This week Joseph Medill in Washington sent to the Chicago *Press & Tribune* an editorial arguing that Lincoln could be elected President that year and Seward couldn't. Seward read it, hunted up Medill, and as Medill told it: "Seward 'blew me up' tremendously for having disappointed him, and preferring that 'prairie statesman,' as he called Lincoln. He gave me to understand that he was the chief teacher of the principles of the Republican party before Lincoln was known other than as a country lawyer in Illinois." The background instigators of Lincoln's appearance at Cooper Union were a faction long opposed to Seward and Weed; they were pleased to see Seward's stature cut down a little; they may have crossed their fingers when Lincoln asked for "harmony, one with another" and said, "Even though much provoked, let us do nothing through passion and ill temper."

Lincoln spoke for his party in New England and visited his boy, Robert, in school at Exeter, New Hampshire. At Hartford, the report ran, he cited one-sixth of the population of the United States looked upon as property, as nothing but property. "The cash value of these slaves, at a moderate estimate, is $2,000,000,000. This amount of property value has a vast influence on the minds of its owners, very naturally. The same amount of property would have an equal influence upon us if owned in the North. Human nature is the same—people at the South are the same as those at the North, barring the difference in circumstances."

Shoe factory workers on strike said they couldn't live on their wages of $250 a year. Douglas laid the strike on "this unfortunate sectional warfare"; Lincoln replied, "Thank God that we have a system of labor where there *can* be a strike." Thus at Hartford. At New Haven, the *Daily Palladium* reported him: "I do not pretend to know all about the matter . . . *I am glad to see that a system of labor prevails in New England under which laborers* CAN *strike* when they want to [Cheers,] where they are not obliged to work under all circumstances, and are not tied down and obliged to labor whether you pay them or not! [Cheers.] I *like* the system which lets a man quit when he wants to, and wish it might prevail everywhere. [Tremendous applause.] . . . I don't believe in a law to prevent a man from getting rich; it would do more harm than good. So while we do not propose any war upon capital, we do wish to allow the humblest man an equal chance to get rich with everybody else. [Applause.]"

He made speeches in Providence, Concord, Manchester, Dover, New Haven, Meriden, Norwich, and finally in Bridgeport on March 10, usually to "capacity audiences," several times escorted by brass bands and torchlight processions of cheering Republicans. About midway he wrote his wife, "I have been unable to escape this toil. If I had foreseen it, I think I would not have come east at all." He was hard put to make nine speeches "before reading audiences who had already seen all my ideas in print." He turned down invitations to speak in Philadelphia, Reading and Pittsburgh, being "far worn down." He thanked James A. Briggs for a $200 check for the Cooper Union speech, begged off any more speaking dates, but on March 11 did go with Briggs to hear Beecher preach in Brooklyn and to attend the Universalist Church of Edwin H. Chapin in New York. The next day he took the Erie Railroad for Chicago and two days later was home in Springfield, arriving, said the *Journal*, "in excellent health and in his usual spirits."

Chapter 14

"Mary, We're Elected"

William H. Seward, eight years older than Lincoln, leading all other candidates for the Republican presidential nomination, was a New Yorker of Welsh-Irish stock, a slim, middle-sized man, stooped, white-haired, with a pointed nose, a slouching walk, a plain conversational tone in public speaking, "eyes secret but penetrating, a subtle, quick man, rejoicing in power." His friend and manager, Thurlow Weed, publisher of the Albany *Evening Journal*, ran a Seward publicity bureau, was in touch with large special interests and made free use of money in promoting Seward.

When governor of New York, Seward had brought into effect laws requiring jury trial for fugitive slaves, with defense counsel fees paid by the state. In the U.S. Senate, replying to Webster, Seward had said, ". . . there is *a higher law* than the Constitution, which regulates our authority over the domain." In October 1858 he spoke of the slavery issue as not "the work of fanatical agitators," but rather, "It is an *irrepressible conflict* between opposing and enduring forces, and it means that the United States must and will, sooner or later, become either entirely a slaveholding nation, or entirely a free-labor nation."

Southern voices and papers called him "monstrous and diabolical," some of his own advisers telling him he had gone too radical. He had retreated into explanations that he wasn't as radical as he sounded, but a stigma hung on him. While Lincoln went on month after month quoting from his House Divided speech, Seward refused to refresh memories about his "higher law" and "irrepressible conflict." Lincoln's speech had a mystic songlike quality while Seward's was bare intellectual doctrine.

Handsome, portly, overdignified Salmon P. Chase of Ohio, antislavery, radical, had twice been governor and served a term as U.S. Senator; he would get delegates from Ohio and elsewhere but didn't seem formidable. Judge Edward Bates of Missouri would have that state's delegates and a scattered following from elsewhere. He was 67, had married a South Carolinian's daughter who bore him 17 children. He had been a Whig Congressman and his backers said that as a Free-Soil Whig from a Border Slave State he would avert secession. He was smallish, bearded, a moderate Old Line Whig who kept a diary that whispered to him he would be President. In 1856 he had been a leader in an Old Line Whig convention at Baltimore which endorsed the American [Know-Nothing] party and he didn't know the full force of German editors and political leaders who had axes out for him and would throw a fierce strength against him.

John McLean, an Ohio Democrat, appointed associate justice of the U.S. Supreme Court by President Jackson, was in the running, his dissenting opinion in the Dred Scott case being in his favor. He was 75, and Lincoln wrote to Trumbull, "I do not believe he would accept it [the nomination]; . . . If he were ten years younger he would be our best candidate." McLean's health was failing and he was to die within a year, but he was mentioned in reckonings that did not include Lincoln.

Before mid-May the Lincoln-Douglas debates book, at 50 cents in paper or $1.00 clothbound, was to go into four editions; the pamphlet reprints of the Cooper Union speech were selling at one cent the copy, and there was a growing legend spreading wider of the tall homely man who was log-cabin born and had been flatboatman and rail splitter, struggling on to where his speech and thought were read nationwide. All this had created an aura about Lincoln that in the few weeks now left before the national Republican convention in May was to be the more effective because it was no forced growth. It had a way of dawning on men, "Why, yes, come to think of it, why not Lincoln? The more you look at him the more he is the man."

He had in 1859 traveled 4,000 miles to make 23 Republican speeches. He had covered more ground over America than any others of his party mentioned for President; born in Kentucky, he had traversed the Mississippi River in a flatboat to New Orleans, had lived in the national capital, had met audiences over all the Midwest as far out as Kansas, in New York City, and across New England. He had purposely in public hidden his hopes and strengths as a candidate and coming weeks would tell the results. He had followed this course long before John Wentworth's advice of February 6: "Look out for *prominence*. When it is ascertained that none of the prominent candidates can be nominated then ought to be your time."

Lincoln wrote to an Ohio delegate, of the coming Chi-

cago convention, that Seward "is the very best candidate
we could have for the North of Illinois, and the very *worst*
for the South of it." With Chase of Ohio it would be the
same, while Bates of Missouri would be the best for the
south of Illinois and the worst for the north. And Judge
McLean, if 15 or even 10 years younger, would be stronger
than either Seward or Bates. "I am not the fittest person to
answer the questions you ask [about candidates]. When not
a very great man begins to be mentioned for a very great
position, his head is very likely to be a little turned."

With Trumbull he would be "entirely frank," writing,
"The taste *is* in my mouth a little." He repeated for Trumbull his view of the Seward, Chase and Bates followings
in Illinois. Three small-town newspapers in Illinois had
nominated Trumbull for President; the taste was a little in
his mouth too and while he regarded himself as one of the
darker dark horses, he favored McLean as against Lincoln,
who had secured his election as U.S. Senator.

To another Ohio delegate Lincoln wrote: "Our policy,
then, is to give no offence to others—leave them in a mood
to come to us, if they shall be compelled to give up their
first love. This, too, is dealing justly with all, and leaving
us in a mood to support heartily whoever shall be nominated." In a Bloomington speech in April, he thrust at
the Douglas logic: "If I cannot rightfully murder a man, I
may tie him to the tail of a kicking horse, and let him kick
the man to death."

Mark Delahay, as the Lincoln leader in Kansas, asked
for money, Lincoln replying: "Allow me to say I can not
enter the ring on the money basis—first, because, in the
main, it is wrong; and secondly, I have not, and can not
get, the money. I say, in the main, the use of money is
wrong; but for certain objects, in a political contest, the
use of some, is both right, and indispensable." He could
make a distinct offer: "If you shall be appointed a delegate
to Chicago, I will furnish one hundred dollars to bear the
expences of the trip." In a second letter after Kansas elected
a pro-Seward delegation he wrote to Delahay, "Come along
to the convention, & I will do as I said about expenses."

Into the state Republican convention at Decatur on May 9

came John Hanks carrying two fence rails tied with flags and streamers, with the inscription, "Abraham Lincoln, the Rail Candidate for President in 1860: Two rails from a lot of 3,000 made in 1830 by Thos. Hanks and Abe Lincoln—whose father was the first pioneer of Macon County." Shouts followed: "Lincoln! Lincoln! Speech!" He thanked them with a sober face. Cheers: "Three times three for Honest Abe, our next President." Shouts from the convention: "Identify your work!" "It may be that I split these rails," and scrutinizing further, "Well, boys, I can only say that I have split a great many better-looking ones."

Thus the Rail Candidate was brought forth, and the nickname of Rail Splitter. The idea came from Richard Oglesby, a Decatur lawyer, Kentucky-raised, a plain and witty man, who shared Lincoln's belief in the people. He had hunted out John Hanks and planned the dramatization of Lincoln as "the Rail Splitter." Far more important was it that the convention instructed its delegates to the Chicago convention to vote as a unit for Lincoln; 7 of the 22 delegates personally preferred Seward, and Orville H. Browning's choice was Bates.

Two weeks earlier, at the national Democratic convention in Charleston, South Carolina, where the Douglas delegates held a majority control, but lacking the necessary two-thirds to nominate their hero, slavery men had split the party, and two separate wings of it were to hold conventions in June. The answers of Douglas to Lincoln in the Freeport debate and his break with the Buchanan administration had lost nearly all former trust of the South in him. William Lowndes Yancey of Alabama, tall, slender, with long black hair, spoke in a soft, musical yet tense voice for the minority. "The proposition you make, will bankrupt us of the South. Ours is the property invaded—ours the interests at stake . . . You would make a great seething caldron of passion and crime if you were able to consummate your measures." Ten days of speeches, ballots, wrangles, brought adjournment to Baltimore in June. Now it was taken as certain that there would be two Democratic parties in the field, one Northern, the other Southern, and Republican victory in November almost sure.

On May 9 in Baltimore was organized the new Constitutional Union party with a short platform calling for the maintenance of the Constitution, the Union and law enforcement. For President they nominated John Bell of Tennessee, a former Whig Congressman and U.S. Senator, for Vice President, Edward Everett, a former Secretary of State and president of Harvard University. Not much was expected from them; their platform was not merely simple but too simple.

Illinois delegates were outfitting with silk hats and broad-cloth suits for the Chicago Republican convention May 16. Lincoln was saying, "I am a little too much a candidate to stay home and not quite enough a candidate to go." Judd and others had made a special point of getting the convention for Chicago. They told the national committee that holding the convention in an eastern city would "run a big chance of losing the West." Chicago had become a symbol for audacity, enterprise and onward stride. Its population of 29,000 in 1850 had become 80,000 in 1855, and 109,000 in 1860; it betokened the "great Northwest" that had wrought transformations in American national politics. Its trade in hogs, cattle, wheat, corn, farm machinery, and the associated finance and transportation, made it the depot and crossroads for thousand-mile prairies. Out of it ran 15 railway lines with 150 railroad trains a day; on May 16, 1860, they had brought an estimated 40,000 strangers and 500 delegates to the convention. At the corner of Lake and Market Streets the Sauganash Hotel had been torn down, and a huge rambling lumber structure, to hold 10,000 people, had been put up and named the Wigwam. Chicago girls and women, with the help of young men, had made the big barnlike interior gay and brilliant with flags, bunting and streamers of red, white and blue.

Judge David Davis had adjourned the Eighth Circuit courts, took over the entire third floor of Chicago's finest hotel, the Tremont House, paying a rental of $300 for spacious Lincoln headquarters and rooms for his staff of Lincoln hustlers, evangelists, salesmen, pleaders, exhorters, schemers. Jesse Fell, once a Pennsylvanian, could mix with and interpret the pivotal Keystone delegates. Judd, as a railroad lawyer of close association with a Pennsylvania delegate who was a railroad lawyer, could make honest promises to the powerful interests who wanted a Pacific railway and other benefits. Leonard Swett, as a young man from Maine, might break, as he did, the Seward unity of that state's delegates. Richard J. Oglesby, as a Whig Free-Soiler raised in Kentucky, would do his best with his rough hearty jargon among the Kentucky delegates and those from Missouri. John M. Palmer, a loyal Democrat until the Kansas-Nebraska Bill, would be effective among former Democrats, while Gustave Koerner, the German-born refugee, would be a demon at breaking down the chances of Bates who in 1856 had lent his name to the Know-Nothings.

Judge Stephen T. Logan, William H. Herndon, Ward Hill Lamon, who knew Lincoln from close association, could testify where needed in personal talk with doubtful delegates. Helping on many errands and interviews would be the lawyers William W. Orme of Bloomington and Nathan M. Knapp of Winchester. Illinois state treasurer, William Butler, at whose house Lincoln once boarded, and Ozias M. Hatch, Illinois secretary of state, were no greenhorns in politics, and Jesse K. Dubois, state auditor, was about the closest coadjutor of the shrewd chief manipulator, Judge Davis. A born trader and man of affairs, Davis owned 10,000 acres of land in Iowa, many farms and tracts in Illinois, and was often rated a millionaire.

In the parlor of the Lincoln headquarters were cigars and wine, porter, brandy, whisky, for any delegate or important guest; the total bill, $321.50, was paid by Hatch and Lamon. They called in delegates and held quiet private talks or made speeches to groups; Thurlow Weed at his Seward headquarters in the Richmond House was using the same methods. Medill and Charles H. Ray of the *Tribune* were on hand with ideas and their influence. Weaving from caucus to caucus were Andrew G. Curtin of Pennsylvania and Henry S. Lane of Indiana; each was running for governor in his state and each solemnly positive that their states would be lost if Seward was nominated. The same gospel of gloom about Seward came from David Dudley

Field, George Opdyke and other New Yorkers who had come on to stop Seward. Innocent-faced Horace Greeley went hither and yon saying he had only goodwill toward Seward but the man to carry the country was Bates. A long roll could be called of the delegates who day and night buttonholed others and told them Seward couldn't carry the doubtful states of Pennsylvania, New Jersey, Indiana and Illinois.

From the midwest states people had swarmed into Chicago, proud and curious about the first great national convention to be held so far west. New York had sent a thousand to shout and cheer for Seward; among them was Tom Hyer, the champion heavyweight prize fighter. Pennsylvania sent 1,500 marchers to see the big show and help Pennsylvania. A Wisconsin delegate had to register at a cheap hotel where, after inspecting the bed, as he told it, "I spent the rest of the night in a chair, as sure as my name is Carl Schurz." Processions with brass bands and bright nobby uniforms marched, cheering candidates. During the three days of the convention the crowd outside the Wigwam was two and three times the size of the one inside; relays of orators made speeches. A thousand saloons had customers making holiday and hullabaloo. Mark Delahay wrote two rambling, boozy letters to Lincoln, reporting in his way that the confusion was confounding.

Delegate Knapp wrote to Lincoln May 14: "We are laboring to make you the second choice of all the Delegations we can where we can not make you first choice. We are dealing tenderly with delegates, taking them in detail, and making no fuss . . . brace your nerves for any result."

The day before the convention opened, May 15, Davis and Dubois wired Lincoln: "We are quiet but moving heaven & Earth. Nothing will beat us but old fogy politicians." The next day Judd's message was: "Dont be frightened. Keep cool. Things is working." On the afternoon of May 17 the platform was adopted in a sweep of yells and cheers. The Seward men then wanted to ballot on candidates; a motion to that effect was made but the chair said "the tally-sheets had not been prepared" and on a quick motion to adjourn and by a light unrecorded vote, Chairman George Ashmun announced the motion prevailed and the convention was adjourned. The moment was fateful; Seward men believed they could have nominated their man that afternoon. That May 17 the main Lincoln backers worked all night and clinched important deals. Davis telegraphed Lincoln: "Am very hopeful. Dont be Excited. Nearly dead with fatigue. Telegraph or write here very little."

Dubois and other Lincoln men went into conference with the Pennsylvania and Indiana delegations. "We worked like nailers," said Oglesby. Ray of the *Tribune* came to his chief, Medill. "We are going to have Indiana for Old Abe, sure." "How did you get it?" asked Medill. "By the Lord, we promised them everything they asked." Caleb B. Smith was to be Secretary of the Interior and William P. Dole, Commissioner of Indian Affairs; Indiana would vote a solid block for Lincoln on the first ballot. Pennsylvania with its block of 54 delegates wearing white hats would vote for Simon Cameron, as a favorite son, on the first ballot, and then were willing to go elsewhere. Judge Davis dickered with them; Dubois telegraphed Lincoln the Cameron delegates could be had if Cameron was promised the Treasury Department. Lincoln wired back, "I authorize no bargains and will be bound by none."

A message from Lincoln was carried to Chicago by Edward L. Baker, editor of the Springfield *Journal;* it was a copy of a newspaper with markings of Seward speeches, with Lincoln's marginal notes, "I agree with Seward's 'Irrepressible Conflict,' but I do not endorse his 'Higher Law' doctrine," and then Lincoln's underlined words, "Make no contracts that will bind me." Why Lincoln should send such cryptic messages to old companions who were losing sleep, spending money and toiling fearfully to make him President was anybody's guess. He may have believed that in the rush and heat of events some corrupt bargain might be made, and he would have these messages to show. Definitely, too, out of his many years of close association with him he knew Davis' mind, will and conscience, and such peremptory messages from him would not stop the judge from a resolved purpose to nominate Lincoln.

What happened next was told by Whitney: "The bluff Dubois said, 'Damn Lincoln!' The polished Swett said, 'I am very sure if Lincoln was aware of the necessities—'" The critical Logan expectorated, 'The main difficulty with Lincoln is—' Herndon ventured, 'Now, friend, I'll answer that.' But Davis cut the Gordian knot by brushing all aside with, 'Lincoln ain't here, and don't know what we have to meet, so we will go ahead, as if we hadn't heard from him, and he must ratify it!' "

In that mood they went to the Pennsylvania managers. When they were through they came down to the lobby of the Tremont House, where Medill of the *Tribune* had been smoking and thinking about a remark of Lincoln's that Pennsylvania would be important in the convention. As Medill saw 300-pound Judge Davis come heaving and puffing down the stairs about midnight, he stepped up to the judge and, as he told it later, asked him what Pennsylvania was going to do. And Judge Davis: "Damned if we haven't got them." "How did you get them?" "By paying their price."

Then came Ray, who had sat in and heard. And Medill asked his editor how Pennsylvania had been nailed down. "Why," said Ray, "we promised to put Simon Cameron in the Cabinet. They wanted assurances that we represented Lincoln, and he would do what we said." "What have you agreed to give Cameron?" asked Medill. "The Treasury Department." "Good heavens! Give Cameron the Treasury Department? What will be left?" "Oh, what is the difference?" said Ray. "We are after a bigger thing than that; we want the Presidency and the Treasury is not a great stake to pay for it."

And so, with three state delegations solid, and with odd votes from Ohio and other states, the Lincoln men waited for the balloting, seeing to it, however, that the convention seating committee carefully sandwiched the Pennsylvania delegation between Illinois and Indiana.

When the platform was adopted the day before, leaving out mention of the Declaration of Independence, old Joshua R. Giddings arose, and said it was time to walk out of the Republican party. Then young George William Curtis of *Harper's Weekly* stood up and shamed the convention; the principle of the equality of men was written in and Giddings stayed on.

Seward victory was in the air; champagne fizzed at the Richmond House. Straw votes on all incoming railroad trains had given Seward overwhelming majorities. Michigan, Wisconsin, Minnesota, were a unit for Seward, as were the New York, Massachusetts (except four who were for Lincoln) and California delegations. Horace Greeley wired his New York *Tribune* that Seward seemed sure to win. Lincoln workers were saying with clenched fists and blazing eyes that the Republicans were beaten at the start if Seward headed the ticket. They scared a definite element who wanted to win; and again there were antislavery men such as Bryant of the New York *Evening Post* who believed Seward to be the same type as Daniel Webster, much intellect, little faith, none of the "mystic simplicity" of Lincoln.

Lamon had been to the printers of seat tickets. Young men worked nearly a whole night signing names of convention officers to counterfeit seat tickets so that next day Lincoln men could jam the hall and leave no seats for the Seward shouters. Hour on hour the bulk of the 40,000 strangers in Chicago kept up noise and tumult for Abraham Lincoln, for Old Abe, for the Rail Candidate. Judd had fixed it with the railroads so that any shouter who wished could set foot in Chicago at a low excursion rate. Men illuminated with moral fire, and others red-eyed with whisky, yelled, pranced, cut capers and vociferated for Lincoln.

On the first two days of the convention's routine business the Seward men were allowed by the Chicago managers to have free run of the floor. But on May 18, when sunrise saw thousands milling about the Wigwam doors, the Lincoln shouters were shoved through the doors till they filled all seats and standing room; hundreds of New York hurrah boys couldn't squeeze in. Lamon and Fell got a thousand men recruited for their lung power; they had been given tickets and were on hand. They watched their leaders, two men located on opposite sides of the Wigwam. One of them, Dr. Ames of Chicago, it was said, could "on a calm day" be heard clear across Lake Michigan. The other one, brought by Delegate Burton Cook from Ottawa, could give out with a warm monster voice. These two Leather Lungs watched Cook on the platform; when he took out his handkerchief they cut loose with all they had and kept it up till Cook put his handkerchief back. They were joined by the thousand recruits picked for voice noise.

Nomination speeches were in single sentences. Judd said, "I desire, on behalf of the delegation from Illinois, to put in nomination, as a candidate for President of the United States, Abraham Lincoln, of Illinois." Here Cook took out his handkerchief. "The idea of us Hoosiers and Suckers being outscreamed would have been bad," said Swett. "Five thousand people leaped to their seats, women not wanting, and the wild yell made vesper breathings of all that had preceded. A thousand steam whistles, ten acres of hotel gongs, a tribe of Comanches might have mingled in the scene unnoticed."

Seward had 173½ votes, Lincoln 102, and favorite sons and others the remainder of the votes on the first ballot. On the second ballot, Lincoln jumped to 181 as against Seward's 184½. On the third ballot, of the 465 votes Lincoln swept 231½ while Seward dropped to 180. Medill of the *Tribune* whispered to Cartter of Ohio, "If you can throw the Ohio delegation for Lincoln, Chase can have anything he wants." "H-how d'-d'ye know?" stuttered Cartter, Medill answering, "I know, and you know I wouldn't promise if I didn't know."

Cartter called for a change of four votes from his state to Lincoln. Other delegates announced changes of votes to Lincoln. As the tellers footed up the totals, and the chairman waited for the figures, the chatter of 10,000 people stopped, the fluttering of ladies' fans ended, the scratching of pencils and the clicking of the telegraph dot-dash dash-dot-dash could be heard. The 900 reporters from everywhere in America clutched their pencils.

The chairman spoke. Of 465 votes, 364 were cast for the candidate highest, and "Abraham Lincoln, of Illinois, is selected as your candidate for President of the United States."

Chairmen of state delegations arose and made the nomi-

nation unanimous. The terrific emotional spree was over.
Strong men hugged each other, wept, laughed and shrieked
in each other's faces through tears. Judge Logan stood on a
. table, brandished his arms and yelled, swung wild his new
silk hat and on somebody's head smashed it flat. Inside
and outside the Wigwam it was a wild noon hour; hats,
handkerchiefs, umbrellas, in the air; brass bands blaring;
cannon explosions on the roof getting answers from city
bells, riverboat and railroad whistles.

Hannibal Hamlin, the Maine senator, a former Democrat, was nominated for Vice-President, and thanks voted
to the convention chairman, George Ashmun of Massachusetts. Seward's manager, Thurlow Weed, pressed the temples of his forehead to hold back tears but the tears came.
Greeley wrote it was a fearful week he hoped never to see
repeated. "If you had seen the Pennsylvania delegation,
and known how much money Weed had in hand, you
would not have believed we could do so well as we did . . .
We had to rain red-hot bolts on them, however, to keep
the majority from going for Seward."

Knapp telegraphed Lincoln: "We did it. Glory to God,"
and Fell: "City wild with excitement. From my inmost
heart I congratulate you." Swett warned, "Dont let any one
persuade you to come here," Dubois and Butler saying:
"Do not come without we telegraph you," Judd more brief:
"Do not come to Chicago," and Koerner briefest of all:
"Dont come here."

On May 18 Lincoln walked from home to his office and
was talking with two law students when the office door
burst open and the *Journal* editor, Baker, told him of the
first ballot in Chicago. They walked to the telegraph office,
found no later news, and at the *Journal* office met a crowd
shouting good news would be coming. Lincoln slouched in
a chair but straightened up at the next news of his big gains
on the second ballot. And when the wires sang that his
nomination had been made unanimous, he knew that a
great somber moment had come to him and the firing of
100 jubilant guns made a shadowed music. He read a flurry
of gay telegrams, shook hands all round, then went home

to tell the news and see his wife's face beam and glow. In the afternoon he shook hands with many callers.

Bonfires of boxes, barrels and brushwood lighted up the Sangamon River country that Friday night. A brass band and a cheering crowd at the Lincoln house surged to the front porch and called for a speech. He saw the honor of the nomination not for him personally but as the representative of a cause; he wished his house big enough so he could ask them all inside. Shouts and yells of hurrah parties broke on the night till the gray dawn of the morning after.

Judge Davis answered a question on what the wild week cost: "The entire expense of Lincoln's nomination, including headquarters, telegraphing, music, fare of delegations, and other incidentals, was less than $700."

Elements that Lincoln had described as "strange and discordant, gathered from the four winds," had formed a powerful party of youth, wild banners, pilgrims of faith and candlelight philosophers, besides hopeful politicians. Industrial, transportation and financial interests found this party promising. Pennsylvania, New York, New England, were satisfied as to both the tariff and the outlook for opening up the Great Plains to settlement and trade. "A Railroad to the Pacific Ocean is imperatively demanded by the interests of the whole country; the Federal Government ought to render immediate and efficient aid in its construction," read the Republican platform plank.

Hordes of politicians had hitched themselves to the Republican party seeing it as a winner; the Government was spending $80,000,000 a year; offices, contracts and favors lay that way; in their connections these politicians had manufacturing and mercantile interests, iron, steel, coal, oil, railroads and steamboats.

In its platform promises on tariff, on land and homestead laws, on farm and factory legislation to benefit workingmen, industry and business, the Republican party had a sincerity, was attending to issues in degree long neglected or evaded. Various practical interests saw to it that their political workers had front seats, committee places and influence in the new party. Before one issue all others shrank, that of union and the wage-labor system as against disunion and slave labor. Carl Schurz had yelled, to a storm of cheers, "We defy the whole slave power and the whole vassalage of hell." A cadence of exasperation, a strain of revolutionary rumble and mutter, rose, died down, and rose again.

The man in Springfield picked to carry the banner stood at moments as a shy and furtive figure. He wanted the place —and he didn't. His was precisely the clairvoyance that knew terrible days were ahead. He had his hesitations. And he was in the end the dark horse on whom the saddle was put. He could contemplate an old proverb: "The horse thinks one thing, he that saddles him another."

The notification committee at his house formally told Lincoln he was nominated for President. He formally replied, and later, after reading the platform, sent a letter of acceptance. He would co-operate, "imploring the assistance of Divine Providence."

In June the adjourned Democratic national convention met in Baltimore, and after bitter and furious debates, nominated Douglas of Illinois for President and Herschel Johnson, a Georgia unionist, for Vice-President. Delegates from 11 slave states walked out, bolted their old party, and nominated John C. Breckinridge of Kentucky for President and Joseph Lane of Oregon for Vice-President. They rejected with scorn and hate Douglas' "popular sovereignty" and his leadership; they believed with John Randolph who 40 years earlier had advised secession, saying, "Asking a state to surrender part of her sovereignty is like asking a lady to surrender part of her chastity." When Stephens of Georgia was asked what he was thinking, "Why, that men will be cutting one another's throats in a little while. In less than twelve months we shall be in a war, and that the bloodiest in history."

To Judge Davis came many letters asking how Lincoln, if elected, would deal with patronage and offices, with party factions, with coming issues and events. Davis requested Lincoln to guide him in answering such letters. Lincoln wrote May 26 for Davis "the body of such a letter as I think you should write . . . in your own handwriting," adding whatever assurances Davis might "think fit." The letter for Davis' use was vastly implicative, luminously shrewd yet wise, comprehensive yet brief, as an indication in that hour of the mingled peace and turmoil in Lincoln's mind and conscience. It read:

> Since parting with you, I have had full, and frequent conversations with Mr. Lincoln. The substance of what he says is that he neither is nor will be, in advance of the election, committed to any man, clique, or faction; and that, in case the new administration shall devolve upon him, it will be his pleasure, and, in his view, the part of duty, and wisdom, to deal fairly with all. He thinks he will need the assistance of all; and that, even if he had friends to reward, or enemies to punish, as he has not, he could not afford to dispense with the best talents, nor to outrage the popular will in any locality.

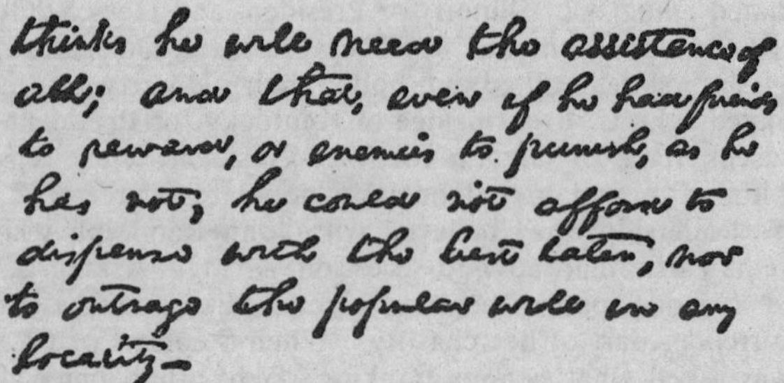
thinks he will need the assistance of
all; and that, even if he had friends
to reward, or enemies to punish, as he
has not; he could not afford to
dispense with the best talent, nor
to outrage the popular will in any
locality—

From original letter written by Lincoln to David Davis

Judge Davis kept close track of the Midwest campaign, and August 24 wrote from Bloomington to Thurlow Weed that he had been in Indiana and found the Republican party in danger of losing that state. "They believe that with

$10,000 the State can be carried . . . The election may run itself, as it is doing in a great many States, but, depend upon it, without pecuniary aid, there can be neither certainty nor efficiency." Among those keeping Lincoln in touch with the campaign machinery were Davis, Swett and Judd. Errands between Illinois, New York and Pennsylvania were indicated in a letter of Swett to Thurlow Weed: "We should be exceedingly glad to know your wishes and your views, and to serve you in any way in our power. I say this freely for myself because I feel it, and for Judge Davis, because, although now absent, I know his feelings. Of course, nobody is authorized to speak for Mr. Lincoln."

Wide-Awake clubs of young men in uniforms marched in torchlight processions. Seward spoke across the Northern States; Lincoln went to the railway station to pay him a cordial greeting when he passed through Springfield. Batteries and flotillas of orators spoke. They argued, threatened, promised, appealed to statistics, passions, history. But the high chosen spokesman of the party had little or nothing to say. He wrote a few letters, and shook hands with orators, politicians and reporters who came by the dozen and score to the house on Eighth Street. He spoke August 8 when railroads, buggies, horses and ox wagons brought 50,000 people to Springfield. He greeted them; the "fight for this cause" would go on "though I be dead and gone." He ended: "You will kindly let me be silent."

Follet, Foster & Company announced a biography of Lincoln, *authorized* by him, which brought his outburst, "I have scarcely been so much astounded by anything, as by their public announcement . . . I certainly knew they contemplated publishing a biography, and I certainly did not object to their doing so, *upon their own responsibility*." He had even helped them. But, "At the same time, I made myself tiresome, if not hoarse, with repeating my protest to Mr. Howard, their only agent seen by me, my protest that I *authorized nothing*—would be *responsible for nothing.*"

Five hack biographies sprouted in June. Later came more pretentious and competent biographies, bound in boards, one by William Dean Howells, the best by D. W. Bartlett, a 354-page volume with a steel engraving of Lincoln. Six editions were printed of the New York *Tribune*'s impressive *Political Text Book for 1860,* 248 pages of the most notable speeches and documents of all parties. In campaign literature the Republicans far surpassed the Democrats. Medals and coins were struck, one medal praising soap on one side and the candidate on the other. Requests for autographs flooded in. Wendell Phillips was asking, "Who is this huckster in politics?" Seward was saying, "No truer defender of the Republican faith could have been found."

Newspapers came, estimating Lincoln as "a third-rate country lawyer"; he lived "in low Hoosier style"; he "could not speak good grammar"; he delivered "coarse and clumsy jokes"; he was descended from "an African gorilla." Letters asked his view on this or that. And secretary John G. Nicolay sent all the same answer; his positions were well known when he was nominated; he must not now "embarrass the canvass."

Slimy, putrid and reeking, was an article in the Macomb, Illinois, *Eagle,* in August 1860, printing what it claimed to be "an extract of a speech made by Mr. Lincoln in 1844." It quoted Lincoln as saying:

> Mr. Jefferson is a statesman whose praises are never out of the mouths of the Democratic party . . . The character of Jefferson was repulsive. Continually puling about liberty, equality, and the degrading curse of slavery, he brought his own children to the hammer, and made money of his debaucheries. Even at his death he did not manumit his numerous offspring, but left them soul and body to degradation and the cart whip. A daughter of this vaunted champion of democracy was sold some years ago at public auction in New Orleans.

To one who sent him a clipping of it, Lincoln wrote, "I do not recognize it as anything I have ever seen before, emanating from any source. I wish my name not to be used; but my friends will be entirely safe in denouncing the thing as a forgery." To a Boston group who invited him to a Jefferson birthday festival he had declined, writing:

Those claiming political descent from him have nearly ceased to breathe his name everywhere . . . soberly, it is now no child's play to save the principles of Jefferson from total overthrow in this nation . . . The principles of Jefferson are the definitions and axioms of free society . . . All honor to Jefferson—to the man, who, in the concrete pressure of a struggle for national independence by a single people, had the coolness, forecast, and capacity to introduce into a merely revolutionary document, an abstract truth, applicable to all men and all times, and so to embalm it there, that to-day, and in all coming days, it shall be a rebuke and a stumbling-block to the very harbingers of re-appearing tyrany and oppression.

John Locke Scripps, a Chicago *Tribune* editor, had a long interview with Lincoln, and on his request Lincoln wrote for his use a 2,500-word autobiography. From this Scripps wrote a 32-page close-print pamphlet titled "Life of Abraham Lincoln." Scripps wrote to a brother, "I have been getting out a campaign Life of Lincoln for the million which is published simultaneously by us [the Chicago *Tribune*] and by the *New York Tribune*." Though Scripps was rushed, and wrote against time, he produced a little book packed with a charming readable story having documents and dignity. A million copies at five cents apiece meant millions of readers now had a few answers to, "Who and what is Abraham Lincoln, his folks, his ways, his looks, his home, his beliefs and policies?" His education? "He was never in a college or an academy as a student, and was never, in fact, inside of a college or academy building until after he had commenced the practice of the law. He studied English grammar after he was twenty-three years of age; . . . he studied the six books of Euclid after he had served a term in Congress, and when he was forty years of age, amid the pressure of an extensive legal practice." He knew about hard work from "splitting rails, pulling the cross-cut and the whip-saw, driving the frower, plowing, harrowing, planting, hoeing, harvesting." He knew about sports. "In wrestling, jumping, running, throwing the maul and pitching the crow-bar, he always stood first among those of his own age."

Scripps in his book quoted Douglas as saying in one debate in 1858, "Lincoln is one of those peculiar men who perform with admirable skill everything they undertake." And Scripps wrote further: In many cases where "a poor client" had "justice and right on his side," Mr. Lincoln charged no fee and sometimes quietly slipped the client a five or ten dollar bill. His Mexican War record, his bill to abolish slavery in the District of Columbia, the debates with Douglas were elaborately documented. And personally, his six-feet-four-inch frame "is not muscular, but gaunt and wiry. In walking, his gait, though firm, is never brisk. He steps slowly and deliberately, almost always with his head inclined forward, and his hands clasped behind his back." At rest, his features were not handsome, "but when his fine, dark-grey eyes are lighted up by any emotion, and his features begin their play, he would be chosen from among a crowd as one who had in him not only the kindly sentiments which women love, but the heavier metal of which full-grown men and Presidents are made." As to religion, "He . . . is a pew-holder and liberal supporter of the Presbyterian Church in Springfield, to which Mrs. Lincoln belongs." Scripps believed of Lincoln, "He has an exquisite sense of justice." On only this one point was Lincoln found "exquisite." Of the millions who read the pamphlet biography, many sat brooding, inquiring, thoughtful, about this fabulous human figure of their own time.

In this summer of 1860 Lincoln saw a powerful young political party shaping his figure into heroic stature, coloring his personality beyond reality. From hundreds of stump orators and newspapers came praise and outcry for "Abe," "Old Abe," "the Rail Candidate," "the Backwoodsman," "Honest Abe," "the Man of the People," the sagacious, eloquent Man of the Hour, one who starting from a dirt-floor cabin was to move into the Executive Mansion in Washington.

What men there had been who had gone up against the test and gone down before it! What heartbreaking challenge there was in the act of heading a government where vast sensitive property interests and management problems called for practical executive ability, while millions of people hungered for some mystic bread of life, for land, roads, freedom. They were the titanic, breathing, groaning, snarling, singing, murmuring, irreckonable instrument through which, and on which, history, destiny, politicians worked— The People—the public that had to be reached for the making of public opinion.

Chicago politicians were saying Lincoln seemed to be in "rough everyday rig" in his pictures. Lincoln had written he would be "dressed up" if Hesler, the Chicago photographer, came to Springfield. And Hesler made four fine negatives of Lincoln in a stiff-bosomed, pleated shirt with pearl buttons. Volk, the sculptor, arrived, had a rose bouquet from Mrs. Lincoln, and presented her with a bust of her husband. A round stick was needed for Lincoln's hands while Volk made casts. Lincoln stepped out to the woodshed and returned to the dining room whittling a broom handle. The edges didn't need such careful whittling, Volk remarked. "Oh, well, I thought I would like to have it nice." Sitting for one portrait, as the likeness emerged Lincoln said, "There's the animal himself."

Douglas stumped the country in what seemed for him a losing fight; he went on tireless, men amazed at the way he wore out, went to bed, and came back fighting. At Norfolk, Virginia, in late August he told an audience of 7,000 that he wanted no votes except from men who desired the Union to be preserved. On a slip of paper handed him was the question whether, if the South seceded, he would advise resistance by force. To this he flashed, "I answer emphatically that it is the duty of the President of the United States and all others in authority under him to enforce the laws of the United States as passed by Congress and as the courts expound them . . . In other words, I think the President of the United States, whoever he may be, should treat all attempts to break up resistance to its· laws as Old Hickory treated the Nullifiers in 1832." At Raleigh, North Carolina, he said he would "hang every man higher than Haman" who resisted Constitutional law. No Illinoisan would ever consent to pay duty on corn shipped down the Mississippi. "We furnish the water that makes the great river, and we will follow it throughout its whole course to the ocean, no matter who or what may stand before us."

At places in the North he favored "burying Southern disunionism and Northern abolitionism in the same grave," saying, too, that if Old Hickory were alive he would "hang Northern and Southern traitors on the same gallows." The Pacific railway and other dreams would never come true "unless you banish forever the slavery question from the halls of Congress and remand it to the people of each state and territory."

In Cedar Rapids, Iowa, on news in October of Republicans sweeping Pennsylvania, Douglas turned to his secretary, "Mr. Lincoln is the next President," adding, "We must try to save the Union. I will go South." In Tennessee, Georgia and Alabama, he spoke to large crowds, often amid threats and jeers of thugs and rotten fruit and eggs meant to reach his head. In Atlanta, Alexander Stephens, though Douglas was not his first choice for President, introduced Douglas with warm praise. Harassed and in sinking health, Douglas spoke in the Deep South with passion and storm in his voice of the love he held for the Union and his scorn of those who would break up the Union. Mr. Lincoln in Springfield must have been deeply moved when he read some of these Douglas speeches.

Letters kept coming to Lincoln—what would he do with slavery if elected? Would he interfere? Would it not be wise now to say plainly he wouldn't interfere? One he had answered, "Those who will not read, or heed, what I have already publicly said, would not read, or heed, a repetition of it." He wrote to a pro-Douglas Louisville editor, "I have *bad* men also to deal with, both North and South,—men who are eager for something new upon which to base new misrepresentations,—men who would like to frighten me, or, at least fix upon me the character of timidity and cowardice."

He wrote Swett about a matter concerning Weed and others, his main point in one sentence, "It can not have failed to strike you that these men ask for just, the same thing—*fairness*, and fairness only." But he ended the letter, "Burn this, not that there is any thing wrong in it; but because it is best not to be known that I write at all."

When the notification committee had called, he soberly brought them a pitcher of ice water. Mrs. Lincoln was all ready with bottles of champagne but Koerner warned that wouldn't do; it would be told against them. Lincoln loosened the stiff occasion by calling on a tall judge to stand up and measure height with him.

The campaign came to its last week. As the summer and fall drew on he was to those who met him the same friendly neighbor as always—but with more to think about. He shook hands with Whitney in a big crowd, and a half-hour later, seeing Whitney again, he shook hands and called him by name. "He didn't know me the first time," said Whitney.

Millions of people had by this time read his words of two years ago in the House Divided speech. They struck the soft, weird keynote of the hour. "If we could first know *where* we are, and *whither* we are tending, we could then better judge *what* to do, and *how* to do it."

Twice, since he had first so spoken, the corn had grown from seed to the full stalk and been harvested. In a book he had carried, it was told, "All rising to power is by a winding stair." As he went higher it was colder and lonelier. The last leaves were blowing off the trees and the final geese honking south. Winter would come and go before seed corn went into the ground again.

Early reports on election evening, November 6, gave Douglas 3,598 votes and Lincoln 3,556 in Sangamon County while in Springfield Lincoln had 1,395 against 1,326 for Douglas. From nine o'clock on he sat in the Springfield telegraph office. Lincoln with friends stepped across the street to where the Republican Ladies' Club had fixed a supper. The ladies rushed him. "How do you do, Mr. President?" Hardly were the men seated when a messenger rushed in waving a telegram. New York had gone Republican. Lincoln's election was clinched.

In the streets, and around the Statehouse, crowds surged, shouting themselves hoarse. The jubilee was still going as

Lincoln walked home to say to a happy woman, "Mary, we're elected." The local *Journal* was saying, "Our city is as quiet as a young lady who has just found out that she is in love."

In Mobile, Alabama, Douglas had told a large audience that their rights would be far safer in the Union than outside. In the office of the *Register* he read dispatches. They told him only what he had expected. He tried to read the coming events in the light of his knowing from high sources that scores of powerful Southern leaders had their plans for secession on the election of Lincoln. He knew what his course would be. He had told the South what it would be. He was tired and sad but he had spent his life in storms and was ready for the next one.

The national count gave Lincoln 1,866,452 votes; Douglas, 1,376,957; Breckenridge, 849,781; Bell, 588,879. Lincoln had majorities in 17 Free States, Breckinridge carried 11 Slave States, Bell 3 Slave States. In the electoral college Douglas had only the 3 votes of New Jersey and the 9 of Missouri. The total electoral college votes looked a little silly, giving dim light on the popular balloting, with Lincoln, 180; Breckinridge, 72; Bell, 39; Douglas, 12. In a total of some 4,700,000 votes the other combined candidates had nearly a million more votes than Lincoln. Fifteen states gave him no electoral votes; in ten states of the South he didn't get a count of one popular vote. He was the most sectionally elected President the nation had ever had and the fact would be dinned into his ears.

Events marched and masked their meanings. Facts were gathering motion, whisking into new shapes and disguises every day. Dream shapes of future events danced into sight and out of sight, faded and came again, before a whirligig of triple mirrors.

Chapter 15

The House Dividing

Lincoln's election was a signal. The Atlanta newspaper, *Confederacy*, spoke for those who had visions of violence: "Let the consequences be what they may—whether the Potomac is crimsoned in human gore, and Pennsylvania Avenue is paved ten fathoms deep with mangled bodies, or whether the last vestige of liberty is swept from the face of the American continent, the South will never submit to such humiliation and degradation as the inauguration of Abraham Lincoln." This was in part bravado and blowoff and in part hope and determination.

Equally flaring and vivid in Boston was Wendell Phillips, speaking for an abolitionist faction: "Let the South march off, with flags and trumpets, and we will speed the parting guest . . . All hail, disunion! . . . Let the border states go. Then we part friends. The Union thus ended, the South no longer hates the North . . . The laws of trade will bind us together, as they do all other lands." Mildly the innocent-faced Greeley chimed in, "Let the erring sisters depart in peace."

In North Carolina, the Raleigh *Banner* spoke for a small segment of the South: "The big heart of the people is still in the Union. Less than a hundred politicians are endeavoring to destroy the liberties and usurp the rights of more than thirty millions of people. If the people permit it, they deserve the horrors of the civil war which will ensue."

South Carolina legislators voted to raise and equip 10,000 volunteer soldiers; Georgia voted $1,000,000 and Louisiana $500,000 for guns and men. Robert Toombs was saying: "It is admitted that you seek to outlaw $4,000,-000,000 of property of our people . . . Is not that a cause of war?" But was secession the safest immediate way of managing this property? Jefferson Davis had hopes and doubts. And Alexander Stephens had written, "I consider slavery much more secure in the Union than out of it if our people were but wise."

In the day's mail for Lincoln came letters cursing him for an ape and a baboon who had brought the country evil. He was buffoon and monster; an abortion, an idiot; they prayed he would be flogged, burned, hanged, tortured. Pen sketches of gallows and daggers arrived from "oath-bound brotherhoods." Mrs. Lincoln saw unwrapped a painting on canvas, her husband with a rope around his neck, his feet chained, his body tarred and feathered.

A Tennessee woman wrote of her dream about how to keep out of war. Another suggested he should have all his food tasted. Still another letter told Lincoln to resign at the inaugural and appoint Douglas as the new President.

A chemist and metal-worker, A. W. Flanders of Burlington, Iowa, in letters to Nicolay, explained with intelligent detail that he could have made secretly a shirt of mail, of flexible chain armor, "plated with gold so that perspiration shall not affect it. It could be covered with silk and worn over an ordinary undershirt." Flanders would "be very happy to get this done for Mr. Lincoln," but his kindly and generous offer could not be accepted.

On the way to Chicago November 21 Lincoln made a two-minute speech at Bloomington, referred to the expressed will of the people, and, "I think very much of the people, as an old friend said he thought of woman. He said when he lost his first wife, who had been a great help to him in his business, he thought he was ruined—that he could never find another to fill her place. At length, however, he married another . . . and that his opinion now was that *any woman would do well who was well done by.*"

In Chicago, as he had arranged by letters, he met Vice-President-elect Hamlin and Joshua Speed. He wasn't sure he had ever before met Hamlin but he had heard him speak in the Senate. Hamlin couldn't remember having met Lincoln but he had heard him in the House in a speech that had "auditors convulsed with laughter." People so crowded in on the two important men in the Tremont House that they went for their conference to a private home. Lincoln wished in appointments to hold a balance between Whigs who had turned Republican and Democrats who had turned Republican. He would trust Hamlin to name the New England member of his Cabinet for Secretary of the Navy, giving Hamlin three names he inclined to favor, Hamlin deciding on a former Jackson Democrat, Gideon Welles, a Hartford editor.

They both favored Seward for Secretary of State. Lincoln soon after wrote one short letter notifying Seward he would appoint him Secretary of State and a longer letter giving Seward Lincoln's belief "that your position in the public eye, your integrity, ability, learning," made the appointment "pre-eminently fit." These two letters Lincoln sent to Hamlin, writing, "Consult with Judge Trumbull; and if you and he see no reason to the contrary, deliver the letter to Governor Seward at once. If you see reason to the contrary, write me at once." Trumbull wasn't eager about Seward but he consented; so Hamlin delivered Lincoln's two letters to Seward, and Seward, after pretending to think deeply about it, accepted.

With Joshua Speed, Lincoln discussed the outlook in Kentucky, possible appointments there, and casually asked Speed how he was fixed for money, income, wherewithal. Speed flashed back that he knew why Lincoln was asking such a question and he didn't need any office Lincoln could offer him, which pleased them both.

The trains into Springfield on a single day would unload hundreds of passengers, arriving to see the President-elect. Some carried shining faces; they just wanted to look at him and tell him they hoped to God he'd live and have good luck. Others, too, carried shining faces, singing, "Ain't we glad we joined the Republicans?" They said they nominated and elected him President, and inquired about post offices, revenue collectorships, clerkships, secretaryships. They wore him. Behind their smiles some had snouts like buzzards, pigs, rats. They were pap-seekers, sapsuckers, chair-warmers, hammock-heroes, the office-sniffing mob that had killed Zach Taylor, that had killed Tippecanoe Harrison. They wore Lincoln—worse than the signs of war.

The office seekers watched Lincoln's habits, waylaid him, wedged in, and reminded him not to forget them. If personally refused, they sent appeals again to Lincoln's ear through friends. One who kept coming, by one device and another pressing claims on Lincoln, was Judge Davis. As Whitney told it: "Lincoln inveighed to me in the bitterest terms against Judge Davis' greed and importunity for office, and summarized his disgust in these words, 'I know it is an awful thing for me to say, but I already wish some one else was here in my place.'"

Smart alecks came, often committees of them, guffawing at their own lame jokes, with thrusts of familiarity at Lincoln as though they might next be tickling him in the ribs. Whitney saw Lincoln one afternoon, with smiling humor, usher the last member of such a committee out of the door, and Whitney remarked, "I wish I could take as rose-colored a view of the situation as you seem to." Lincoln's smiles had all crept back into the leathery fissures of his face, as he told Whitney: "I hope you don't feel worse about it than I do. I can't sleep nights."

Strong-hearted, black-eyed Hannah Armstrong came, the widow of Jack, the mother of Duff. Lincoln took her two hands. They talked, homely and heart-warming talk. He held the hands that had been good to him, so long ago, when he was young and the sap ran wild in him. And as she was going: "They'll kill ye, Abe." "Hannah, if they do kill me, I shall never die another death."

The gray-bearded, quiet-mannered Judge Edward Bates on invitation visited Lincoln, and consented to be U.S. Attorney General, "a fine antique," ran one comment. Against Indiana and Illinois factions, Lincoln kept a convention pledge to appoint Caleb B. Smith of Indiana, a garden-variety spoils politician, to be Secretary of the Interior. Norman B. Judd, the Republican state chairman, wanted this or some other Cabinet place but couldn't swing it; Judge Davis worked against him and so did Mrs. Lincoln in writing Davis a letter of bitter dislike for Judd.

Thurlow Weed came from Albany, on Swett writing him

that Lincoln wanted to see him about Cabinet matters. They talked politics and issues in general. Would Bates of Missouri do for Attorney General? Yes, Weed was sure; he paid tribute to Bates' personal reliability. Telegrams had come from prominent Republicans trying to head off appointments Weed might seek, Lincoln told the New York leader.

Lincoln had long trained himself to put men at their ease while pumping them with quiet questions, learning by asking, and asking with keen, soft persistence. He knew that Weed was in touch with such men of power as A. T. Stewart, leading New York merchant, and August Belmont, New York representative of the Rothschilds, international bankers, and one of the northern capitalists to whom the South was in debt $200,000,000. Also Lincoln learned in elaborate detail how Weed hated and feared radicals North and South and favored all possible conciliation and appeasement of the South.

Salmon P. Chase, newly elected U.S. Senator from Ohio, came by invitation. Lincoln said he "wasn't exactly prepared" to appoint Chase Secretary of the Treasury, but if he did, would Chase accept? Chase wouldn't promise. He'd think it over. And he went away to line up friends to put pressure on Lincoln to appoint him.

Simon Cameron came and after long talks left with a letter signed by Lincoln:

> I think fit to notify you now, that by your permission, I shall, at the proper time, nominate you to the U.S. Senate, for confirmation as Secretary of the Treasury, or as Secretary of War—which of the two, I have not definitely decided. Please answer at your own earliest convenience.

Cameron's enemies brought evidence to Lincoln intended to show that Cameron was "the very incarnation of corruption" and his fortune "acquired by means forbidden to the man of honor." Lincoln wrote Cameron another letter; things had developed which made it impossible to take him into the Cabinet. Would he write a letter publicly declin-

ing any Cabinet place? And Cameron's answer was a bundle
of recommendations outnumbering the opposition three to
one; Lincoln later wrote Cameron that he wouldn't make a
Cabinet appointment for Pennsylvania without consulting
him.

Donn Piatt, an Ohio journalist, left Springfield to say,
"Lincoln told us he felt like a surveyor in the wild woods of
the West, who, while looking for a corner, kept an eye over
his shoulder for an Indian."

Henry Villard earlier had written of Lincoln: "More than
once I heard him 'with malice aforethought' get off purposely some repulsive fiction in order to rid himself of an
uncomfortable caller. Again and again I felt disgust and
humiliation that such a person should have been called
upon to direct the destinies of a great nation." Villard later
still, reporting for the New York *Herald*, judged the President-elect "a man of good heart and good intentions," but
"not firm." Weeks passed and he definitely saw Lincoln as
"a man of immense power and force of character and natural talent . . . a man to act and decide for himself . . . tremendously rough and tremendously honest and earnest."
Thus judgments, in favor and against, shifted as the winds
shift.

"Resistance to Lincoln is Obedience to God!" flared a
banner at an Alabama mass meeting; an orator swore that
if need be their troops would march to the doors of the
national Capitol over "fathoms of mangled bodies."

Against Southern advice that South Carolina wait till
President Buchanan's term ended, Robert Barnwell Rhett
and his forces had manipulated the precise dramatic event
of secession. As a Congressman of six terms and a U.S.
Senator of one term, as editor of the Charleston *Mercury*,
as lawyer and churchman, as manager of the Charleston
Bible Society, as vice-president of the Young Men's Temperance Society, as secretary of the Charleston Port Society
for promoting the Christian gospel among seamen, as the
father of 12 children, the driving motive of Rhett's life was
to win secession and Southern independence, build a confederacy on the cornerstone of African slavery, and restore

the African slave trade outlawed by the U.S. Constitution as of 1808. Rhett organized "minutemen" and vigilance committees, to make sure of delegates pledged to secession. He wrote the ordinance of disunion, and in secret session the convention's 169 delegates in St. Andrew's Hall at Charleston, December 16, 1860, passed it without debate in 45 minutes. A newly adopted flag brought a great shout, rocked the hall, and from lowlands to upcountry were bells, bonfires, torchlights, parades, shotgun salutes and cries of jubilee. One by one the six other Cotton States of the lower South joined South Carolina in leaving the Union.

Senators and Representatives from the South spoke sad and bitter farewells to Congress; U.S. postmasters, judges, district attorneys, customs collectors, by the hundreds sent their resignations to Washington. Of the 1,108 officers of the U.S. Regular Army, 387 were preparing resignations, many having already joined the Confederate armed forces. The U.S. mint at New Orleans and two smaller mints were taken over by the Confederate States, as were post offices and customhouses. Governors of seceded states marched in troops and took over U.S. forts that had cost $6,000,000.

Reports flew that Southern forces would seize Washington, Lincoln to be sworn in at some other place. Twenty-two carloads of troops were starting from Fort Leavenworth across Missouri for Baltimore. Cameron of Pennsylvania was saying, "Lincoln, if living, will take the oath of office on the Capitol steps." Dr. William Jayne of Springfield wrote to Trumbull, "Lincoln advised he would rather be hanged by the neck till he was dead on the steps of the Capitol than buy or beg a peaceful inauguration." Newly organized artillery companies were drilling in Chicago. A thousand Negro slaves were throwing up fortifications in Charleston, South Carolina. Governor Yates notified the legislature, "Illinois counts among her citizens 400,000 who can bear arms." Five million dollars and a hundred thousand troops would be offered by their state, Pennsylvania legislators were saying.

"The Revolution" was the top headline under which a New York daily paper assembled the news of the country. Nine columns were required on one day to report declarations of Southern conventions, and resignations from the Army, Navy and training academies. Stephens of Georgia had dug into history. "Revolutions are much easier started than controlled, and the men who begin them, even for the best purposes and object, seldom end them."

The New York *Herald,* circulating 77,000 copies daily, earning profits of $300,000 a year, advised in an editorial, "A grand opportunity now exists for Lincoln to avert impending ruin, and invest his name with an immortality far more enduring than would attach to it by his elevation to the Presidency. His withdrawal at this time from the scene of conflict, and the surrender of his claims to some national man who would be acceptable to both sections, would render him the peer of Washington in patriotism." And the *Herald* added: "If he persists in his present position . . . he will totter into a dishonoured grave, driven there perhaps by the hands of an assassin, leaving behind him a memory more excrable than that of Arnold—more despised than that of the traitor Catiline."

Senator Jefferson Davis, pale and just risen from a sick-bed, in January spoke his words of parting: "I offer you my apology for any thing I may have done in the Senate, and I go remembering no injury I have received." His regrets coupled to a warning: "There will be no peace if you so will it." Swiftly, on Davis' walking out forever, Senator William M. Gwin of California would vote $100,000,000 for a Pacific railway. But Crittenden of Kentucky said that, with the Union "reeling about like a drunken man," he could not see a Pacific railway. "Build up the Union first; then talk about building up a railroad."

If Lincoln should try to retake the seized forts, he would have to kill in sickening numbers, said John Y. Brown of Kentucky. "From the blood of your victims, as from the fabled dragons' teeth, will spring up crops of armed men, whose religion it will be to hate and curse you." "Very well, sir," said Thaddeus Stevens. "Rather than show repentance for the election of Mr. Lincoln, with all its consequences, I would see this Government crumble into a thousand atoms."

Lincoln delivered remarks such as, "Please excuse me . . .

from making a speech," and, "Let us at all times remember that all American citizens are brothers of a common country." He indicated in letters to Trumbull, Washburne and others at Washington they must stand for no further spread of slavery. "On that point hold firm, as with a chain of steel," he counseled, and warned, "The tug has to come, & better now, than any time hereafter." His close friend, Edward D. Baker, now U.S. Senator from Oregon, told the Senate that Lincoln would respect the Fugitive Slave Law. Also, Lincoln told friends privately that the forts seized by the seceded states would have to be retaken. But as to public declarations of policy on this and that, he was waiting.

Congressman William Kellogg of Canton, Illinois, one of the few most favored by Lincoln in patronage, held a long conference with Lincoln in Springfield January 21. Then Kellogg went to Washington, spoke for a mild compromise in his bill for extension of slavery into all new territories to be formed south of 36° 30′; he was howled down by the radicals of his party, and read out of the party by the Chicago *Tribune*—as both he and Lincoln had probably expected. One result of this Kellogg proposal was that the Unionist Democrats of southern Illinois, Indiana and Ohio, near the Slave State borders, could say to their people that when the Southern States left the Union, there was still a chance for slavery extension into the western territories. Then, too, the Slave States of Missouri and Kentucky had a fresh argument for staying in the Union. The action was mazy.

In the very air of the City of Washington was coming a sense of change, of an impending program to be wrought out on historic anvils in smoke and mist, of old bonds and moorings broken, of a formerly confident and dominant class giving way to an element a little raw and new to government and diplomacy, young and strange in its champing and chafing.

In the White House Buchanan suggested gently, "The election of any one of our citizens to the office of President does not of itself afford just cause for dissolving the Union." He could meditate on his serving as a private in the War of

1812 nearly 50 years before, of his horseback ride through bluegrass Kentucky, his temptation to settle in law practice there, and his going back to Lancaster, Pennsylvania. Elected a Congressman, he lived on, a bachelor, always reserved as to women. An estate of $300,000, out of 40 years of public officeholding, gave him little ease now, nor the comment "Buchanan has a winning way of making himself hateful."

He argued that seceded states had no right to secede, yet the Federal Government had no right to use force to stop them from seceding. He urged, however, the right of the Federal Government to use force against individuals, in spite of secession, to enforce Federal laws and hold Federal property. Yet his words lacked action to give them force. He wrote letters, negotiated, conferred, sent messengers, employed moral suasion against an organization making elaborate preparations to use guns. To Congressman Morrill of Vermont he was like an old man chuckling to his rowdy sons, *"Don't,* but if I were you I would, and I can't help it if you do."

One comfort to him was his niece, Harriet Lane, robust, with golden-brown hair, violet-blue eyes, a graduate of the Visitation Convent near Washington. A warship had been named for her, also a race horse, a flower, a fashionable gown and many a newborn girl child. "No American woman ever had more offers of marriage than Harriet Lane." Her uncle wrote the caution, "Never allow your affections to become interested, or engage yourself to any person, without my previous advice." They were chums; she shared as no others did his political secrets, with his warnings often not to tell others, for they "must tell it or burst."

While a hurricane was preparing, these two careful persons lived with their mild secrets in the White House. "Be quiet and discreet and say nothing"—the written advice of the old man to his niece was his own guiding motto. Once he termed himself "an old public functionary." "I at least meant well for my country," ran a line of his January message to Congress. To many he seemed half apparition, ready for the graveclothes that would swathe a past epoch.

Now they snarled in dog-fight tones in the halls of Con-

gress. Now the radical abolitionist Ben Wade of Ohio kept a
sawed-off shotgun in his desk. "Better for us that the fruitful
earth be smitten and become dry dust," mourned Tom Corwin. "Better that the heavens for a time become brass and
the ear of God deaf to our prayers; better that Famine with
her cold and skinny fingers lay hold upon the throats of our
wives and children . . . than that we should prove faithless
to our trust . . . and all our bright hopes die out in that
night which knows no coming dawn." This was a psalm for
the people to hear. To Lincoln he sent an epistle for Lincoln's eye only:

> . . . I cannot comprehend the madness of the times.
> Southern men are theoretically crazy. Extreme North-
> ern men are practical fools. The latter are really
> quite as mad as the former. Treason is in the air
> around us everywhere. It goes by the name of patri-
> otism. Men in Congress boldly avow it, and the public
> offices are full of acknowledged secessionists. God
> alone, I fear, can help us. Four or five States are gone,
> others are driving before the gale. I have looked on this
> horrid picture till I have been able to gaze on it with
> perfect calmness. I think, if you live, you may take
> the oath.

His dark words were addedly profound coming from the
best wit and storyteller in Washington.

Only the hard of hearing had not heard of the Crittenden
Compromise that winter. All territory north of the southern
boundary line of Missouri to the Pacific Ocean would be
free soil forever, and all territory south of that line would
be slave soil forever, by Constitutional amendment, said the
Crittenden Compromise; Congress would be forbidden ever
to abolish slavery or interfere with it in Slave States or in
the District of Columbia; the U.S. Government would pay
slaveowners for slave property lost through action of mobs
or law courts in the North. Thus Crittenden would bargain
with the seceded states hoping they would stay in the Union.
Who could blame Old Man Crittenden of Kentucky for this
plan from his head, and heart? Of his two strong sons, Tom

was for the Union and the Constitution and George was for secession and the Confederacy. And he wept over the House Divided.

Behind his compromise rallied Douglas, Edward D. Baker, Edward Everett, Thurlow Weed, August Belmont, Cyrus McCormick, many powerful newspapers, including the New York *Herald*, and such authentic and lovable advocates of peace as Tom Corwin. Petitions in its favor came to the Senate chamber in bales and stacks. The Crittenden Compromise marched up the hill, then down again; the forces against it had been long in growing and breeding. Behind each event operating for peace came another to cancel it.

General Winfield Scott, 75-year-old Virginian, military head of the U.S. Government, with headquarters in Winder's Building opposite the War Department, most often was to be found resting on an office sofa. At Chapultepec, Vera Cruz, Cerro Gordo, in the Mexican War he had held his saddle and ordered long marches and storming attacks and mapped the campaigns and run the armies. Six feet five inches tall, 300 pounds in weight, in shining gold braid and buttons, in broad epaulets and a long plumed hat, when he walked he seemed almost a parade by himself. Small boys waited of a morning to see him come out of his house and move like six regiments toward a waiting carriage. What with age, dropsy, vertigo and old bullets to carry, he could no longer mount a horse. To Scott's request for men and guns to garrison nine Southern forts against seizure, Buchanan wrote that to grant it would show on his part "a degree of inconsistency amounting almost to self-stultification." An Illinois Congressman presented his respects to General Scott with word from the President-elect, "Tell him, confidentially, I shall be obliged to him to be as well prepared as he can, to either hold or retake the forts, as the case may require, at and after the inauguration."

With inauguration day a few weeks off, letters warned Lincoln he would be killed before he reached Washington. He sent Thomas S. Mather, adjutant general of Illinois, to Washington to sound Winfield Scott on his loyalty. Mather came back to report he had found the Mexican War hero propped up with pillows, in bed, an old worn man with flesh in rolls over face and neck. His breathing heavy, he half choked and wheezed out the words: "Say to him that, when once here, I shall consider myself responsible for his safety. If necessary I'll plant cannon at both ends of Pennsylvania Avenue, and if any show their hands or even venture to raise a finger, I'll blow them to hell."

Delegates at Montgomery, Alabama, on February 4 organized a provisional government named the Confederate States of America, electing Jefferson Davis of Mississippi as President and Alexander Stephens of Georgia as Vice-President. Second to Robert Barnwell Rhett as a torch of revolution was William Lowndes Yancey of Alabama. And yet, in the seats of high power sat neither Yancey nor Rhett. Yancey and other extremists would have liked Rhett to be President. But a moderate element took the power, men who would rather have waited, who would have held a convention and presented demands to the North. In their newly adopted constitution they struck directly at Rhett, Yancey and the slave traders, and bid for international good will by expressly forbidding the African slave trade for all time.

Conventions in North Carolina and Arkansas deliberated, and joined the Confederacy. In Tennessee the voters balloted 105,000 to 47,000 in favor of secession, Union votes coming heavy from the mountaineers. In Virginia, three to one of 130,000 voters were in favor of "the Mother of Presidents" going into the Confederacy, the mountaineers chiefly being Unionist. In Texas, Governor Sam Houston refused to call the legislature and tried to stop secession, but was bowled over.

The California Senator, James A. McDougall, once an Eighth Circuit lawyer in Illinois, jingling his Mexican spurs like sleigh bells, his trousers thrust in his boots and his boots lifted on his senatorial desk, could see "as many minds as men and no end of wrangling," and was only sure, "I believe in women, wine, whiskey, and war." The less lush Henry Adams of Massachusetts was writing a brother, "No man is fit to take hold now who is not as cool as death."

It was sunset and dawn, moonrise and noon, dying time and birthing hour, dry leaves of the last of autumn and springtime blossom roots.

Chapter 16

"I Bid You an Affectionate Farewell"

When a Brooklyn hatter one January day presented Lincoln with a black silk hat, he turned to say, "Well, wife, if nothing else comes out of this scrape, we are going to have some new clothes." Such attentions pleased Mrs. Lincoln. She had a sprightly manner of saying, "We are pleased with our advancement." In the hustle of deciding what to take along to the White House, when asked about many things to be done or not done, she would sometimes burst out, "God, no!" One winter morning she was burning papers in the alley when Jared P. Irwin, a neighbor, asked if he could have some of them. She said he was welcome and Irwin scraped from the fire several of the most interesting letters written by Mr. and Mrs. Lincoln to each other.

Pressure came on her to give her husband the names of men he should appoint to offices, with reasons why. Of one woman for whose husband she got a fat office, Mrs. Lincoln told another woman, "She little knows what a hard battle I had for it, and how near he came to getting nothing." She spoke of fears about her health, would mention "my racked frame" to other women, and say she hoped the chills she suffered from in earlier years would not return to Washington. She might find Washington a city of tears and shadows. She would go there with new clothes, fresh ribbons, and see. She made a trip in January to New York City, there meeting Robert, who came down from Harvard. She had as good a time as possible for her, choosing and buying gowns, hats, footwear and adornments becoming to one to be called "the First Lady of the Land."

Ordering things to wear, she could write instructions, "I am in need of two bonnets—I do not wish expensive ones, but I desire them of very fine quality and stylish." She wrote specifications to the milliner. "One bonnet, I wish fine, very fine, pretty shape. This I desire, to be trimmed with black love ribbons—with pearl edge. I cannot have it without the latter . . ." Villard wrote for the New York *Herald* January 26 of the President-elect "delighted" at the return of Mrs. Lincoln and Bob from the east. "Dutiful husband and father that he is, he had proceeded to the railroad depot for three successive nights in his anxiety to receive them, and that in spite of snow and cold. Mrs. Lincoln returned in good health and excellent spirits; whether she got a good scolding from Abraham for unexpectedly prolonging her absence, I am unable to say; but I know she found it rather difficult to part with the winter gayeties of New York." Villard noted, too, that Robert, fresh from Harvard, dressed in an elegance in "striking contrast to the loose, careless, awkward rigging of his Presidential father."

Lincoln rode to Mattoon, missed connections with a passenger train, and took the caboose of a freight train to Charleston. With a shawl over his shoulders, and his boots in slush, mud and ice, he picked his way in the late evening dusk alongside the tracks the length of the freight train to the station, where a buggy was ready. Friends took him to the house where he stayed overnight. Next day he drove eight miles out to an old farm. Sally Bush Lincoln and he put their arms around each other and listened to each other's heartbeats. They held their hands and talked, they talked without holding hands. Each looked into eyes thrust back in deep sockets. She was all of a mother to him. He was her boy more than any born to her. He gave her a photograph of her boy, a hungry picture of him standing and wanting, wanting. He stroked her face a last time, kissed good-by and went away. She knew his heart would go roaming back often, that even when he rode in an open carriage in New York or Washington with soldiers, flags and cheering thousands along the streets, he might just as like be thinking of her in the old log farmhouse out in Coles County, Illinois.

The sunshine of the prairie summer and fall months would come shifting down with healing and strength; between harvest and corn-plowing there would be rains beating and blizzards howling; and there would be the silence after snowstorms with white drifts piled against the fences, barns and trees.

Lincoln cleaned out files, threw away useless odds and ends. Manuscripts he wished to preserve and didn't want to be encumbered with in Washington, he put into a carpetbag and gave to Elizabeth Todd Grimsley, whom he called "Cousin Lizzie." His "literary bureau," he termed it, and told Mrs. Grimsley to watch it with care but if he should not return to Springfield she might dispose of the manuscripts as she pleased. Among them were two drafts of his lecture "Discoveries and Inventions."

His regular secretary was a trusted, reliable, accurate, scrupulous young man, sober as a work horse, earnest as the multiplication table; he had freckles and reddish hair; a young Bavarian from the *Pike County Sucker*. This was John G. Nicolay, secretive, dependable, often carrying messages not to be written but whispered.

The other or second secretary, not strictly engaged as such, was going to Washington. Lincoln had said, "We can't take all Illinois with us down to Washington, but let Hay come." A keen and whimsical lad, John Hay. He had been class poet at Brown University, graduated, gone home to Warsaw, Illinois, then to Pike County, and later to Springfield to study law with his Uncle Milton, who had an office on the same floor as Lincoln & Herndon. He wrote notes in French to a sweetheart, and had a handsome, careless elegance all the girls in Springfield liked.

Between seven and twelve o'clock on the night of February 6, there came to the Lincoln home several hundred "ladies and gentlemen," wrote one correspondent, "the political elite of this State, and the beauty and fashion of this vicinity." It was the Lincolns' good-by house party. The President-elect stood near the front door shaking hands and nearby was Bob and Mrs. Lincoln and four of her sisters.

On one farewell day, as Lincoln was meeting people in Johnson's Block opposite the Chenery House, there came to him an old farmer, in butternut jeans, who had ridden horseback many miles since daybreak. And the old man was bent and worn with age, and nearly blind. He had known the Armstrongs and what Lincoln did for Duff Armstrong. And he came and put his old eyes close to Lincoln's face, peered and studied the lines of the face, burst into tears, and murmured, "It *is* him—it's the *same.*" And after mentioning the Duff Armstrong case, he shook the hand of the President-elect and said solemnly two or three times, "God preserve you, Mr. Lincoln."

"Lincoln is letting his whiskers grow," men were saying in January, when his upper lip and cheeks were shaved but a stubble left on the chin. Then in February hair had grown over jaws, chin and throat, the upper lip shaven. This facial design was wrought by William Florville, a Haitian-born colored man, known as "Billy the Barber" whose shop in Springfield dated back to 1831. For more than 20 years he had shaved and done the haircuts of Lincoln while Lincoln handled several real-estate title cases for Billy who owned town lots and a farm. In his house was celebrated, it was said, the first Catholic mass in Springfield. He wrote for the Springfield *Journal* droll and charming praise of his razor skill, had keen humor, and Lincoln while being shaved undoubtedly picked up new funny stories.

Why Lincoln took to whiskers at this time nobody seemed to know. A girl in New York State had written begging him to raise a beard. An October letter from New York signed only "True Republicans" pleasantly but seriously asked him to "cultivate whiskers and wear standing collars." But something more than these random wishes guided him. Herndon, Whitney, Lamon, Nicolay, heard no explanation from him as to why after 52 years with a smooth face he should now change.

At sunset the evening before the day set for starting to Washington, Lincoln and Herndon sat in their office for a long talk about their 16 years as partners. Then Lincoln slumped on a sofa and looking up at the ceiling, mentioned that many a time after a Herndon drunk, people tried to get him to drop his partner and he told them that for all of his shortcomings he believed in Herndon. Thus Herndon wrote of it. Herndon said afterward: "I could have had any place for which I was fitted, but I thought too much of Lincoln to disgrace him. And I wanted to be free, drink whisky when I pleased." Herndon had one request, however, that Lincoln would speak to Governor Yates and have him reappointed state bank examiner, to which Lincoln agreed. As Lincoln gathered a bundle of papers and stood ready to leave, he told Herndon their partnership would go on, their "shingle" stay up. As they walked down the stairs Lincoln said he was "sick of office-holding already" and "I shudder when I think of the tasks that are still ahead."

In a dusty third-story locked room over the store of his brother-in-law, C. M. Smith, Lincoln, with a few books and documents he consulted, had hidden away from all callers while he worked on his inaugural address for March 4, in Washington, amid the cannon to be planted by General Scott. Two printers, sworn to secrecy, had in January set up and run off 20 copies of the address. Weeks had gone by. Nobody had told or been careless. The inaugural text was still a well-kept secret.

Lamon was called from Bloomington and told: "Hill, it looks as if we might have war. I want you with me, I must have you." And Lamon was going along, banjo, bulldog courage and all.

A queer dream or illusion had haunted Lincoln at times through the winter. On election evening he had thrown himself on a haircloth sofa at home, soon after the telegrams reported him President-elect. Looking into a bureau mirror across the room he saw himself full length, but with two faces. It bothered him; he got up; the illusion vanished; but when he lay down again there in the glass were two faces again, one more pale than the other. He got up again, mixed in the election excitement, forgot about it; but it haunted him. He told his wife and she too worried.

A few days later he tried it once more and the illusion of the two faces again registered to his eyes. But that was the last; the ghost since then wouldn't come back, he told his wife, who said it was a sign he would be elected to a second term, and the death pallor of one face meant he wouldn't live through his second term.

Lincoln took walks alone. Whitney ran across him in a section of Springfield where he had no business, unless to be walking alone. His arms were full of papers and bundles of mail. Where was he going? "Nowhere in particular," he told Whitney.

Clothes, furniture, books, the household goods were packed in boxes and trunks. The family took rooms a few days in the Chenery House; the old home was leased, horse, buggy and cow sold off, the German-language paper turned back to Canisius.

At the hotel Lincoln had roped his trunks himself, and had written, "A. Lincoln, The White House, Washington, D.C." on cards he fastened on the trunks.

A cold drizzle of rain was falling February 11 when Lincoln and his party of 15 were to leave Springfield on the eight o'clock at the Great Western Railway station. Chilly gray mist hung the circle of the prairie horizon. A short locomotive with a flat-topped smokestack stood puffing with a baggage car and special passenger car coupled on; a railroad president and superintendent were on board. A thousand people crowded in and around the brick station inside of which Lincoln was standing, and one by one came hundreds of old friends, shaking hands, wishing him luck and Godspeed, all faces solemn. Even the huge Judge Davis, wearing a new white silk hat, was a somber figure.

A path was made for Lincoln from the station to his car; hands stretched out for one last handshake. He hadn't intended to make a speech; but on the platform of the car, as he turned and saw his home people, he took off his hat, stood perfectly still, and raised a hand for silence. They stood, with hats off.

Then he spoke slowly, amid the soft gray drizzle from the sky. Later, on the train he wrote with a pencil about half of his speech, dictating to Nicolay the remainder of his good-by words to Springfield: "My friends—No one, not in my situation, can appreciate my feeling of sadness at this parting. To this place, and the kindness of these people, I owe every thing. Here I have lived a quarter of a century, and have passed from a young to an old man. Here my children have been born, and one is buried. I now leave, not knowing when, or whether ever, I may return, with a task before me greater than that which rested upon Washington. Without the assistance of that Divine Being, who ever attended him, I cannot succeed. With that assistance I cannot fail. Trusting in Him, who can go with me, and remain with you and be everywhere for good, let us confidently hope that all will yet be well. To His care commending you, as I hope in your prayers you will commend me, I bid you an affectionate farewell."

Bells rang, there was a grinding of wheels, the train moved and carried Lincoln away from his home town and folks. The tears were not yet dry on some faces when the train had faded into the gray to the east.

At Tolono station, the last stop in Illinois, he said, "I am leaving you on an errand of national importance, attended, as you are aware, with considerable difficulties. Let us believe, as some poet has expressed it:—'Behind the cloud the sun is still shining.' I bid you an affectionate farewell."

And there were voices, "Good-by, Abe."

END OF VOLUME I